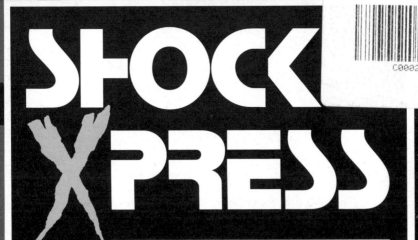

SHOCK XPRESS

2

Edited By
STEFAN JAWORZYN

Editorial Consultant:
Stephen Jones

TITAN BOOKS
LONDON

SHOCK XPRESS 2

ISBN 1 85286 519 9

Published by
Titan Books Ltd
19 Valentine Place
London
SE1 8QH

First edition March 1994
10 9 8 7 6 5 4 3 2 1

Printed and bound in England by Hillman Printers (Frome) Ltd,
Frome, Somerset.

British Library Cataloguing-in-Publication Data. A catalogue record for
this book is available from the British Library.

Picture credits:
Allied Artists, Alpha Films, American International, Art House
Productions Ltd, Astra Video, Aurora Books, BFI Stills, Posters and
Designs, Border Films, Box Office Spectaculars, Inc, Brent Walker Films
Ltd, Jörg Buttgereit, The Cannon Group, Carribean Films, Columbia
Pictures, Compton Film Distributors, Connoisseur Films Ltd, Copenhagen
Film + Video Festival, Corgi Books, DCA Pictures, Entertainment in Video,
Eros, Exclusive Films, Extasy Video, Gala Films/Kenneth Rive, Goodtimes
Video, Richard Gordon, Alberto Grimaldi-PEA, Jerry Gross, Grove Press,
Guild Film Distribution Ltd, Harry Novak Films, Hillcrest Productions,
Intropics Video, Lindsay Shonteff Film Productions Limited, Lynx Video,
MGM Inc, Miracle Film Releasing, Miracle Films, Monarch Film
Corporation, Monogram, New World Pictures, Palm Springs Enterprises,
Panther Books, Paramount Pictures, Pietro Pascuttini, Penguin
Productions, Perfect Features, Planet Films, PRC, Protelco, Rank Film
Distributors, S.F. Films, Springboard Video, Steve Postal Productions, Jack
Stevenson, Target International Pictures, Tigon Pictures, Trans-Lux, 20th
Century-Fox, United Artists, United International Pictures, Universal,
Warner Bros Ltd, Warner Bros Television Distribution, Western Visuals,
Wingnut Films Ltd.
Any omissions will be corrected in future editions.

Front cover photo:
The Black Cat © 1990 World Picture s.r.l. and 21st Century Film
Corporation.

Back cover photos:
Top: *The Chair* © 1988 Angelika Films/Urban Entertainment (Medusa
Pictures).
Middle: *Army of Darkness* © 1992 De Laurentiis/Introvision (Guild Films).
Bottom: *Evil Dead II* © 1987 Rosebud Releasing/Renaissance Pictures
(Palace Pictures).

CONTENTS

For Christa

ACKNOWLEDGEMENTS:

Art House Productions, The Associates/Alison Packman, Aurora Books, BFI Stills Library, Nigel Davies, Mariangela Giordano, Mick Hamer, *Horror and Science Fiction Films*/Donald C. Willis, David Hyman, *Leonard Maltin's Movie and Video Guide*, *Monthly Film Bulletin*, Steve Roe, *Shock Cinema* and Lindsay Shonteff.

Special thanks to David Barraclough for his support through all stages of this project.

Copies of *Shock Xpress 1* are still available from all good bookshops or through Titan Books Mail Order. To order copies of the book, or for a catalogue of all Titan's film and TV publications, please send a large stamped SAE to Titan Books Mail Order, 19 Valentine Place, London SE1 8QH.
Please quote reference SX2.

Some back issues of *Shock Xpress* are also still available. All enquiries should be addressed to *Shock Xpress*, c/o Titan Books. Please enclose a SAE or IRC.

XPRESSWAY TO YOUR SKULL

Three fucking years... And to think we thought the two year gap between the last issue of *Shock Xpress* magazine and the first book seemed a long time...

So what, exactly, has occurred in between? Well, amongst the endless hate-filled trivialities passing for 'events' (or even 'existence') in these parts, I've been trying to dream up an explanation for this volume's delays (and the multitude of nightmares attendant to the first volume) that wouldn't take at least another two books to detail... But considering such agonising minutiae is all too much effort (and would also detract from the quintessential 'mystery' of *SX*, ahem...), so I guess I'd better think of something else...

Yet I find myself curiously vacant when finally attempting to emit my anticipated bilious rant... Whatever deluded (and by now entirely predictable) pronouncements I make on the state of Britain's pathetic psychopathology will doubtless be irrelevant by the time of publication, and unless you've been in a crack coma (or voted Tory...) for the last few years you'd have to be a tad fucked up not to have noticed the 'decline' (let's be charitable) in the overall standard of 'living' in this doomed country... But however predictable and whinging my comments may be, they still seem more relevant (to me, anyway, and I don't care a fig what anyone else thinks) than droning on about some worthless spaghetti 'masterpiece' of rubber dummy mutilation or infantile Japanese animation that would insult a child's intelligence. And you know, when some of my business associates ask, "Yo, Mis' Shock mofo, how come y'all don't do no shit for that crappy book o' yo's no mo'?", I fondle my goatee and several hours after they've nodded off conclude "and, my good man, what's more I CAN'T THINK OF A SINGLE CONSTRUCTIVE THING TO SAY ABOUT MODERN MOVIES!" Sure, that's not actually true, but when the loser you're addressing isn't experiencing consciousness *per se*, what difference does it make? (Please don't think I'm being politically incorrect for dumping on the semi-conscious: some of my best friends — and contributors, come to think of it, not that I've met many of them as I'm far too fat and 'sick' to leave the house — inhabit a world untroubled by sordid reality...)

Oh well, I've already forgotten what I was talking about, but those of you foolish enough to peruse this 'introduction' hoping for an explanation of what *Shock Xpress* is or why the contents are as they are, or perhaps some whimsical reminiscence concerning my discovery of what fun it was to soil my britches at scary movies before I could even say "pass the crack pipe", are not about to achieve enlightenment, or even experience satisfaction. Instead you should be *grateful* that I've restricted my ranting to a single page in order to indulge (*name deleted*) in an extra thousand words' worth of navel contemplation...

And that is just about it... But consider: *Shock Xpress* is now FOR ADULTS ONLY. 'They' (politicians, sectors of the media, the religious right...) want to influence and/or restrict your ability to speak freely, read freely, view freely, think freely, even *fuck* freely. As they get nearer to achieving their objectives maybe it's time to do something other than watch movies. Good luck trying to figure out what it could be... ∎

Stefan Jaworzyn, January 1994

"And what's more, it's a proven scientific fact that the Chuckie doll is responsible for single parent families, unemployment, higher taxation..." BLAT! The unbelievable truth proves too much for a Tory media expert.

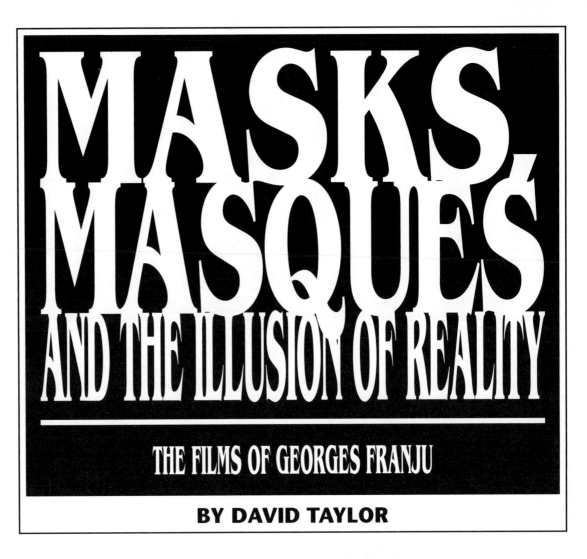

MASKS, MASQUES
AND THE ILLUSION OF REALITY

THE FILMS OF GEORGES FRANJU

BY DAVID TAYLOR

"What pleases me is that which is terrible, tender and poetic."
– Georges Franju

Picture the scene: the Cameo Cinema, Edinburgh on 2 September 1959. Despite protestations from some of his committee members, Don Elliot, the administrative director of the Edinburgh Film Festival, went ahead with plans to screen the world première of Georges Franju's *Les Yeux sans Visage*.

The Festival had already attracted controversy the previous week by showing the American film *The Savage Eye*, a pseudo-documentary directed by Ben Maddow, Sidney Meyers and Joseph Strick which charted the attempts of a divorcee to adjust to single life in Los Angeles. Its grim, unglamorised portrait of seedy bars and strip clubs, plastic surgeons and faith healers, had been defended on the grounds that it presented an accurate depiction of West Coast low life.

Les Yeux sans Visage had no such credentials. It was a horror film, pure and simple. One only had to glance at the plot synopsis to see that: having been responsible for the grotesque scarring of his daughter Christiane in a car accident, the pioneering surgeon Dr Genessier is prepared to go to any lengths to restore her beauty, including kidnapping and murdering other young women in order to graft their skin onto his daughter's face. He is eventually torn to pieces by the dogs on which he experiments and his daughter wanders off into the night.

Reaction to the film was predictable. It was reported that three people fainted during the notorious skin graft sequence and there were numerous walk-outs. Critic Dilys Powell, reviewing the film in *The Sunday Times* on 6 September, dismissed it as 'deliberately revolting.' *The Edinburgh Evening News* dubbed it 'cold-blooded.' Even the Cameo's manager, J. K. S. Poole, proclaimed that it was "A lousy film...with a gimmick." Franju himself added fuel to the fire when, on hearing of the fainting episodes, he commented that now he knew why Scotsmen wore skirts.

Don Elliot defended the screening of the film: "It is not the policy of the Film Festival to look for horror films, but when we get one by a director with a reputation such as Georges Franju we have to give it very careful consideration. He is one of the most brilliant French film directors and that is the committee's justification for presenting it. They do so with a certain amount of concern for the public, but any festival, if it has to deal not only with the pleasant facts of life, must face up to the situation by showing films of an unusual nature."

The ubiquitous Tony Tenser, then official representative of Miracle Films, which had picked up the UK distribution rights to *Les Yeux sans Visage*, pointed out

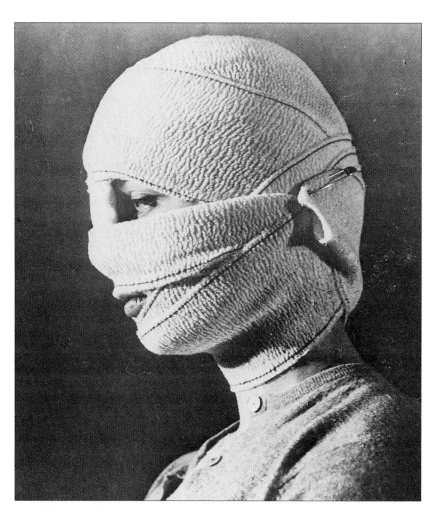

that things could have been worse. "The French conception of horror is less than ours. They think the British can take more horror than they can. But the version they intended for us will never be shown in Britain... The French make the English versions of sexy films less sexy than their own, but the English versions of horror films they make more horrific... When we saw the version intended for Britain we thought it was a bit much altogether. So we sent for the French version and put English subtitles on it." He added that the British Board of Film Censors had insisted on cuts before the film could be put on general release.

(Although most sources state that two minutes were eventually cut from *Les Yeux sans Visage* by the BBFC, this is untrue. In fact, all that was removed from the film was two shots. Miracle Films were instructed to shorten the skin graft sequence at the point where the skin is physically lifted away from the face and to remove the final shot of Christiane's gradually deteriorating face from the time lapse sequence, which shows her flesh beginning to reject the transplant. Although many sources state that the climactic savaging of Dr Genessier by his blood-crazed hounds was extensively cut, it certainly was not done so by the UK censors. It has also been reported that further cuts were made to the film for its US release, under the title *The Horror Chamber of Dr Faustus*, although this writer cannot verify or deny such assertions.)

It was almost a year before *Les Yeux sans Visage* was released in UK cinemas, as *Eyes without a Face*, though it appears there were initial plans to release it as *Horror Chamber of Dr Faustus*. Despite the long delay since its

(Previous page) Francine Bergé in **Judex**.

(This page) **Les Yeux sans Visage.**

HILLCREST PRODUCTIONS present

PIERRE BRASSEUR

ALIDA VALLI

HORROR CHAMBER OF Dr FAUSTUS

ALL ENGLISH DIALOGUE 'X'

Edith Scob in **Les Yeux sans Visage** *(above) and in* **Thérèse Desqueyroux** *(right).*

Edinburgh screening, none of the controversy had abated. The mainstream critics were almost uniformly hostile to the film.

'WHY did they let this film come in?' screamed the headline in the *Birmingham Evening Despatch* of 5 August 1960. Critic Ivor Jay followed up this rhetorical question with a three column attack on the film and its makers: 'To write about this movie objectively is more than usually difficult. It is even impossible. I don't intend to try. You may like it. I loathed it.' Jay continued his undeniably subjective rant with: 'It is a sick, unhealthy film. If it has the merits of being beautifully acted and well directed they are virtues which become vices because they increase the movie's power to shock. When talents are directed solely towards the creation of nausea it is a shameful business... I am no advocate of censorship, but for once I sincerely regret that a foreign film — this one — ever got a licence to be shown in this country... To use the words 'credits' above the list of scriptwriters, cameramen, directors, etc is to perpetrate a sardonic joke. This film is to nobody's credit.'

The most lamentable effect of the continuing controversy was that it finally overshadowed both the film and its maker. Any sort of retrospective reappraisal of *Les Yeux sans Visage* outside of the specialist film press was not forthcoming. Despite the fact that his subsequent film, *Pleins Feux sur l'Assassin* (1960), was the most commercial film of his career and was given a showcase once again at the Edinburgh Film Festival, it failed to secure a UK release. Later films, including the award-winning *Thérèse Desqueyroux* (1962), were relegated to art house screenings only. Having been pulled briefly into the public's view for one film, Franju remained a relatively anonymous fig-

ure outside of France for the rest of his career.

Even today, when obscure cult items are being 'rediscovered' almost weekly, Franju's films are seldom screened, with the exception of *Les Yeux sans Visage* which remains a mainstay of the horror movie circuit. He is conceivably the only major French film director for which few people are aware of the bulk of his work and even fewer have seen it.

"I remember one day when I was tiny I found myself before a wardrobe with a mirror... I opened it and because the wardrobe was damp the inside was infested with mushrooms... The sight startled me and has probably established a certain mechanism in my sense of the bizarre." — Georges Franju

Franju was born at Fougères in Brittany on 12 April 1912, one of twin brothers. He spent much of his youth shirking his education, preferring to sit under trees and read the exploits of Fantômas (of whom more later) and works by de Sade and Freud. After leaving school, he worked for an insurance company and packed crates in a noodle factory before entering military service in Algeria. On his return in 1932, he studied theatre design and worked on sets for both the Folies Bergère and the Casino de Paris.

This early appreciation of the aesthetics of the theatre is reflected in the unerring eye for architecture and interior design that he brought to films as a director. Indeed, in some cases, Franju would shoot in such a way as to enforce a sense of theatricality to his sets or locations, such as the abattoir in his short documentary *Le Sang des Bêtes* (1949): "In fiction, fantasy is usually obtained by giving the artificial the appearance of reality. In our films we set out to restore to documentary realism its actual quality of apparently artificial decor. We managed it by shooting buildings from directly in front or else we chose houses with sharp profiles and avoided any sense of depth... and we often waited several days for the weather to be simultaneously diffuse and dense in the sky, or else for everything to be lit up with that particular, local colour which strikes one as a freak of the sunlight..."

In 1934 he met up with fellow aspiring film-maker Henri Langlois and, by borrowing money from the Langlois family, they made their first short film, entitled *Le Métro*, a straightforward documentary about the workings of the Paris underground system. For Franju it was a false start in film-making, for he was not to return to directing for another fifteen years. In the meantime, he formed a film club which he named Le Cercle du Cinema and edited a film magazine, named *CINEMAtographe*, which was to only last for two issues.

Then, in 1937, Franju and Langlois made a lasting contribution to the film world by devising and inaugurating the Cinémathèque Française, which was to grow into one of the most respected film archives in the world. The following year Franju was elected the executive secretary of La Fédération des Archives du Film, the international federation of film archives. After the liberation of Paris, he became secretary-general of L'Institut de Cinématographie Scientifique.

It is perhaps ironic that Franju should spend so much of his life saving films from extinction at the cost of producing his own body of work. Yet in one sense it is only through understanding his deep love and respect for past film-makers that one can begin to appreciate what he was trying to achieve himself.

If one considers Franju's work within the much

wider context of French film history, one can see that he is a somewhat anachronistic figure. The emergence of film-makers such as Alain Resnais, François Truffaut and Jean-Luc Godard in the '50s heralded the arrival of the *nouvelle vague* in French cinema. Although Franju's work was contemporaneous with this movement, he did not consider himself part of the avant-garde. Rather, he allied himself with both German and French expressionistic cinema and the surrealist movement, saying: "I was asked which...was the most intensely poetic film and I quoted Buñuel; which was the most beautiful horror film, and I quoted Murnau; which was the most intensely graphic film, and I quoted Lang."

A fourth, and perhaps the single most important, influence on Franju was the great French expressionistic director, Louis Feuillade. Although he is virtually unknown today, Feuillade was one of the most prolific and popular directors of silent films in France. He began his career writing scripts for Pathé Studios in 1905, later moving to the Gaumont studios. In all, he reckoned to have written over 800 scripts for one- or two-reel silent films and directed around 700 of them. His most important works, however, were his serials, which included *Fantômas*, *Les Vampires*, *Judex*, *Tia Minh* and *Barabbas*. Despite their primitive techniques and melodramatic plots, Feuillade's films caught the imagination of both the public and fellow artists. Luis Buñuel cited him as an influence on his early films and Alain Resnais praised the way he "creates mystery and evokes dreams by the use of the most banal elements of daily life."

Franju, too, acknowledged his debt to Feuillade by remaking *Judex* and dedicating his film to the director of the original. This was more than a simple homage or a slavish imitation. Franju took the theories instigated by Feuillade, along with those of Murnau, Lang and Buñuel, and transformed them into something uniquely his own, informed by his own sense of aesthetics and personal philosophy.

He wanted to create films which, in the great expressionistic ideal, elicited as strong an emotional response from the viewer as an intellectual one.

> *"Kafka becomes terrifying from the moment it's documentary. In documentary I work the other way round."* — Georges Franju

Although you would think that Franju's documentary films were, by definition, the antithesis of fantasy, they formed an essential step in the development of his own personal film aesthetic.

Like all documentarists, Franju sought to explore the truth behind reality. To make his audience see, not just look.

To this end, he employed the techniques of the surrealists by imbuing meaning through the juxtaposition of apparently disassociated images. The perfect example of this is *Hôtel des Invalides* (1951), which was his own favourite of his documentaries. He had been approached by the custodians of the Hôtel des Invalides, the French military museum which also housed a retirement home for war veterans, to prepare a short film which could be used as a record of the museum. When they saw the completed film, they were scandalised and it was never used for the purpose for which it had been intended.

With the film, Franju had conspired to make a subversive statement about the nature of war and its effects. He would cut from a half-suit of armour to a

legless invalid, from a bust of Napoleon to a wounded veteran, whilst the narration intoned that "legend has its heroes, war its victims." Other images were more abstractly disturbing, such as a child peering intently at the helmet of a suit of armour, shot side-on to give the impression of confrontation, or birds spiralling like vultures over the rooftops of Paris.

Emmanuele Riva reflects in **Thérèse Desqueyroux**.

In another documentary, *Notre Dame, Cathédrale de Paris* (1957), Franju showed aspects of this elaborate bastion of the Catholic faith that few people were aware of. Pausing only to remark on the number of empty seats to be found in the cathedral, he carried the viewer out to the seldom-seen rear prospect, where piles of broken gargoyles were tossed after they had crumbled from the parapets. Then it was up to the towers themselves where, he explained, pigeons frequently battered themselves to death by flying into the edifice of the cathedral or else clustered together in the bell towers to starve or freeze to death.

Even the minor documentaries became opportunities for Franju to alter his viewers' perspectives on their respective subject matter and promote his own political or social opinions. In *Les Poussières* (1954), a short film intended to be used to inform factory workers of routine safety precautions, he managed to twist the message round until it ended up condemning the factory owners for being responsible for the unsafe conditions which made such precautions necessary. And in his tour around a provincial steelworks in *En Passant par la Lorraine* (1950), which was intended as a morale booster for French industry after the dark days of the Second World War, he took time to pause and consider the fatalities which had occurred due to unsafe working practices.

Franju was, in short, no great respecter of authority, whether it be political, military, religious or industrial. The actor Philippe Noiret, with whom Franju later worked on *Thérèse Desqueyroux*, went so far as to describe him as "a man apart, something of an anarchist." Franju, however, rejected this claim. Although he would admit that "Anything said against the military

A trip to the slaughterhouse... **Le Sang des Bêtes**.

imagination for the most ordinary action to become imbued with disquieting meaning, for the decor of everyday life to engender a fantastic world.'

In *La Première Nuit*, a rich young schoolboy decides to forgo his usual chauffeur-driven trip home in order to pursue the object of his affections, a pretty young blonde schoolmate, into the underworld of the Paris Métro. Losing sight of the girl in the turmoil of the rush hour, the boy is forced to spend a night underground, hopping from train to train and endlessly prowling the labyrinthine corridors of the transport system. As he is worn down by fatigue, the Métro becomes increasingly threatening and phantasmagorical. It will be morning before the young boy will make good his escape and once again rise blinking into the sunlight.

What is perhaps most affecting about *La Première Nuit* is its gradual progression from reality to fantasy. Franju doesn't resort to special effects or cheap tricks to create the hallucinatory world of the Métro, he simply heightens our awareness of space by utilising ever more acute angles and unusual perspectives, as well as amplifying sound for effect. The Métro's cavernous corridors, antiseptic decor and gently swinging, creaking lights all contribute to the viewers' growing disorientation. In one mesmerising sequence, the young boy looks up from his seat in an empty carriage to find the young blonde girl gazing at him impassively through the window of a train on the opposite platform. There is a slightly queasy, dislocated feel to the boy's yearning as both trains pull out of the station in the same direction, swaying sensuously against each other before being swallowed up by their respective tunnels, hers rising up towards the light, his deeper into the bowels of the earth.

Whilst the film owes a debt to the works of Jean Cocteau, it also seems relevant to view *La Première Nuit* as partly autobiographical. Its location immediately recalls the Franju/Langlois collaboration *Le Métro*, with the young boy's romantic awakening being a metaphor for the artistic awakening of Franju himself.

In the final shot of the film, the young boy has finally escaped from the Métro to find his way home. The city he emerges to is, however, not the same one that he descended from; the grey urban sprawl has been transformed into a tree-lined boulevard. The young boy vanishes down the road, the tree tops overhead echoing the vaulted ceilings of the Métro station below. The inference is clear: the boy does not view the world through the same eyes. He has reached a turning point.

As, indeed, had the director.

"You can't set out to make films with the intention of being poetic. Or if I say I'm going to make a philosophical film, I'm just being ridiculous. What I'll make is a film from which philosophical conclusions can be drawn." — Georges Franju

Franju's first feature film, *La Tête contre les Murs* (1958), came about almost by accident. The actor Jean-Pierre Mocky had written an adaptation of Herve Bazin's novel of teen rebellion and was shopping around for a director. Having been unable to interest anyone on his shortlist, which included Alain Resnais, he made a snap decision to settle on Franju.

La Tête contre les Murs tells the story of François Gerane (Mocky), a rebellious teenager from a broken middle class home. When François breaks into his father's office to steal money and perform an act of

and the priesthood is well said," he also stated, "I am (even) the opposite of an anarchist, because from the moment where what's needed is collective action, I detest everything that's individual."

Nevertheless, it was his individual view which he brought to bear in his documentaries. These films were not an attempt to chart life as it was lived, but to promote life and society as Franju saw it. Even his notorious trip round the slaughterhouse at Villette, *Le Sang des Bêtes*, which many critics consider to be a film without a subversive manifesto, is a film of its time. For the generation for whom the Liberation was still a fairly recent memory and for whom fresh meat would still be considered something of a luxury, the images of the dispossessed citizens of Paris sifting through the rubbish heaps around the abattoir in search of trinkets to sell would have displayed a side of Parisian life every bit as upsetting as the image of a white horse kneeling, almost in supplication as a bolt is fired through its skull. There was no question as to which 'side' Franju was on. As he said himself: "I am always on the side of the victims."

"Any screen image has an immediate presence. Whatever you do, a film is always in the present tense. The past is spontaneously reactualised by the spectator. That's why anything artificial ages quickly and badly. Dreams, poetry, the fantastic must emerge from reality itself. Every film is a documentary, even the most poetic." — Georges Franju

In 1958, Franju made his first fictional film. Entitled *La Première Nuit*, it was only twenty-one minutes in length and was based on a screenplay written by Marianne Oswald and Remo Forlani. In an epigraph to the film that would be equally at home at the beginning of any of his movies, Franju stated: 'It only requires a little

wanton vandalism, he is threatened with prison. His despotic father, however, is anxious to avoid the scandal of a trial and so he volunteers to have has son incarcerated in a lunatic asylum. The asylum itself turns out to be little more than a medieval torture dungeon, where the insane are held under restraint and are both physically and mentally mistreated by the staff. François escapes and is kept in hiding by his Parisian girlfriend Stéphanie (Anouk Aimée). When the authorities begin to close in on them, he sacrifices himself to avoid implicating her and returns to the asylum, this time for good.

By all accounts, the shoot was an unhappy experience. Franju had to accept the screenplay as written because there was no time for revisions. The film overshot its budget, partly due to inclement weather conditions (it was shot in winter) and partly because of Franju's decision to film within the environs of a working psychiatric hospital at Dury. This situation both distressed and depressed the cast and crew. Franju later acknowledged that spending all day within the asylum before retiring to their respective hotels had taken its toll, commenting that "if we'd slept in the asylum, we'd still be there."

On release, the film met with a mixed reception. Franju's focusing on the more barbarous aspects of the mental health system repelled the audience and was derided by the authorities as being hopelessly outdated (the original novel is specifically set in 1934), as drug therapy had precluded the need for force in modern psychiatric treatment. Nevertheless, the film was praised for its almost tactile atmosphere of decay and loneliness, as well as for its performances. Jean-Luc Godard enthused of the cast: "They don't act. They quiver."

Whilst there is no doubt that the film is melodramatic in its treatment of insanity, this was intentional, a blurring of the dividing line between reality and fantasy. The film 'works' if considered as being from the narrative perspective of young François himself. Which is to say, we are seeing his view of life within the asylum. To deny the film its excruciating sequences of human degradation would be to render it meaningless, since a more reasoned approach would have diluted both the anti-authoritarian stance adopted by Franju on behalf of his main character and made a mockery of the sacrifice which Francois makes to protect Stéphanie.

Whatever its shortcomings, La Tête contre les Murs gave Franju the chance to get his grounding as a feature film director and to begin assembling his own repertory of cast and crew, with whom he was to collaborate on some of his later films. There was director of photography Eugen Schüffan (changed to Eugene Schuftan in the USA), who was to work on such classic American films as The Hustler and another notable film about insanity, Lilith. There was composer Maurice Jarre, who Franju had plucked from obscurity to provide the soundtrack for Hôtel des Invalides and whose giddy, playful musical themes highlighted the basic unreality of the film. And there was actor Pierre Brasseur, who played the head of the asylum.

Most importantly, however, there was a young actress called Edith Scob, who had an unforgettable cameo as a madwoman. It would be tempting to view the doll-like Scob as the little blonde girl of La Première Nuit grown up. Certainly she came to occupy a very special place in Franju's universe, signifying the romantic ideal to which his characters (and thus, inevitably, he himself) aspired. As Franju once put it,

"She gives the unreal reality."

"Fever, yearning, fear, hope... I found all this in the beautiful eyes of Edith Scob. But I was always troubled by them. Troubled in the presence of this young, sweet girl. Because sweetness was an emotion which her face never expressed." — Georges Franju

After completing La Tête contre les Murs, Franju asked novelist Jean Redon to write a screenplay for his book Les Yeux sans Visage, with a view to bringing it to the screen.

Franju certainly had his work cut out trying to convince both producers and the French censors that this scenario was filmable. "When I shot Les Yeux sans Visage I was told: 'No sacrilege because of the Spanish market, no nudes because of the Italian market, no blood because of the French market and no martyrised animals because of the English market.' And I was supposed to be making a horror film!"

With the exception of any explicit nudity, Franju managed to include just about everything he had been warned against. And the film still carries an oblique erotic charge, partly through Scob's sensitive portrayal of lost innocence (a performance made all the more remarkable for being delivered from behind a featureless eggshell mask for the most part) and partly through Alida Valli's depiction of Genessier's ruthless medical assistant Louise, a leather-clad vamp gazing hungrily at the young Parisians from whom she must select the next victim to supply the skin for her mentor's experiments. There is also more than a hint of sexual perversity in the relationship between Christiane and her father.

The gore quotient in Les Yeux sans Visage is tame by

*The author, restrained by editorial assistants after being told to cut another 25,000 words from his article. (**La Tête contre les Murs**, actually.)*

modern standards, although Georges Klein's primitive make-up techniques stand up remarkably well, mainly because Franju is wise enough to use them sparingly. What remains most affecting about the film is its aura of loneliness and despair. The grey winter landscapes and brittle monochrome photography conjure up an environment every bit as hostile as the asylum at Dury or the abattoir at Villette. The use of masks — Christiane's ersatz face, Genessier's surgical masks, the victimised Edna's bandage wrappings — further serves to dehumanise the characters. Only their eyes, full of fear and pain, or wild with madness, betray their intrinsic humanity.

Yet *Les Yeux sans Visage* is not, as some critics have maintained, an essentially pessimistic work. Unlike *La Tête contre les Murs*, where François eventually is forced to capitulate to authority, Christiane empowers herself and rebels against it. Her comment that "My face scares me; my mind scares me even more..." is less an indication of her own descent into madness than a recognition of her own revolutionary impulses. This reading is supported by the coded symbolism of the characters' names: Genessier, with its echoes of Genesis, being the creator and Christiane translating into Christian man or his creation. The third part of this irreligious trinity is formed by Genessier's other 'creation', Louise, his dark angel Lucifer.

Thus, when Christiane silences Louise forever and frees the hounds to savage her father, she is explicitly rejecting the constraints of authority, which is simultaneously parental, autocratic and religious. That this is the only way in which she can regain her innocence is indicated by her releasing the doves that will accompany her into the night, her true face revealed to the world. Like man absolved of sin, she has returned to the Garden.

Franju explored these themes again in the non-fantasy oriented *Thérèse Desqueyroux*. In that film, based on the novel by François Mauriac, Emmanuele Riva plays Thérèse, a rural housewife slowly being suffocated by her drab bourgeois lifestyle. In an act of wilful anarchy, she seeks escape by slowly poisoning her husband. When her crime is discovered, she is incarcerated, but her husband refuses to press charges and thus she is compelled to return home with him. Yet home is no less a prison than the one she has been released from; her husband's family confine her to her room and she begins to deteriorate both physically and mentally. It is only when his cruelty is exposed to society that she is allowed to escape to a new life in Paris.

If *Thérèse Desqueyroux* was more 'acceptable' to filmgoers because it contained none of the explicit sadism or overt sexual overtones found within either *La Tête contre les Murs* or *Les Yeux sans Visage*, it lost Franju a lot of support among his former champions in the *nouvelle vague* precisely because of its 'good taste.' Nevertheless, the film is notable less for its thematic values than for Philippe Noiret's portrayal of Thérèse's despotic husband Bernard as a rather vain, pompous and boring individual. What has been described as 'the banality of evil' has seldom been better captured on the screen. Riva also delivers a sterling performance as a woman driven first by frustration, then by her own instinct for survival, to reject the role carved out for her by society. She received the Best Actress award for her performance at the Venice Film Festival.

Pierre Brasseur as a miserable old git in **Pleins Feux sur l'Assassin**.

"A closed door is very distressing... because you don't know what's on the other side." — Attributed to Georges Franju by Jean Louis Castelli

For the screenplay of *Les Yeux sans Visage*, Franju had approached the writing team of Thomas Boileau and Pierre Narcejac to help polish the dialogue. The two writers were old friends who had already established an immense following around the world for a series of offbeat crime novels or *policiers*. Taking the traditions of the classic detective novels of Arthur Conan Doyle and Agatha Christie, they then gleefully turned the stock characters and plot devices on their head to generally subversive effect. Many of their novels were turned into films, most notably *Les Diaboliques* (Henri-Georges Clouzot), *Vertigo* (Alfred Hitchcock) and *Faces in the Dark* (David Eady). The vein of black irony running through *Les Yeux sans Visage* is undoubtedly due to the efforts of the two writers.

Once *Les Yeux sans Visage* was completed, Franju decided to adapt an original screenplay by Boileau and Narcejac. The result was *Pleins Feux sur l'Assassin*.

The film revolves around an article of French law that stipulates a missing person will not be assumed dead until five years after their disappearance. Knowing this to be the case, the dying Count of Kéraudron (Pierre Brasseur) contrives to hide his corpse behind a two-way mirror in one of the rooms of his château, so that his detested family will be unable to claim their inheritance. When said family are informed by the Count's lawyers that they will be responsible for the upkeep of the château for the five years until they can sell it and divide the spoils, their only recourse is to try and raise money by transforming the property into a tourist attraction and mounting a *son et lumière* show in the forecourt. (*Son et lumière* is a theatrical show with no actors, the story being narrated through the use of sound and lighting effects.) No sooner have plans been made for the show, than an unknown assassin begins to kill off members of the family one by one.

In public, Franju expressed enthusiasm for the project: "It's a ghost story without a ghost. What I shall

enjoy is making emptiness live." In private, however, he was at war with the producers, who were worried that it would generate the same sort of controversy as *La Tête contre les Murs* and *Les Yeux sans Visage*. To this end, they insisted on script approval, eliminating potential problem areas such as a proposed lesbian subplot. Franju was also hampered by having to utilise actors with proven box-office drawing power, such as Jean-Louis Trintignant, rather than his usual rep players. As Franju later said, "You can't build anything on an avalanche of concessions."

The finished film is an enjoyable, if unremarkable 'locked room' whodunnit. Despite the producers' earnest efforts, Franju manages to make his presence both seen — he makes a fleeting cameo appearance in the audience for the *son et lumière* performance — and felt — most notably by introducing a note of anarchy at a solemn Catholic funeral, having the coquettish Micheline (Dany Savale) switch on a transistor radio and broadcast a gormless pop tune to interrupt the proceedings. It is also fascinating to see Franju handling comedy, as in the scene where Jean-Marie (Trintignant) confronts Micheline, who he has secreted in one of the château's towers until after the reading of the will, sneaking back to her hiding place having raided the larder for a midnight feast. Their delightful squabble over the food, culminating in a tug of war over a Camembert cheese, proves something of a revelation for a director noted for his solemnity.

In the final estimation, however, the film is more miss than hit and one can only imagine what might have been had Franju been given *carte blanche* to complete the film in his own inimitable way. Certainly he would have made more of the concept that it is the château itself performing the murders, in response to the invasion of its grounds. He would also undoubtedly have livened up the murder sequences, rather than having all but one occur off-screen. There are numerous other hints of the film that was never made — scenes set within circles of standing stones, an old owl which guards the way into the château's tower, the legend narrated by the *son et lumière* show — all just loose ends left dangling at the film's rather perfunctory conclusion.

One positive aspect of the film was that it gave Franju the opportunity to work for the first time with director of photography Marcel Fradetal, who had served as an assistant cameraman on Carl Dreyer's *Vampyr*, which Franju much admired. They were to work together on all of Franju's subsequent feature films, with the exception of *Thérèse Desqueyroux*.

The story of what happened to *Pleins Feux sur l'Assassin* after its general release is infinitely more interesting than the film itself. For many years it was believed to be lost, as neither negative nor any positive prints could be found (an irony considering Franju's work in saving prints of films at the Cinémathèque Française). When questioned about the film, Franju himself could offer no clues as to its whereabouts. After his death, the negative was finally recovered. Like the body of the Count of Kéraudron, it was right under everyone's noses, mistakenly filed away under its working title, *Le Château des Mystères*, in the original processing laboratory. Bernard Queysanne, Franju's former assistant, was given the job of preparing a new print. Having remained unseen in the UK since its début at the Edinburgh Film Festival in 1962, it was given a belated second screening at the French Institute in London in 1993.

"*Feuillade's realism is all the more beautiful because he wasn't trying to be aesthetic...*"
— Georges Franju

Man with bird's head. Channing Pollock in **Judex**.

Fantômas was the fictional creation of writers Marcel Allain and Pierre Souvestre and whose first eponymous adventure had proved to be an enormous success when published in 1911. The book charted the cliffhanging exploits of a French arch-criminal and master of disguise known only as Fantômas and the efforts of the intrepid Inspector Juve to track down and bring to justice this shadowy figure. Although the preposterous plots of the thirty-two Fantômas adventures strained the credibility of even the most forgiving reader, they succeeded purely through the sheer charisma of the title character. Fantômas could be anyone he pleased, changing identity the way that most people change their underwear, and his true identity remained a total mystery. What's more, the reader could never be quite sure of his ultimate motives; each crime hinted at

Judex. *(Right)* *Théo Sarapo carts off Edith Scob. Francine Bergé looks on.*

(Below) The Singing Nun she's not... Francine Bergé administers to Edith Scob.

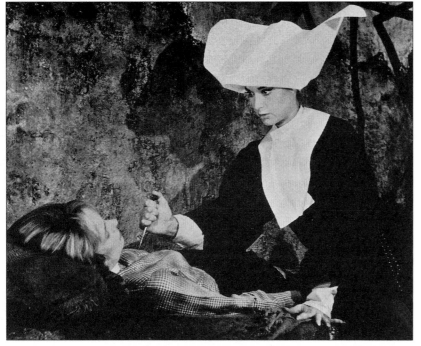

some grand master plan which the villain had devised, yet not even the intrepid Juve could come close to discovering the scheme. This awareness of an even greater mystery yet to be revealed lent an extra *frisson* to the palpable aura of paranoia which the novels engendered. It was this element of anarchy slowly unravelling the fabric of society which so delighted the surrealists, who immediately proclaimed the Fantômas novels to be totally in sympathy with their artistic credo.

The film-maker Louis Feuillade had been reprimanded by the French Ministry of the Interior for making the serials of *Fantômas* and the very similar *Les Vampires*, about a gang of criminals led by the shadowy figure of Irma Vep, on the grounds that the films glamourised criminality. To placate them, he created *Judex*, wherein the cryptic, multi-faced lead character is a force for good rather than evil.

When Franju announced plans to remake *Fantômas*, he was advised against it. The censors, presumably wary of Franju's intentions despite the 'good taste' displayed in both *Pleins Feux sur l'Assassin* and *Thérèse Desqueyroux*, weren't taking any chances and suggested he remake *Judex* instead. Franju railed against the decision: "Fantômas strangles, he poisons, he asphyxiates, he dissolves in acid, he shoots... And what does Judex do? Instead of torturing the dreadful banker Favraux, he awaits a carrier pigeon!" (This was in reference to an event in the script where Judex chooses discretion as the better part of valour.) Nevertheless, working in conjunction with scriptwriter Jacques Champraux, Feuillade's great-grandson, Franju "seized the opportunity."

Despite Franju's initial reservations about the project, he found himself in sympathy with the film. One suspects that this is mainly because he spends less time with the hero Judex (Channing Pollock) than with the scheming villainess Diane Monti (Francine Bergé). The result is certainly one of his finest films, as well as an individual and highly influential masterpiece of fantasy cinema.

Judex not only draws from the films of Feuillade,

but from other disparate echoes from Franju's youth, including Lewis Carroll and de Sade. Having instructed director of photography Marcel Fradetal to film in a pictorial style "somewhere between earth and sky," the film is imbued with a strange dreamlike and fetishistic quality. Witness the scene where the feline Monti strips out of her disguise of a nun's habit to reveal the skin tight black cat-suit beneath, a gleaming stiletto strapped to her hip. Or the remarkable masquerade sequence, where the camera slowly pans up the smart dinner-suited figure of Judex to reveal an elaborate mask depicting a noble bird of prey, before abruptly disclosing the dead dove lying cradled in his outstretched hand. Or the sequence where Judex's night-crawlers scale the sheer brick wall of the house where the virginal Jacqueline (Edith Scob) is being held prisoner. The convoluted plot of *Judex*, revolving around the attempts of the hero to exact revenge on a corrupt banker and bring the wicked Diane Monti to justice, plays second fiddle to its elaborate set pieces.

Despite the censor's best (*sic*) intentions to avoid glamourising villainy, Franju had the last laugh. After the incorruptible Judex has rejected the sexual advances of Diane Monti and she has plunged to her death in their climactic roof-top fight, Franju abruptly cuts to her spreadeagled figure on the ground below. There we find one of the film's symbols of innocence, a young boy who has aided Judex in his mission, silently weeping over her crushed figure. Even in death, the appeal of the villain is stronger than that of the hero.

Franju and Champreux came together again two years later to make *Rencontre avec Fantômas* (1965), a television documentary that charted the history of the extraordinary fictional creation. It was never broadcast outside of France.

"For me...content is a matter of the human condition...and that centres on certain things which I think ought to be asserted...among these is a hatred of the military and a hatred of priests..."
— Georges Franju

Franju's final two films for the cinema were both literary adaptations. The second, and lesser, of these was *La Faute de l'Abbé Mouret* (1970), based on the novel by Emile Zola. Although the subject matter — a Catholic priest rejects his vows to the Virgin Mary and succumbs to the temptations offered by a free-spirited country girl — was in sympathy with Franju's own beliefs of following one's natural instincts rather than those inflicted by society, it was an uncomfortable film. Franju seemed unhappy working in colour rather than monochrome, so much so that the 'sensual' pastoral interludes were overshadowed by the far harsher scenes depicting the monastic life endured by Mouret (Francis Huster) within the church. As the feral girl, Gillian Hills was less than effective and one mourns the fact that the actress for whom the role was originally intended, Brigitte Bardot, had not been on hand to deliver some of her more kittenish eroticism. The end of the film, where Hills is 'punished' by literally smothering to death in wild flowers, was a betrayal of all that Franju stood for.

Far more successful was Franju's adaptation of Jean Cocteau's novel about World War One, *Thomas l'Imposteur* (1964). One can detect the influence of Cocteau's work on Franju's films as far back as *La Première Nuit*, yet this was their first direct collaboration. Cocteau

himself had approved of Franju as a director, because he said that he preferred to be betrayed by him than by anyone else.

The title character is Guillaume Thomas (Fabrice Roleau), a sixteen year-old boy who is too young to fulfil his romantic dreams of becoming a war hero. That is until he innocently discovers people are prepared to believe him when telling them that he is the nephew of the celebrated General de Fontenoy. From that moment onward, he becomes immersed in the lie, joins forces with the altruistic Princesse de Bormes (Emmanuele Riva) in ferrying wounded soldiers back from the front and uses his 'family name' to smooth their passage with the authorities. He becomes so indispensable to the war effort that even when his deception is uncovered, no one dares to reveal his secret. Finally he realises his ambition to fight in the trenches. One day, crossing enemy territory under the mistaken belief that he is going to pick up new orders for his division (the message that awaits him is actually a love letter from his fiancée), he is shot by the enemy. Even as he dies, he is unable to relinquish the fantasy that has become his life, endlessly repeating to himself that he must fake death if he is to survive.

It is interesting to compare the novel of *Thomas l'Imposteur* with the film. The elements one assumes to be Franjuvian — one of the soldiers nicknames himself Fantômas; a wounded veteran tells the story of another crippled soldier who was considered so unlucky that no one in the hospital would go near him, until he became literally overgrown with fungus; the wounded

(Below) **Thomas l'Imposteur** — *Fabrice Rouleau.*

soldiers to be taken back to hospital are selected by pitchfork, as those that scream loudest are the likeliest to survive — are actually taken directly from the novel. On the other hand, the elements which one suspects are Cocteauesque — Thomas shooting at his own reflection in a mirror; a Paris fête which replicates the conditions on the front line; a blazing horse careening through a town square — are actually Franju's inventions. The brief glimpse of Edith Scob, her character identified in the book simply as the anaesthetist's assistant, is a genuinely enigmatic moment in the film.

Common to both novel and film is the central conceit of war as pure theatre. "Ah, the actors prepare," whispers the Princesse de Bormes as she gazes out onto the battlefield. The irony being that both she and Thomas are themselves both acting out their respective roles, he through his all-consuming lie, she

The army of zombies in **L'Homme sans Visage**.

through her self-indulgent transformation into an angel of mercy. Inevitably, their lies are shown to be just part of a far greater deception being inflicted on the world. Everyone in the story is a liar, from the Princesse des Bormes' daughter Henriette (Sophie Dares), who has convinced herself that she is in love with Thomas, to the newspaper editor who prints nothing but fake reports because that is what people want to read. History itself has become a masquerade.

By the end of the film, fantasy and reality have become interchangeable. "Now he was in Fairyland," whispers the voice-over narration of Jean Marais as Thomas jumps up onto the battlefield, bombs bursting overhead like fireworks, and begins running gleefully across no man's land, *en route* to his own extinction.

"...in him, make-believe and reality were one."
— Jean Cocteau, *Thomas l'Imposteur*

After *La Faute de l'Abbé Mouret*, Franju drifted into television work. Few of these productions have been seen outside of France, although a glance down the credits reveals some intriguing projects, including *La Ligne d'Ombres* (1971), an homage to Joseph Conrad.

The only film from Franju's television period to receive any sort of foreign distribution was *L'Homme sans Visage* (1974), starring Jacques Champreux, Gayle Hunnicutt, Gert Frobe and Josephine Chaplin, a *Fantômas*-like thriller about a criminal mastermind out to steal the treasure of a twelfth century sect descended from the Knights Templar. With the help of an army of zombies, he wages war with the descendants of the cult. *L'Homme sans Visage* was originally filmed as an eight-part serial with a total running time of 448 minutes. After its initial telecast, a truncated 105 minute version was issued to cinemas and released abroad under the titles *Shadowman* and *Nuits Rouge*. The short version was, needless to say, a travesty.

Franju's final television film, *Le Dernier Mélodrame* (1977), was based on an outline by Pierre Brasseur and charted the final days of a strolling theatre company. This film marked the last time that Franju was to work with Edith Scob, although they were briefly reunited in 1979 at a retrospective of *Judex* at the ninth Festival de Paris du Film Fantastique.

A few years before his death in 1987, Franju received an honorary nomination as artistic director of the Cinémathèque Française.

That Franju never really received the recognition he deserved in his lifetime is perhaps unsurprising. His films were often too brutal and his themes too personal for a general audience. Watching his films today, one is aware that they are the work of someone not quite at home in his era. Perfectly acceptable events for the time — Genessier's skullduggery abruptly interrupted by a airplane passing overhead, Judex observing his prisoner on a closed circuit television — seem nevertheless anachronistic in Franju's world. It is not an overstatement to say that a viewer unaware of the films' dates of production would probably have difficulty placing them within the context of modern cinema. Or put another way, Franju's work is genuinely timeless.

Whatever his shortcomings, Franju helped keep alive for future generations an era of film that could easily have slipped into obscurity, both through his films and through his work as an archivist. Indeed, had he never exposed a single frame of film to the light, he would have earned his place in the history of the cinema. ■

SHADOWMAN A JACQUES CHAMPREUX • GAYLE HUNNICUTT
(L'HOMME SANS VISAGE) JOSEPHINE CHAPLIN • GERT FROEBE
Directed by: GEORGES FRANJU

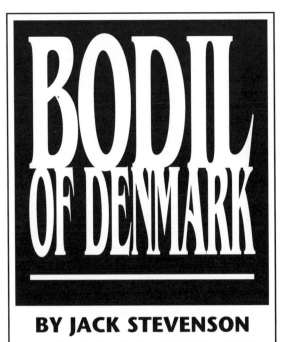

BODIL OF DENMARK

BY JACK STEVENSON

'...to make everybody feel a bit more at ease, we started with a few outdoor shots of Bodil riding her stallion on the beach and along a gorgeous country lane flanked by beautiful, blooming yellow mustard fields. We had her dress in her own spanking white riding breeches, jodhpurs, knee-length riding boots and duck-billed riding cap. In cutting we used this footage for the opening of the Bodil sequence, to make the contrast with the later animal sequences all the more striking while at the same time saying, "Look, here is a girl who not only makes porno films with animals and lives in a filthy, smelly house, but who can also dress up nicely, is a good rider and is nice and sensitive a girl as any other."'

Phyllis and Eberhard Kronhausen, *The Sex People*, 1975.

Bodil Joensen was born in Denmark in 1945, but her birth as an *outré* porno celebrity would officially occur in March 1969, the year Denmark passed its celebrated anti-censorship legislation, freeing all pictorial representation. All written text had been 'freed' since the passage of a similar law in 1967. The 1969 legislation had two related effects.

Firstly, it gave economic sanction to the newly forming Danish hardcore porno industry, officially anointed soon after with Sex 69, a sex trade fair held in Copenhagen, so popular it had to turn away 1,000 people a day. By the early '70s, pornography would rank second after agriculture as Denmark's largest export commodity.

Erotic cinema in America and Europe had for some years been inching towards hardcore explicitness, but in the US a confusing patchwork of local obscenity statutes would inhibit the formation of an 'industry' for roughly another two years. Now, suddenly, on the cusp of the '60s, when all Western societies seemed to be questioning the sexual *status quo*, here was a country with 'no holds barred'!

Secondly, Denmark, like its fellow Scandinavian countries, was blessed with an abundance of good-looking women, and now with the 'Freedom Law' the rest of the world began to idealise it as some sort of liberated paradise of sexual freedom — an open, natural society, far more enlightened than uptight countries like America or Germany (who would quickly become the biggest buyers of Danish product).

Whatever the reality, Denmark was suddenly hot property. People were curious.

Throughout 1969, 1970 and 1971, a swarm of sex researchers, documentarians and independent filmmakers, armed with their new freedom, descended on Denmark, along with professional photographers from the USA and Europe, in search of product, subject matter and myth.

Bodil was to be their most exotic find. They larded their 'studies' of Danish sexual freedom with noble talk of enlightenment and personal expression, while Bodil herself went about it with all the naive enthusiasm of a small town girl about to become one of the

Bodil — just a regular girl with a peculiar fondness for animals...

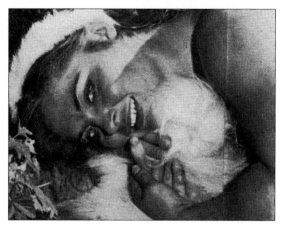

That's it for the udder one...Bodil and friend make an unk unk unk*ing noise...*

most exploited 'actresses' in the history of cinema, and also one of the most enigmatic.

The Movies

Bodil was featured in numerous films produced in the busy 1970-72 period, everything from full-crew 35mm productions to amateur shorts shot with hand-held 8mm and 16mm cameras. As was generally the practice in hardcore, footage was commonly bought and sold and subsequently mixed into any number of productions, rendering an attempted 'definitive' filmography irrelevant if not futile...

Ole Ege, a Danish film-maker and ex-photographer, co-produced one of the most unique films starring Bodil. Starting out in the sex magazine field in the 1950s, Ege would eventually turn his energies to film, and in 1968 formed Marmalade Films, his own production company specialising in 8mm porno shorts. Today, Ege heads the Copenhagen Erotic Museum which houses his extensive collection of vintage erotic photographs and artifacts.

In 1970, Ege was introduced to Shinkichi Tajiri, a Japanese-American who inhabited a castle in Holland and taught at the Art Academy in Berlin. (Tajiri is still well known in Berlin in avant-garde circles.) He had already shot a 16mm short entitled *The Viper*, which had been awarded a prize at Cannes. He suggested to Ege that they make a film about Bodil. Ege was repulsed by bestiality, but Tajiri managed to sway him. They paid Bodil 2,000 Danish Kroner; Ege filmed and Tajiri acted as soundman. The sound equipment malfunctioned, so the planned live-sound dialogue with Bodil was replaced with classical music: Beethoven's *Pastorale*. The result was a twenty minute colour documentary, shot in 16mm and entitled simply *Bodil, a Summerday in 1970*. The film won a top prize at the Wet Dream Festival in Amsterdam that year.

Ege recalls the film, shot on Bodil's farm in northwest Sealand, a three hour drive from Copenhagen. "Tajiri and I drive around with Bodil, who has a sperm supply, to the farmers in the neighbourhood. Her van has a sign saying 'Dreamlight covers Odsherred' — the name of her horse and the area, respectively. The boar or the stallion is in the truck, the farmers give her a hand at the mating and Bodil enjoys the activities, burning one cigarette after another. When she plays her erotic game with the dog or the horse, it is not only a sexual curiosum, it is an erotic play with animals she loves and who are devoted to her." Ege, like many others who dealt with Bodil, found her genuinely likable.

The first half of *Bodil, a Summerday in 1970* is replete with scenes of Bodil wrestling and coaxing her charges while her skimpy work dress rides halfway up her backside. This is intercut with shots of her naked, riding her horse around a field. Her past is also explored as the camera scans over family portraits and photos. We see Bodil as a child and as a schoolgirl, Bodil with brothers and sisters, with her parents, in group shots with classmates at graduation. There are several black and white photos of a young Bodil with her favourite Collie dog standing apart from other people. At the age of twelve or thirteen, her dog licked her between the legs and that was the start of it. She wanted to become a vet, but never finished her education, and went into animal husbandry instead.

As a twenty-five year old woman in *...Summerday*, she is on the heavy, raw-boned side but with a certain buxom, broad-faced beauty. In a shocking yet somehow natural turn, the film's second half displays explicit bestiality as Bodil performs with dog, horse and hog. The classical soundtrack tends to give the film an intermittently majestic, overblown, bizarre and poetic feel, yet forces the viewer to draw impressions based on the visual images alone. The hand-held *ciné-verité* style camerawork gives the film an authentic, intimate resonance. It holds up well today, unlike many of the pseudo-documentaries so prevalent at the time, which now appear dated and ridiculously transparent.

It's also a film of seemingly irreconcilable contradictions: a sympathetic treatment of what most consider abhorrent and perverted — a non-exploitative take on a subject loaded with exploitative potential.

Ege made another film soon after entitled *Pornography*. It was scored with a jazz soundtrack by Dexter Gordon and employs a personal, underground-style approach. *Pornography* comprised four segments, one of which starred Denmark's now infamous 'Animal Girl', Bodil. Ege possesses the only known print, and showed it at the Erotic Museum cinema shortly after it opened in summer 1992.

The Girl and the Boar was another short film of Bodil shot by Ege. This may or may not have been the segment used in both *Pornography* and *Sexual Liberty Now*. Ege recalls that Bodil wasn't hard to find in those days and was willing to be a model. "Lots" of film-makers employed her, he says. Bodil had a well-rehearsed repertoire of sexual acts with an unchanging cast of animal companions and there is very little variation from film to film. She needed no 'direction' — the film-makers simply set up and shot...

But to appreciate the accomplishments of *...Summerday*, it should be seen alongside its brain-damaged twin, *Animal Lover*, perhaps the crudest and rudest exploitation film ever.

Animal Lover surfaced in America in 1971, imported by Alex De Renzy who, along with fellow San Franciscans Jim and Art Mitchell, pioneered the US hardcore scene in late 1969.

Since his visit to Copenhagen for Sex 69, De Renzy had contacts in Denmark and an interest in Danish product. As noted, Denmark was suddenly in style and numerous were the films of the period dealing with Danish sexuality: *Sexual Freedom in Denmark*, *A Day with Ilse*, *Dagmar's Hot Pants*, *Wide Open Copenhagen*, *Pornography in Denmark* and so forth. De Renzy's first major success was, in fact, *Censorship in Denmark — A New Approach*, a film containing on the street interviews and other documentary nuggets.

In the finest tradition of porno cinema, *Animal Lover*

dogs climax in your mouth?" he indelicately continues. She chokes on her anguish...admits she made love to dogs orally. Eventually freed, she is dumped penniless and near-naked on a desolate road, forced to resort to prostitution in order to purchase a ticket back to America.

The 'victimised' girl was no doubt an actress hired for the film, but it's all pretty dramatic and revolting nonetheless. The misfortunes of 'fallen women' have proven big box-office ever since the the turn of the century, when White Slave Trade scandals were all the rage, but this section of *Animal Lover* must rank as one of the most misguided, ghastly and hideous attempts at titillation ever. What kind of human being could find this arousing?

The film then inexplicably cuts into the Danish production, which De Renzy further lengthens with four 'on the street' interviews filmed in Copenhagen — probably shot during the making of *Censorship in Denmark*. An off-screen interviewer (De Renzy?) asks passers-by — half of whom turn out to be American tourists — what they think of pornography. Denmark's rotund, "largest producer of pornography" is interviewed in his bookshop while Gitte, an attractive and embarrassed blonde clerk, is verbally prodded into showing the cameras a sampling of hardcore magazines.

Bodil's stock repertoire of sex acts is almost identical to those shown in the other films, but here there are more close-ups and zoom shots, and the scenes last longer, with little camera movement. The colours on the print I viewed were bright and lurid. This is pure pornography, shorn of any 'scientific' or artistic rationalisation. For the merely curious it becomes a relentless, almost brutal experience and recalls the old adage of 'Be careful what you ask for, you might get it.'

Some people still remember *Animal Lover*'s short run at De Renzy's Screening Room cinema in 1971 — the show was reportedly shut down by an outraged public two weeks after it opened. This in America's most liberated city in an era of almost radical permissiveness. However, it played elsewhere on the burgeoning, new

(Above) The sleazy, incoherent 'expert' from **Animal Lover**. *Would you buy a coat-hanger abortion from this man?*

(Left) Bodil and 'Svend Nielsen'.

(Below) One of the many early '70s smut 'classics' to flood the market... Whither **Wide Open Copenhagen**?

(in its American version anyway) is a patchwork conglomeration of several films. The core footage is a self-contained, forty minute film produced in Denmark in 1970 by Willy Børgstrom and Grøndahl Films, directed by Freddy Hansen and photographed by Paul Møller. It opens with an introduction by a Danish narrator who identifies himself as Svend Nielsen. Svend then proceeds to interview "our little farm girl, Bodil" as the two sit on chairs outdoors, Bodil flanked by Lassie, her beloved Collie. Nielsen questions Bodil in Danish and gives somewhat different answers back to the camera in English, occasionally mixing up the two languages. His command of English was little better than Bodil's own, which appears to be non-existent — unusual for a Dane. Nielsen concludes the interview with an awkward plea for total human freedom, citing the 1969 Freedom Law and promising the viewers that they are about to see things they have never dreamed of in their wildest imaginations. They proceed to the barn where Bodil performs with horse, dog and boar.

Evidently De Renzy needed to stretch the film out to feature length and tacked on a twenty minute 'lecture' to the opening. An unnamed 'expert' attempts to contextualise bestiality in an historically valid, naturalistic vein. The result is quite the opposite and what we get instead is one of the most appallingly inept and bizarre performances of fraudulent expertise ever filmed.

The lecture is delivered in a halting fashion by a scurrilous looking, moustachioed fellow wearing thick glasses and a red polka dot tie. He appears to be about fifty-five and could pass for a seller of junk automobiles or a coat-hanger abortionist. Aimlessly citing facts, figures and examples from history, our host emerges from behind his desk and lurches ahead without the aid of notes. He unravels...he rambles on the verge of incoherency, repeats himself, loses track — staring into the camera — and mispronounces words. He refers to the "film you're about to see" and it seems to be a different film entirely.

Next he conducts an interview with a young lady whom he introduces as a secretary from San Mateo, a suburb south of San Francisco. He sits side-saddle on the couch, socks exposed as trouser legs ride halfway up to his knees, she in a chair, face hidden in shadow.

She tells her story of travelling to Marrakesh. Snatched off the street by sadistic Arab men, she's enslaved in a sex compound for months and repeatedly raped by "whoever wanted me." She witnesses a girl raped by dogs who bleeds to death, the dogs lapping up the blood... "Did *you* have sex with dogs?" he prods through her sobs provoked by the memory. "Did the

DAGMAR'S **HOT PANTS** ✗   Starring **Diana Kjaer** : **Robert Strauss**   **Anne Grete**   A TRANS-AMERICAN FILMS-UNICORN ENTERPRISES PICTURE   🐐 A TIGON PICTURES RELEASE   Color by Movielab

product-hungry circuit of West Coast porn theatres. Kenneth Turan and Stephen Zito reported in *Sinema*, their 1973 book, that the film had been 'successful in finding at least a limited audience.' But the film had a resonance beyond mere audience counts and box-office grosses and would become the stuff of underground legend.

Other films appropriated footage of Bodil for shock effect, such as *Sexual Liberty Now*, which used only the startling and rumoured-to-be-dangerous scenes of her coupling with a hog.

The most well known film featuring Bodil was *Why?* (*Hvorfor Gør De Det?* [Why Do They Do It?], 1971), produced by American sex researchers Phyllis and Eberhard Kronhausen who were living in Denmark in the early '70s. Previous to this the Kronhausens had produced an anthology of 1920s and '30s hardcore stag films entitled *Porno Pop*. They would also become known for their exceptional collection of erotic art displayed at the San Francisco Museum of Erotic Art (which can be seen pictured in the 1974 hardcore film *Sip the Wine*) and for publishing *The Sex People* in 1975.

Bodil is the focus of the third segment in the three-part *Why?*, which deals with 'the psychology and sociology of the Danish live sex show business as it flourished in 1970 and 1971', as the Kronhausens describe it in *The Sex People*. Bodil, a 'live sex performer'? Indeed she was — for the cameras if not the public...

Bodil's scenes were once again filmed at her farm in Odsherred. (In her interview in *Animal Lover*, Bodil says that her dream is to someday own her own farm with all the animals around her, indicating she was not the owner of the often-photographed premises shown in so many porno films and magazines.) Bodil performs with her bull Sofus, her dog Lassie and with Dreamlight, her stallion whom she can only fondle due to the physical impossibility of human/horse copulation. "You can't do it with a stallion, he'd split you apart," she wistfully remarks. She found it necessary to feed Sofus and Lassie Yohimbene, an aphrodisiac widely used in Africa in its root form. She would knead soft bread into a ball and add in two pills, which she fed to the animals.

By this time Bodil had a boyfriend who worked as a guard at a nearby prison. He helped her transport the animals and practiced bestiality himself. They even had sex with each other, as captured on film in *Why?* — two human beings having heterosexual intercourse!

In form and structure, *Why?* was yet another of the episodic 'educational documentaries' that were all too numerous — and usually suspect — in 1970 and '71 before narrative hardcore dramas gained prominence with *Deep Throat* and *Behind the Green Door*. Yet it was one of the most honest, well-produced and factually grounded of the 'white coaters'.

Bodil

Contradictions. Here was a simple country girl who tells Svend Nielsen her desire in life is just to get her own farm and live quietly with all her animals around her, and in the next breath attempts (unsuccessfully) to feign a hard, experienced tone when she tells him she's been in the porno business a full year now. She clearly welcomed the attention of the porno industry and became a willing and accessible 'model', yet she was anything but a jaded porn star. Bestiality was the most natural thing in the world to her, but she wasn't above making money from the photo and film shoots and becoming a star after her own fashion. Her magazines can *still* be purchased in adult bookshops that stock bestiality material!

While her workmanlike attitude and enthusiastic willingness comes off as raw or as downright simple-mindedness to some, to others it exudes a certain innocence or even charm. Most of those who met her describe her as a sweet if rather strange young lady.

But it is Bodil's earnest, innocent demeanour while performing the most taboo of sexual acts that shocks people as much as the acts themselves. They are forced to think, 'Who *is* this woman?', which disrupts the anonymous fantasy that is integral to pornography as an interactive discipline. Others are put off by her aggressiveness, because they want to see the girl get raped by the animals — not the other way around. Undeniably it's part freak show, part porn performance.

Bodil first became 'known' in her rural neighbourhood when her magazines were distributed there. In 1970, she told Svend Nielsen that her neighbours understand what she's doing and act friendly towards her; they understand it's a way for her to make money. Nielsen paraphrases a passage in a magazine that testifies to the easy-going atmosphere, describing how the local butcher gives her bones to take back for her dog.

Evidently all this would change quickly, as roughly a year later the Kronhausens' film crew was denied permission to even park in the lot of a restaurant across the road from Bodil's farm. In a very short space of time, Bodil would become one of the most ostracised and controversial of all Danish porno models, actors and performers — perpetual target of rumours that she was feeble-minded, in prison or had committed suicide.

The rumours came true, in part, in the early 1980s when Bodil committed suicide after a period of depression.

Most of what we can discern about Bodil comes from small details and nuances that glimmer through the maw of porno left as her legacy: Bodil wearing her customary headband and Cleopatra eye make-up, which Kronhausen observed heightened the bizarre impression she made and gave her a 'little girl playing a movie star' look... Bodil talking about her mother, who considered sex to be dirty... Her insistence on greeting every member of Kronhausen's crew with a certain awkwardness and stiff handshake... Her locket, observed in *Why?*, which contained a photo of her dog Lassie... ■

(Top) Bodil!

(Middle) Bodil!!

(Bottom) Bodil!!!

(Right) Bodil!!!!

NICKELS AND DIMES AND NO TIME

THE UPS AND DOWNS OF LINDSAY SHONTEFF

BY ALLAN BRYCE

If the name of Lindsay Shonteff is familiar to you, then the chances are that you're either a close friend of the family or a train-spotting genre buff who has it marked down from the credits of his two best-known horror flicks, *Devil Doll* and *Curse of Simba*. However, it may come as a surprise to even the most goggle-eyed, anorak-wearing cineaste that this man has a list of some twenty-four movies to his credit, most of which are harder to find than Lord Lucan's forwarding address. And he's still making pictures today, though they don't actually seem to be showing anywhere...

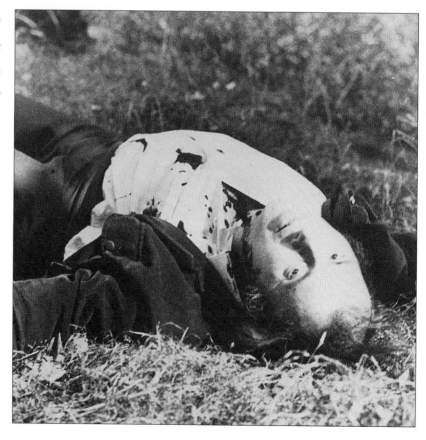

(Previous page) Dead person from **The Fast Kill**.

(Right) 'Dirty Harriet' — Linda Marlowe in **Big Zapper**.

I first became interested in Lindsay Shonteff movies in the early '70s, when I spent an unhealthy amount of time frequenting the lower class of London soft porn cinemas — the sort of places where even the cockroaches wore dark glasses to avoid being recognised. It was there that I sampled the sleazy delights of Shonteff's *The Yes Girls*, with Malcolm Muggeridge's niece, Sally. (Sally was in the film — I didn't take her to the cinema.)

I also got the once-in-a-lifetime chance to attend the London première of *Night After Night After Night*, a cautionary Shonteff tale of a cross-dressing psychotic judge who smudges his lipstick wiping out back-street prossies. Lindsay couldn't make it to the opening, but I enjoyed it immensely, along with two blokes in raincoats and an ice-cream vendor of indeterminate sex. *The Times* ignored it, but the film got a favourable review in *Playbirds*...

The archetypal Lindsay Shonteff movie is a sexy spy spoof, usually starring the sort of people who turn up on *Celebrity Squares* or doing coffee adverts when you could have sworn they were dead. "I really hate making those kind of films," he says. "But they seem to make money." I guess all great artists have to make compromises. Who else but Shonteff could think of casting Cleo Rocos as Miss Juicy Pair or Walter Gabriel out of *The Archers* as a knife-wielding loony? And is it sheer coincidence that Lindsay's biggest star, Tom Adams, went on to small screen superstardom in the Allied Carpets adverts?

It has become quite fashionable in recent times for a critic who is out to make a name for himself to home in on the work of a little known director. They can then churn out a lot of nonsense that nobody can argue with because they haven't seen the movies in question. And if they sing this auteur's praises long and loud enough, then other lost souls will inevitably take up the same clarion cry. It's the celluloid equivalent of joining the church of Jim Jones (though I'd sooner have a Kool Aid with a skull and crossbones on the side than sit through the collected work of Jess Franco).

Anyway... This might at first glance seem to be my bid for pseud status, with all you wanted to know (and a lot more you didn't) about Lindsay Shonteff. But I'm not out to try to convince you that an encounter with one of Lindsay's movies will change your life. That way lies madness. Let's not beat about the bush here: even the man himself admits that the backers of one of his recent movies wanted to commit suicide when they saw the result of his efforts...

The simple fact is that there are a lot of peripheral pleasures to be gleaned from watching Lindsay's movies, especially in these days of factory-line blandness, where the same old plots are recycled into an endless succession of big screen TV movies... See enough of Lindsay's films and you'll begin to appreciate the recurring elements that add that unique Shonteff flavour: the oddball casting, the bizarre locations (Gerrards Cross standing in for Vietnam), the sleazy characters (he doesn't like the word sleazy to be applied to his productions, but if the cap fits...), the constant bouts of explosive violence that go on far too long to be convincing, his imaginative use of widescreen and, of course, the completely incomprehensible plots.

My quest to find the man behind the movies led me

to a smart detached property on a new estate in Berkshire, where Lindsay lives with his wife Elizabeth. After being bowled over by the family Alsatian, I was welcomed into the lounge by the big, friendly, bear-like man whose husky voice retains its Canadian accent despite a lifetime in the UK. There are no film posters on the walls and he has precious little publicity material from his own movies. Perhaps this is indicative of his love/hate relationship with the movie biz. It's obvious he's a bit depressed about his current circumstances. There are no green shoots appearing in the barren wasteland that was once the British film industry.

For years he has been producing movies independently and flogging them off, territory by territory, at international film markets. The latest is a western called *The Gunfighter*, which he has just shot on 35mm, mostly with his own money. With all those movies under his belt, Lindsay might at least have expected to have achieved some measure of financial stability. But his is a familiar story in which the chief ingredients are industry backstabbing and the practiced dishonesty of distributors and studio bosses.

"I've grown weary of making English films that never earn any money in England," he sighs. "It's a closed shop here. The guys who buy and sell live in a festival cocktail party land and don't want to know about much else. They buy films by the yard through agents. Perhaps if they bought some of my movies it might result in more British movies being made with the revenue. But then what right has an unknown film director to complain about his home television market when they can give the bullet to a comic genius like Benny Hill, who was the biggest foreign money earner they ever had...?" That gives you some kind of idea of where Lindsay's coming from.

The best known of Lindsay's pictures is probably *Licensed to Kill*, a snappy 1965 Bond spoof starring Tom Adams as the super-slick secret agent Charles Vine. But I can't imagine that blatantly commercial movies like this, and low budget B-movie programmers like Shonteff's *The Fast Kill* and *Big Zapper*, are ever likely to be the subject of intense intellectual discussion in the bar at the NFT.

Lindsay himself is very self-depreciating about his work. He's the first to admit that a number of his movies have been complete disasters. But to my mind, even the least of them is a lot more fun to sit through than some of the pap that's clogging up video shop shelves at the present.

Shonteff left school at sixteen and went to work in an art studio to help support his family. But movies were always an overriding interest and he saved up the money to make his first, an 8mm short, when he was just eighteen years old. He explains, "I found an actor who was willing to work for nothing and we went out and shot a thing called *The Bum*, about a tramp living in the streets of Toronto. The story is that he robs a blind man and pays for his crime by getting hit with a truck." He chuckles in reminiscence. "That film had all the flaws that you would expect to find in an amateur production: camera angles all over the place and so on..."

So you could say *The Bum* was starting at the bottom. But it was a capable enough effort to gain him some sort of entry into the film business. Explains Shonteff: "I took it to a motion picture company in Ottawa and asked if I could get a job there. The head of the company said I had film sense, which was very kind of him, but the only job he could offer me was

humping and carrying camera equipment." He took that for a few months, then went back to Toronto because he had heard of two guys who were making a feature film called *Ivy League Killers*. He went to see them and volunteered his services to do any job at all. They kept him at his word and he ended up sweeping floors, making coffee, carrying bits and pieces of equipment here and there, and so on.

"Of course that experience was invaluable. I saw a film being put together from inception to completion. And best of all, I had the opportunity of working with the director in the cutting room after he finished shooting the picture. The director was a film-maker named Bill Davidson, and he really knew what he was doing. Anyway, during the shooting, he was directing one particular sequence and when it was finished he shouted, 'Cut! Print it!' Well, the entire crew were looking at each other and laughing up their sleeves, because the scene that he had said to print was just terrible: the acting was pathetic and it just didn't work in any way. They expected him to do it over again.

"But weeks later in the cutting room, he took this particular scene, put it in the movieola, slammed his foot on the foot pedal and zapped straight through the take without even looking at it. When he got to the last ten feet he stopped. He kept about three feet from a take that ran about 300 feet. What he was looking for was a certain reaction from one particular actor in the take. And I guess that no one else saw this reaction at the time except him. Subsequently I've had the same kind of experience on just about every film I've made. I've yet to work with a crew that didn't think they knew more about the art of motion picture making than me, and for these very reasons I don't think that anyone can really know what's happening on a film except the director."

Shonteff developed a great respect for Davidson, who told him: "The only way you can really make a good picture is to disappear for three months in the woods with a camera and a few actors." Davidson was also candid about the financial perils of the industry: "I remember Bill saying to me that he couldn't afford to get shoes for his kids, but the cameraman would probably be able to buy himself a new car from the production. Like a lot of film-makers, he was working for love, but technicians had to be well paid, which I guess is not unreasonable. To most of them it's just a job."

Shonteff wasn't discouraged, though. He moved on

Edina Ronay and the doomed Alan Lake canoodle in **The Swordsman**...

to a similar gopher position on a television western series that was being shot in Toronto. "It was about some pioneers from the 1850s or whatever, and I met Sid Furie there — he's the guy who directed *The Ipcress File*. I told him I was hoping to make a small picture with some money I was going to borrow from my two sisters and my brother. His advice was: 'Don't even think about it, just go out and do it. Because if you think about it, you probably won't *ever* do it.' So I did go out and make a picture, called *The Hired Gun*, which was shot in six days, in black and white. It was pretty terrible, but the gunfights were well staged!"

On the strength of that, the twenty year-old director managed to get a TV pilot based on the Guy de Maupassant short story, 'The Madman'. It was shot in 35mm and ran about thirty minutes. "The initial idea was that it would be extended by two other short pro-

Bryant Halliday demonstrates his star qualities in a couple of Lindsay's classics...

jects to make up an hour and a half. But unfortunately the company backing it ran out of money and couldn't do the other two shows."

In the meantime, Sidney Furie had travelled to England and was working on a film called *The Boys* for up-and-coming production company Gala Films. Out of work and despondent, Lindsay fired off a letter to Furie, expressing his frustration at months of inactivity in Toronto. In reply, Furie suggested he come over to England and said he would do his best to help Shonteff out. "So I packed my bags and came over here," says Shonteff. "And Sid did just that. It took maybe six or seven months of knocking around in cheap hotel rooms, but when you're young it's no problem. In fact it's quite enjoyable. And he did get me a feature. It was *Devil Doll*, a two week picture that came out pretty well."

In fact, *Devil Doll* was shot in twelve days. It was the chilling tale of a ventriloquist's dummy that came to life and murdered people. Many critics have pointed out its obvious resemblance to the scary Michael Redgrave story from *Dead of Night*, though Shonteff tells me that he has never seen this classic Ealing horror movie. "Bryant Halliday was chosen to play the lead because he had money in the project. But in spite of that financial muscle he was perfect for the role. I think he's living in Paris nowadays. It was produced by Dick Gordon, and just recently I gather he's been talking about making *Devil Doll 2*!"

The film did extremely well in foreign sales, and thanks to that, Lindsay got another low budget chiller to direct, called *Curse of Simba* (frequently known as *Curse of the Voodoo*). Shot in eighteen days amid the wilds of Hampstead Heath, it starred Halliday as a big game hunter who is cursed by an African tribal chief when he kills a sacred lion. Back in England he suffers some scary hallucinations, which force him to return to the scene of the crime, where he faces up to and kills his voodoo tormentor, thus ending the curse. Little shown nowadays, the film is nevertheless regarded as superior of its kind, with a nod to the low-key atmospherics of early Val Lewton pictures.

The film business was a fun business to be in in the mid-'60s. There were quite a number of small production companies based in London at the time and Shonteff was approached by one of them — Golden Era — to make a James Bond spy spoof called *Licensed to Kill*. Scripted by Shonteff and Howard Griffiths, it told of how secret agent Charles Vine (Tom Adams) was hired to protect a Swedish scientist (Karel Stepanek) and his anti-gravity machine from a small army of Russian spies and assassins. There were shoot outs in Docklands, plus the usual sleazy tour of West End sex dens, and a classic final scene where a hired killer takes his shoes off to sneak up on our hero — revealing huge holes in his socks. You wouldn't get that in a Bond movie. It went on to make a fortune for US distributor Joe Levine when he retitled it *The Second Best Secret Agent in the Whole Wide World* and got Sammy Davis Jr to sing the title song.

While he was waiting for *Licensed to Kill* to be released, Shonteff also made a low budget drama — again for Golden Era — called *Run with the Wind*. It was the story of a young girl who leaves her lover to start a new relationship with a folk singer (long-haired Shawn Phillips). This overly sentimental film was a box-office failure in England, but sold to the USA and received favourable reviews praising its honesty and efficiency. It also featured a good performance by

Francesca Annis, who Shonteff chose over Shirley Anne Field for the lead role (at the cost of Embassy Films withdrawing from the project).

Licensed to Kill had become the director's most financially successful film to date, and on the strength of it he was approached by a major league producer/screenwriter named John Kohn, who had worked with William Wyler on *The Collector*. "I was real flattered that Kohn would want me to direct a picture for him," says Shonteff. "He took me to Columbia pictures and I got a five picture contract with the studio, and a five-picture contract with Kohn. I thought I had finally made it to the big league."

But it was obvious from the word go that he wasn't going to fit in with the system. "One of the first things I got to do was to direct this screen test at Columbia," says Lindsay. "And I had this young guy there from the studio telling me how I should direct the actors, you know? Telling an actor how to pick up a spoon and open a door. How you open a door is you turn the handle and walk in. Actors know how to do these things. The guy was driving me nuts, so I said '*You do it,*' and I walked."

Lindsay then made what he now considers to be two of the most foolish decisions of his life. Firstly he got himself an agent, and secondly he listened to her advice. "John Kohn was putting together a movie in Hollywood called *Fathom* (*eventually directed by Leslie H. Martinson, with Raquel Welch as a sexy spy*)," explains Shonteff, "and I was going to direct it. At the same time, I was offered a picture in Hong Kong called *Su-Muru* for a producer named Harry Alan Towers, with Frankie Avalon, Klaus Kinski and George Nader. Just going to Hong Kong sounded great to me, and the cast was wonderful. I asked my agent for advice and she said: 'A bird in the hand is worth two in the bush.' So I took the film in Hong Kong.

"Two weeks later, Kohn phoned to say that *Fathom* was on, but I was in Hong Kong, and that was the end of my relationship with John Kohn. Very foolish. I found out later my agent didn't want me to work with Kohn anyway, for her own reasons. I was very young, and influenced very easily."

But at least he got to work with the legendary Harry Alan Towers, and *The Million Eyes of Su-Muru* was a hoot! It was a sort of tongue-in-cheek female Fu Manchu picture, starring Shirley Eaton as the leader of a female organisation bent on enslaving mankind. Shonteff says that making the movie turned out to be a very enjoyable experience: "I liked all the actors and the people I was working with. I saw the script as a straight comedy, with Frankie Avalon and George Nader as kind of a Mutt and Jeff duo. George came up with a lot of funny ideas for the picture, and Klaus Kinski was absolutely fantastic in terms of comedy. He was always coming up with ideas that I incorporated at every opportunity.

"One of them was that when somebody in the movie went to meet his character in a hotel room, the place would appear empty until Kinski made his entrance from under a pile of pillows on the couch! Another one was that his tongue was like a rattlesnake's, and that throughout the whole movie, whenever he saw a pretty girl, he would stick it out and try to lick her! They took all that stuff out, of course. But if you look closely at the film you'll see Kinski's tongue just start to come out and they'll cut to somebody else. He was sort of a crazy guy, but very talented."

Shonteff's problems started when the movie got to

the post-production stage. "When they came to cut the movie, they cut every one of these funny scenes out of the picture, which left a different picture to the one I was making. Then they shot some additional stuff to cover the holes. I think they thought I was a madman, and that didn't help my career too much. But I think it could have been a very funny movie if they'd left it the way myself and the actors had put it together."

To add insult to injury, when Shonteff returned to London he discovered that in his absence he had been offered — and his agent had turned down — a deal with a major agency in Hollywood. "They said they could get me pictures in Hollywood and split the commission with my agent in London. But my agent had replied I wasn't interested." He sighs deeply at the memory. "And at that point I parted company with my agent, and walked straight into the wilderness. At the time I thought I was being incredibly brave. Now I realise I was being incredibly stupid..."

After a very short while he realised he was unemployable, and the only way round it was to employ myself. Luckily, this coincided with a friend of his, who was a cameraman in Canada, coming over to London with a little money that he wanted to invest in a low budget feature. The result was *Clegg*, a gutsy private eye thriller containing lots of violent shoot-outs, beatings and naked women. "It was made for peanuts," says Lindsay, "shot for £6,000 and my blood. The final budget was something like £11,000 for a colour 35mm feature, which meant making a lot of tough deals, paying people very little money and shooting in four weeks. But we finished it and the picture did okay."

In fact it did more than okay. It did so well that the distributors, Tigon, swiftly hired Shonteff to make a modest movie about the permissive pop scene as it was in those swinging days. He came up with a script called *Susy Superscrew*, about pop groups and the groupies that follow them. The censor didn't like the title, so it inherited the working titles of *The Now Child* and then simply *The X Project*, before finally being released as *Permissive*.

"I think it was a pretty good little film," he reminisces. "It was about a young girl who gets involved with a pop group, and it ruins her life. She ends up committing suicide. I used an original pop group called Forever More, and an unknown actress called Maggie Stride who hadn't had much experience but did as much as she could with the role. The film was made on less than £20,000, and I got a pretty good fee out of it."

The profits he made from *Permissive* were put straight back into his next movie, another sexploitation

Woman with cigar, apparently an actress in **Night After Night After Night**...

Fast Kill, a violent robbery actioner that got one of the biggest releases of his movies when it was picked up by Fox and went out as a second feature to the Lee Marvin/Gene Hackman gangster movie, *Prime Cut*.

Shonteff's *Licensed to Kill* star Tom Adams took top billing in this one as a ruthless crook who plans a diamond heist with split second precision. His straightforward scheme involves killing all the cops who arrive on the scene — machine-gunning them gleefully to death in a scene that goes on for about five minutes — and driving at great speed to the airport, where a plane is waiting to carry the crooks to freedom — with the usual round of double-crosses!

Shot in just under four weeks on a minuscule budget (against a backdrop of bleak Docklands locations that long ago fell victim to yuppie property development), Shonteff thinks this was just "an okay film." But it's one of my own favourites, not least for its compellingly weird assortment of characters, all of whom seem to have some sort of perverted skeleton in their closet. Patricia Haines is particularly memorable as a butch lesbian marksman — or should that be marksperson? The blood-spattered climax sees them all knifed/shot/strangled to death — a suitable punishment for murdering our poor, decent boys in blue!

Shonteff's own production company was now in full swing, and he kept rolling along from one film to another, financed mainly by the foreign sales that kept coming in. "I really made a lot of junk," he admits. "But in amongst the junk there were a few good movies."

One of the movies that could have been good was called *Evil Is...*, which was actually filmed in 1969 (just after *Clegg*) but took a while to surface in the fleshpots of Soho under the title of *Night After Night After Night*. Starring Jack May from *The Archers* as a stern judge who turns out to be a Jack the Ripper style murderer, it also featured *Clegg*'s Gilbert Wynne as the policeman who eventually unmasks him.

"I took my name off that movie because the editor told the producer I hadn't shot it as scripted," says Shonteff, explaining why the film is credited to the pseudonymous Lewis J. Force. "Of course I hadn't — I had made it better. About five years later, one of the producers said the film should have been cut the way I shot it, and they would have had a very good film. That was nice to hear..."

Night After Night After Night introduced Shonteff to Linda Marlowe, a fine actress who played one of the supporting roles. He subsequently cast her as the lead in *Big Zapper* and *The Swordsman* (aka *Zapper's Blade of Vengeance*), a pair of lively comic book adventures for adults. 'Some called her Dirty Harriet!' was the publicity tagline, and private eye Harriet Zapper (Marlowe) certainly wielded a more interesting pair of magnums than Clint Eastwood...

Big Zapper was nonsense, but fun. It played like a barmy crossbreed of Hong Kong chop sockey, TV's *The Avengers* and a traditional British sex movie. And the mixture worked, particularly in America, where it scored big at the American box-office, making the top ten in *Variety*'s list of commercial hits in the week it opened. *The Swordsman* was a pretty good sequel which featured Marlowe again, this time crossing swords with the raunchy Edina Ronay and a slimy bad guy, well played by Diana Dors' husband Alan Lake.

"Alan had just come out of prison at the time," explains Shonteff, "and a lot of people said, 'Don't use this guy — he's trouble.' But he was great, just terrific. He was anything but trouble, and he couldn't have

comedy drama called *Take Some Girls*. This told of an attractive young girl (Sue Bond) who comes to London and gets caught up in the seedy world of softcore porno film-making. "I had a lot of very innocent nudity in this one," says Lindsay. "Just girls running across a field with no clothes on. In any event, the distributor took it and retitled it *The Yes Girls*, and the thing ran for over a year in the fleshpits in Piccadilly Circus."

In those days the British government used to hand out something called Eady money, which was paid directly to the film-maker from the box-office as an incentive to make films in the UK. Though Shonteff saw little income from the distributor of *The Yes Girls*, he made enough Eady money from it to finance *The*

been more generous with the other actors. The poor guy blew his brains out a few years later..." (Lake committed suicide following his wife's untimely death from cancer.)

An interesting aside to this movie is that Lindsay later showed me a wonderful sequence that was cut from the film by the BBFC. In it, Lake demonstrates his prowess as a swordsman to a sexy, leather-clad Edina Ronay. They square off against each other in a gym, and after a few swift slashes from Lake's weapon she's standing there naked. He slowly runs the tip of the fencing sword back and forth between her legs, accompanied by lots of lip-licking and orgasmic moaning from Ronay. Then a cruel look crosses Lake's features and he performs a vigorous series of cuts and thrusts. A huge close-up on Edina's muff (very effective in scope) reveals he has carved a neat 'Z' into her pubic hair...

Though the second Zapper movie did well in foreign sales, it sat on a shelf in Wardour Street for nearly a year before being unceremoniously dumped into a few London cinemas as a second feature. Lindsay has his own theory as to the reasons for this.

"It was distributed in the UK through Rank," he explains, "and they just didn't get behind it. It was interesting, because prior to making that movie a guy who had a lot of muscle at Rank wanted a meeting with me to suggest a different girl to play the leading role. Well, I had already cast Linda and was morally committed. I'm not saying this affected Rank's decision to leave the film on the shelf for a year, but you figure it out..."

At least there weren't too many distribution problems on *Spy Story*, which was Shonteff's next movie and his most ambitious film to date. Based on a Len Deighton best-seller and vividly shot (in eight weeks, his longest shooting schedule to date) aboard HMS Belfast, this even played major West End cinemas like the Plaza in Piccadilly. But it was not the commercial blockbuster that Shonteff had hoped for when he first optioned the screen rights. "It was no *Ipcress File*," he says with commendable understatement. Instead, it was a complex movie version of a complex novel, full of existential anti-heroes and cynical power-mongering. It could have done with a guest appearance by a gun-toting Tom Adams to liven it up.

"Looking back on the movie nowadays," says the director, "I realise that instead of shooting the book I should have read the book and thrown it away, then scripted the movie to make it a lot more commercial. Shooting the book as literally as I did had the drawback that it was too talky. There were other problems too: the lab mismatched the negative in a couple of places, and that screwed up a couple of good scenes. But it was just a boring movie."

Undeterred, Shonteff pressed on with *No. 1 of the Secret Service*, yet another variation on the *Licensed to Kill* formula (that had already spawned two sequels directed by others). *No. 1* starred Nicky Henson as secret agent Charles Bind, with Richard Todd as his arch-enemy, the evil Arthur Loveday. Aimi McDonald and Sue Lloyd supplied the glamour. "It was one of my most pleasurable films to make," says Shonteff, "and was also one of our most commercial." It sold well everywhere in the world except England, where there were complications, these being that Rank, the preferred cinema circuit of Hemdale (*No. 1*'s distributors) didn't want to release the film two weeks before the latest Bond picture — or indeed, it seems, ever!

Not one to be frightened off, Shonteff immediately filmed a follow-up called *Licensed to Love and Kill*, this time starring Gareth Hunt as Charles Bind, the Number One agent of the British Secret Service. One of the female characters was named Lotta Muff. *Screen International* called it: "...a lookalike Bond movie complete with bizarre baddies, impossibly fantastic gadgets, dishy dollies and punning tag lines. Not so much of a send-up as an in-joke strip cartoon."

With the profits he made from the foreign sales of *Licensed to Love and Kill*, Shonteff went on to realise a personal ambition by financing *How Sleep the Brave*, his favourite amongst his own movies. "I always wanted to make a film about the Vietnam war," he explains. "All wars fascinate me, but especially Vietnam. I was in Hong Kong making *Su-Muru* when the troops came in there on leave, and I heard some incredible stories from those guys.

"I also remember reading a newspaper article written by a Vietcong officer, and one line in particular stuck in my memory. It said: 'When we killed the first American, another one would break from cover to rescue his friend. So we shot him. Then another would come, and another, all running around trying to protect each other.' I felt that was a great compliment to every soldier, that he would be prepared to die to save his comrades. And when I made *How Sleep the Brave*, I put that quote at the end of the picture."

One of the very few Vietnam war pictures shot in England (along with Kubrick's *Full Metal Jacket*, which had a considerably bigger budget!), *How Sleep the Brave* was filmed in woodland around Gerrards Cross and Knowl Hill in Berkshire. This also enabled Lindsay to get the bus home at night. Unfortunately, it was made and released at a time when nobody in the USA would touch a picture about the Vietnam conflict.

"The whole thing was a festering sore," says Shonteff. "But I sold this film in every European country and did very well with it in Scandinavia, where it was given an award as Best War Film (the jury commented: 'It is up to par with the great predecessors in the genre, honest, well made and realistic'). I really think my picture was right for the time. I was eventually offered a distribution deal years later, after

Platoon came out, but got too greedy about it and didn't know how to handle it, so this became a semi-loser, money-wise."

How Sleep the Brave was filmed in the early '80s, a time when the world was just beginning to wake up to the video revolution. After some years of inactivity, Lindsay decided to have a go at making two small horror movies back-to-back on video. The result was a double bill of *The Killing Edge* and *Lipstick and Blood*, filmed in England on hectic nine-day schedules. The latter was marginally the better of the two — a turgid psychodrama with some half-decent gore effects. But neither was exactly a classic. "They were experiments," he admits. "I wanted to try video, but it is no match for film."

Shonteff's most recently released picture is *Number One Gun*, shot in 1990 on a budget of £85,000, a lot of which was stumped up by Lindsay himself. He worked for free, because there was nothing in there for the writer/producer/director/editor. A semi-remake of *No. 1 of the Secret Service*, it stars Michael Howe as a superspy who comes up against sinister Russian agents and the evil but sexy Cleo Rocos. In one scene, Howe is thrown from a plane and floats to the ground with the help of a parasol. Bad seems too modest a word for it.

"It's a pretty stupid picture," admits the director. "You've got to have a good sense of humour to enjoy it. I was sending up a lot of things. I don't think people know what to make of it. I sold it in a few places, but I think the people who bought it, after they saw it, probably wanted to commit suicide. It has been compared to *Hudson Hawk* (which I loved) and is just as stupid. I'm into that humour, but not those budgets.

"It bombed badly on me and I had sunk all my money into it. That's why I don't have the money to make anything else at the moment. It sold to Korea, Greece, Turkey, Spain, Australia and Portugal, and I have a deal on offer from the USA/Canada. But that's not up to the standard volume of sales we usually do, so it's bad news financially. Funnily, the Russians seem to like it, but they don't have any money to buy it. I may take a couple of Ladas instead..."

He is understandably bitter about his current position. Three decades and at least twenty pictures on from *Devil Doll*, he is still stuck in the world of low budget exploitation movies. The problem is that the cinema is only playing big pictures now. "There is no space left for the independents," he sighs. "When you're making movies with nickels and dimes and no time, it is very, very tough, and you need something very unusual to get into the marketplace..."

Still, a man's gotta do what a man's gotta do. Westerns are becoming popular again, so Lindsay went over to Arizona recently to shoot one. It's called *The Gunfighter* and is the story of an ageing, disillusioned gunslinger who arrives in a small western town having been paid to murder the sheriff there. He waits in the saloon, sinking rotgut whiskey and reviewing his life in flashback before the inevitable showdown.

"It's not just a western," explains Lindsay. "It's about America's Top Gun stance in the world today, and a metaphor for their gun culture. It was something I really wanted to make, and since it will seem to be an American picture, perhaps they'll want to see it in Britain!" He showed me a rough cut, and though it was hard to judge the movie on a tiny twelve inch monitor, I was impressed by its visual qualities. It brings to mind the minimalist Monte Hellman productions of the '60s. But it's a bit worrying to discover Lindsay has risked his mortgage on this picture, particularly as in one scene his cowboy hero says: "I'm going to have some lunch..." Do cowboys have lunch? I'd want to check that little detail if it was my money on the line.

By the time you read these words, *The Gunfighter* will either be gazing down from the shelves of your local video store or — worst case scenario — still sitting on the movieola in Lindsay's garage. The director has earned his own little place in the reference books now, but don't be surprised if his name doesn't appear on the credits of his latest movie. "I've got such a bad reputation that I might use a pseudonym," he admits. And if he can't find a distributor for the film? "No problem," he shrugs. "I can always find a bridge and jump off it..."

I'd like to think he was joking. ∎

LINDSAY SHONTEFF: Filmography

195?: **THE BUM.** (short)
 IVY LEAGUE KILLERS. (as floor-sweeper)
1960?: **THE MADMAN (?).** (TV short, unshown)
1961: **THE HIRED GUN (aka THE LAST GUNFIGHTER, THE DEVIL'S SPAWN).**
 With: Don Borisenko, Tass Tory, Jay Shannon, Michael Zenon
1963: **DEVIL DOLL.**
 With: Bryant Halliday, William Sylvester, Yvonne Romain, Sandra Dorne, Karel Stepanek
1964: **CURSE OF SIMBA (aka CURSE OF THE VOODOO, LION MAN).**
 With: Bryant Halliday, Dennis Price, Lisa Daniely, Mary Kerridge, Ronald Leigh Hunt
1965: **LICENSED TO KILL (aka THE SECOND BEST SECRET AGENT IN THE WHOLE WIDE WORLD).**
 With: Tom Adams, Karel Stepanek, Veronica Hurst, Peter Bull
1966: **RUN WITH THE WIND.**
 With: Shawn Phillips, Francesca Annis, Sean Caffrey, Jack Smethurst
1967: **THE MILLION EYES OF SU-MURU.**
 With: Shirley Eaton, Klaus Kinski, Frankie Avalon, George Nader, Wilfred Hyde-White.
1969: **CLEGG.**
 With: Gilbert Wynne, Gary Hope, Gilly Grant (as Suzy the Slag), Norman Claridge
1969: **NIGHT AFTER NIGHT AFTER NIGHT (original title: EVIL IS...).** (as Lewis J. Force)
 With: Jack May, Justine Lord, Linda Marlowe, Gilbert Wynne
1970: **PERMISSIVE.**
 With: Maggie Stride, Gay Singleton, Gilbert Wynne, Alan Gorrie
1971: **THE YES GIRLS (orig title: TAKE SOME GIRLS).**
 With: Sue Bond, Sally Muggeridge, Felicity Oliver, Jack May
1972: **THE FAST KILL.**
 With: Tom Adams, Susie Hampton, Ray Chiarella, Michael Culver
1973: **BIG ZAPPER.**
 With: Linda Marlowe, Richard Monette, Gary Hope, Sean Hewitt
1974: **THE SWORDSMAN (aka ZAPPER'S BLADE OF VENGEANCE).**
 With: Linda Marlowe, Alan Lake, Jason Kemp, Edina Ronay
1976: **SPY STORY.**
 With: Michael Petrovitch, Philip Latham, Don Fellows, Michael Gwynne, Nicholas Parsons
1977: **NO. 1 OF THE SECRET SERVICE (aka NUMBER ONE OF THE SECRET SERVICE).**
 With: Nicky Henson, Richard Todd, Aimi MacDonald, Geoffrey Keen, Dudley Sutton
1979: **LICENSED TO LOVE AND KILL.**
 With: Gareth Hunt, Nick Tate, Fiona Curzon, Gary Hope, Geoffrey Keen
1981: **HOW SLEEP THE BRAVE.**
 With: Lawrence Day, Luis Manuel, Thomas Pollard, Daniel Foley, Gerrany Quatro
1984: **THE KILLING EDGE.**
 With: Bill French, Marv Spencer
 LIPSTICK AND BLOOD.
1990: **NUMBER ONE GUN.**
 With: Michael Howe, Gary Hope, Gerald Sim, Cleo Rocos
1992: **THE GUNFIGHTER.**

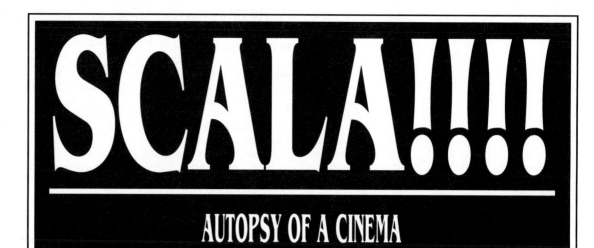

AUTOPSY OF A CINEMA

BY JANE GILES

The secret history of cinemas un-spools like a perverse double bill of a lavish Hollywood epic with a crazed no-budget B-movie. Until June '93 such a programme still existed, at the Scala, the fleapit that lived for the art of the repertory double bill and positively encouraged its punters to have

Cameron Mitchell makes the world a safer place for ski-masked psychos...

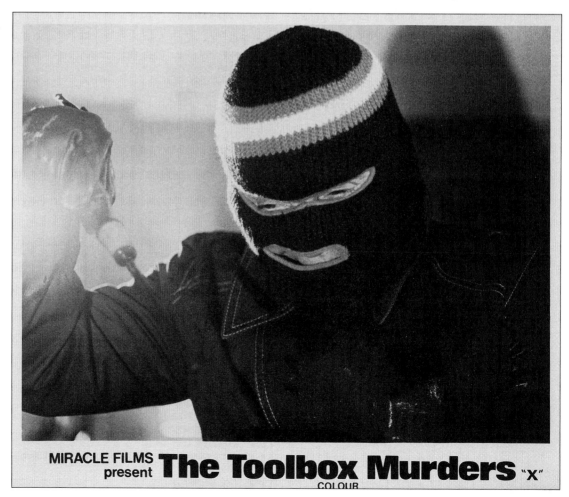

MIRACLE FILMS present **The Toolbox Murders** "X"
COLOUR

sex in the back row while smoking, drinking and filling their eyes with the cutting edge of exploitation cinema. So why did London's favourite cult movie house go dark after twelve years at the King's Cross Cinema?

First, some history. The local passion for moving pictures started in 1896 when Islington inventor Robert William Paul perfected the Animatographe, an apparatus for projecting animated photographs, derived from Edison's Kinetoscope. That year, the Sadler's Wells theatre featured 'Paul's Perfect Palpitating Promethean Photos' to a captivated audience. Home entertainment for persistence of vision addicts consisted of the Filoscope, or flick book, with wild stories such as *Metamorphosis of the Vegetarian*: you *will* believe that prehistoric man evolved from a carrot... This was hardly enough to keep the hoards away from the cheapskate 'penny gaff' shops that began to operate in the 1900s, including the Dreadnought Picture Palace, a former grocery store on Essex Road. Flammable nitrate film and unsafe equipment in over-crowded shop fronts led to the development of purpose built electric theatres licensed by the London County Council to meet the insatiable demands of moviegoers. Soon there were hundreds of thriving cinemas in Greater London, with a total of forty-one in the borough of Islington and six on the Pentonville Road alone. The King's Cross Cinema opened in 1920 as a luxurious Victorian style picture palace with chandeliers, marble mosaic floors, an ornate fireplace and seats for 1,500.

By the 1950s, the King's Cross Cinema was owned by Gaumont, who handed it over to the Odeon chain in the '60s, but moviegoing was in decline and the building wearily lost its former splendour. Reverting to independent ownership in the early '70s, uncensored skin flicks showed by day while Nick Hart Williams' company, The Other Cinema, presented the UK première of *The Battle Of Algiers* by night. Six day shows of second run mainstream films included *Dirty Harry, Z, Shaft, Queimada!* and *On the Buses*. Sundays were reserved for Asian matinees and Greek evening shows. Iggy and the Stooges played live, but rock gigs were a short-lived fixture. The King's Cross Cinema finally closed in 1975 with one last double bill of *The Good, the Bad and the Ugly* and *A Fistful of Dollars*. In 1980, the building was weirdly reincarnated as the Primatarium, headquarters of the British Primate League. Waterfalls, astroturf, jungle murals, slide projection and monkeys live on stage presented the greatest show on earth: the evolution of man. The enterprise failed miserably within a year.

The Scala started life in the late 1970s at The Other Cinema, by then in the West End's Tottenham Street. A management buy out was led by ticket tearer Stephen Woolley and financed by Virgin partner Nik Powell. The usual yawnsome short runs of nice foreign language art films were quickly replaced by an aggressive American-style, daily changing programme advertised on idiosyncratic calender posters. Diverse double or triple bills ranged from Ginger Rogers to Pasolini, all-day punk, Peckinpah, Vertov or Kurosawa. Marathon sessions of *The Prisoner* and *The Avengers* were big hits, as was the celebration of the Golden Turkeys to coincide with the publication of Michael Medved's first book. All-night shows were devoted to Marilyn Monroe, zombies, fifties schlock, seventies exploitation, film noir, Albert Zugsmith and 'celluloid acne'. The occasional first runs included *Eraserhead, Crazy Mama, Pink Flamingos, Wild Angels* and that epitome of the Scala style, *Thundercrack!*, Curt McDowell's

hardcore polymorphous perverse porno horror movie with a sense of humour. With a spit and sawdust public bar out front, the new style repertory cinema thrived. Alongside the older, cineliterate audience was the new post-punk generation, lured by ongoing coverage in the music press and the Scala's promise of moviegoing as an alternative fun night out.

Kicked out of their West End premises by the arrival of Channel 4, the Scala transferred prints, projectors and punters to the circle area of the former Primatarium, now split in two with the old stalls being operated separately as a shadowy snooker club. At 5.15pm on Thursday 9 July 1981 the Scala showed its first film at the King's Cross Cinema: Cooper and Schoedsack's *King Kong* in a double bill with *Mighty Joe Young* as a tribute to the building's former residents. But the monkeys had left their own enduring mark: for months audiences suffocated in the piss-stinking heat of the unclimatised auditorium. Come winter, they froze: the boiler system didn't work either. Management would advise the punters to huddle together at the back of the cinema, not just warmer with better sound quality but a wonderful vantage point as the Scala's enormous auditorium had the steepest rake in London. 'High on atmosphere, low on comfort' — this was one of the more generous accounts of the Scala's eccentric new home. The building shook from basement to roof every time an underground train passed below, providing pleasing moments of synchronicity with the film on screen ('Undergroundaround'). Punters could jack up on three day old black coffee, served cold at the bar. Warren, the big black Scala cat, patrolled the audience. Joy Division and The Pop Group thundered between films while other cinemas were still playing 'Windmills of Your Mind' as intermission music. The auditorium was dimly lit in a glowing red to disguise the beer splats on the huge screen and the collapsing seats stained with...well, never mind. Outside, King's Cross was a rats' nest of pimps, whores and derelict drunks. Inside, the Scala was some kind of celluloid paradise.

Programmed by Stephen Woolley and Jayne Pilling, the new Scala showed well over a hundred films every month, maintaining its commitment to bills of repertory film classics alongside Archival Animated Anarchy, music films, B-movie western conventions and all-day grade-Z marathons. The Scala embraced exploitation films with a god-given vocation. Exclusive revivals

(Above) 'Little' Joe's chopper makes short work of Udo Kier in **Blood for Dracula**...

(Top) Tory MPs enforce the 'get tough' policy for young offenders (Salo).

ranged from *The Men* to *Wild Women of Wongo* and *Les Diaboliques*. First runs included *Multiple Maniacs, Ciao! Manhattan* and *Lucifer Rising*. Powell and Woolley's Palace Pictures operated their burgeoning video and film distribution company out of increasingly cramped offices in the cinema. The Scala presented popular sneak previews of Palace's latest acquisitions, such as *The Evil Dead* and *A Nightmare on Elm Street*. The whole place throbbed with the excited rediscovery of cinema-going.

Each programmer brought their own obsessions to the Scala. When Woolley left in the mid-'80s to concentrate on his career as a film producer, JoAnne Sellar and Mark Valen took over, stepping up the quota of horror movies and gay films respectively. First runs included *Ms. 45, The Driller Killer, The Night Porter, Lonesome Cowboys, From Beyond* and *Straight to Hell*. Repertory shows of Argento, Fulci and Bava made the Scala's name synonymous with Euro horror. Gay cinema found its niche, becoming a core part of the Scala's line-up, while the back of the auditorium became an amiable cruising ground ('Cruisingroundaround'?).

When the major cinema chains slashed their Monday ticket prices to address the traditional weekly dip in attendances, the Scala was unable to compete financially so programmed sexy cult films to win back audiences. Blue Monday remained a regular fixture, starring Russ Meyer's Vixen films, *Salo, Ai No Corrida, Maitresse* and the ever popular *Thundercrack!* It had also proved difficult to draw a crowd on New Year's Day;

unlike the other repertory cinemas in London, the Scala had no local audience, and operating hand to mouth the cinema had to make up for the financial loss of three days' closure at Christmas. Based on the success of the Palace previews and the all-night punters' enthusiastic ability to watch five movies in a row, Sellar started the January 1st Horror Film Festival. Hung-over ushers worked in nauseous misery as a capacity queue of gore-hounds wound twice around the outside of the cinema for previews of the year's new horror films: *The Hills Have Eyes Part 2, Razorback, The Stuff, The Return of the Living Dead, Near Dark, The Lair of the White Worm, Terror at the Opera, Society* and *Santa Sangre*.

In 1984, the Scala defended the horror movies outlawed by Bright's Video Recordings Bill, presenting *The Evil Dead, Tenebrae* and *The Toolbox Murders* amongst an all-day/all-night programme of projected protest. It was a time when the cinema was flourishing; there was a plethora of films available only for the big screen and home video ownership was still comparatively rare. At this time there was also little night-life in London after 1am, due to the restrictions of entertainment licensing. Partly for this reason, the Scala's all-night film shows were enormously popular; there would be a huge gathering of the tribes every Saturday as gangs of punks, bikers, disco bunnies and new romantics participated with the movies on screen. The cinema started to co-host late 'parties' with the Mix, Alice In Wonderland and New Depression; combining films with music and live acts, these club nights were packed. Too packed. The cinema was busted for over-crowding, marking its first appearance in court.

Around this time the Scala got a paint job. A redecoration clause in the lease saw the end of the jungle mural and the arrival of the goofy Hollywouldn't graffiti painted by Yuval and Wigan. This was a rare bit of capital expenditure, as even at the height of its success the Scala could do little more than break even financially. With 500 seats, the cinema was unusually large and expensive to run for a repertory programme, despite ingenious cost cutting exercises and slave labour wages. Unlike other art cinemas in the UK, the Scala existed without a scrap of grant aid from the British Film Institute, Arts Council or its local authority. While this allowed a certain independence, the cinema was always subject to programming by public demand.

The true meaning of repertory is a repeating programme. Amazing but true. Punters would always bitch about the repetition of the repertory programme, while coming back for more. Movies that showed monthly at the Scala tended to be the weird and wonderful exclusives, such as *Café Flesh* and *Pink Narcissus*, or the work of Walerian Borowczyk, John Waters, Andy Warhol and George Kuchar. Others were shown regularly every few months: Tarkovsky, Luis Buñuel, Dario Argento, Dusan Makavejev, Sergio Leone and genre movies. Film tie-ins were made to capitalise on the publicity and public interest around a new release or event. Tributes were programmed on birthdays or deaths of stars and directors. Scanning the papers for news of a celebrity near death, the Scala often mistimed a tribute; both Salvador Dali and Terry-Thomas hung grimly on to life while the pre-printed programme prematurely mourned their deaths. There were regular previews (*Naked Lunch*), seasons (Exterminate All Rational Thought, Little Joe [Dallesandro], *et al*) and personal appearances. When The Cramps attended the Scala's première of *The Return of the Living Dead,* the cinema was decked out with elaborate gravestones in their honour. John Waters anxiously paced the cinema before a preview of his PG-rated *Hairspray* packed with hardcore fans, and fainted with relief when the audience screamed "We love you, Divine!" at the screen. Suitably sick off-West End second runs fell into the Scala's 'bargain bin' thematic double slots. The suggestion box in the foyer spewed forth demands for the uncut, undubbed, unsubtitled *Deep Red* or the unmade *One Saliva Bubble*. Films that exceeded the box-office target would be rescheduled for the following programme until attendance figures indicated that the public had had enough. Audiences voted with their feet for all night Arnie, zombies, Steve Martin, Mad Max, Monty Python and all-day Pedro Almodovar.

In the late '80s, the Scala programme became more polemic. Valen returned to the US while Sellar moved into film production. I found that the ground rules of repertory exhibition had changed. There was no longer a substantial audience for the older classics or even cult favourites such as *Rumble Fish* and *Eraserhead*, as home video had become accessibly cheap and people built up their film collections taped from television. Theatrically, the '70s repertory standards, such as genre movies, the films of Fellini, Herzog, Fassbinder and Godard, were a financial dead loss. Repertory was also diminished as distributors' rights to films expired daily: *Mean Streets*, John Waters' early films, even *Women on the Verge of a Nervous Breakdown* disappeared. The range of movies available only for the big screen narrowed to uncut horror, sex, the avant-garde and off-West End second runs.

The Scala responded by stepping up the programming of rare prints, exclusive presentations, special events and guest appearances. *The Texas Chain Saw Massacre, Apocalypse Now, Girl on a Motorcycle, Je T'Aime, Moi Non Plus, Squirm, Minnie and Moscowitz, Deranged, What?, Trans-Europ Express* and *Towers Open Fire* had not been seen in London for years until the Scala tracked them down. Ghettoised experimental movies such as *Mano Destra* and *The Act of Seeing with One's Own Eyes* (yes Jack!) found a wider audience within programmes of Avant-Garde Erotica and Body Horror. *Henry Portrait of a Serial Killer* was shown exclusively for a year until being picked up for distribution, cut. *Django* dragged his coffin just for us. Some of the best special events staged

*(Left) Another pathetic chopper caption – how about 'Bimbo eats chopper'? Is that offensive enough? (*Nekromantik*).*

at the Scala were the work of obsessive colleagues. *Shock Xpress* went around the clock in 1987, '88 and '89, starring *Nekromantik, Hellraiser, Hollywood Chainsaw Hookers, Monkey Shines, The Stepfather, Slugs, Mongolitos, The Church, The Fly II* and *Bad Taste*. Sweat dripping down the walls, this horror preview festival of relentless dimensions was a runaway success and inspired countless pale imitations. Martial arts promoter Rick Baker attracted audiences from all over the place with his Jackie Chan and John Woo triple bills, plus guest appearances by Donnie Yen, Cynthia Rothrock and Chow Yun Fat. Bal Croce's Psychotronic Films staged 3D specials, Elvis all-night shows and William Castle events, complete with flying skeletons and vibrating seats. Skin Two presented a Bitches, Whips and Heels Dress for Sex special, while Thee Temple Ov Psychick Youth showed *After Cease to Exist*. Over the years, Nick Cave, Lydia Lunch, Gallon Drunk, Dario Argento, Richard Kern, Herschell Gordon Lewis, Penelope Spheeris, Stephen Apostoloff, Genesis P. Orridge, Carolyn Cassady, Johnny Legend, *Thundercrack!*'s Marion Eaton and Sandra Bernhard were all coerced into appearing or performing onstage.

The Scala celebrated its tenth birthday in July 1991 with a preview of Steve Woolley's latest production, *A Rage in Harlem*, and a heaving party. There was the most extraordinary assortment of guests; the Scala had always endeavoured to make everyone feel at home, from gore guys to grannies by way of media types and miscellaneous mavericks. The cinema always brought out a corner of eccentricity. Regular patrons included an elderly 'professor' of shifting origins, who claimed that he visited the Scala daily to express his discernment. There was a bird-like middle aged woman and her hulking son who both loved chainsaw movies, mainly because the blood and thunder films featured fewer "bedroom scenes". This couple called the Scala "Her", explaining, "the Her and the [cinema] cats — they're like people to us". For a while there was a spate of chic Japanese girls coming to see all of the sexy surrealist and avant-garde classics. And there was always the boys with their Forbidden Planet plastic bags. In the audience, staff spotted Francis Bacon, Nic Roeg, Ken Livingstone and numerous music stars too tedious to mention. Shane MacGowan was part of the furniture, despite the fact that Steve Woolley had thrown him out of the Tottenham Street Scala for pissing into the audience during a screening of *Attack of the 50 Foot Woman*. Back at the party, producers, directors, distributors, press and punters raged, celebrating a decade of cinematic decadence. Beer boys looked on benignly while Queer Nation queens snogged on the dance floor. The lovely general manageress forcibly conduct-

15

PSYCHOTRONIC

SCALA PRESENTS

NEKROMANTIK II 4.30 9.10 + TEXAS CHAINSAW MASSACRE 3.00 7.40 + HENRY PORTRAIT OF A SERIAL KILLER 6.10

11

EASTERN HEROES

HONG KONG: CINEMA OVER THE EDGE: A BETTER TOMORROW I 1.00 + A BETTER TOMORROW II 3.00

7

JOANNE SELLAR & NIK POWELL

Gala World Premiere: **DUST DEVIL** in aid of the Save the Scala Fund 8.30. Doors open 7.30. Tickets £10.00 (Party til 1am)

ed the guests through a rousing chorus of 'Happy Birthday' by brandishing the cake knife. Someone reported seeing the stripy Scala cats [John] Huston and Roy [Kinnear] dancing. We toasted to the next ten years.

But by the beginning of 1992, times had really changed. Stung by the escalating consequences of the credit-happy '80s, banks were calling in their loans and the Scala's parent company, Palace Pictures, went spectacularly bankrupt, ending their decade of groundbreaking film distribution and prolific production. To enable Woolley's new company, Scala Productions, to start filming *The Crying Game*, the cinema loaned him its box-office takings every night. Sometimes it was only pennies, as the recession had also kicked in hard to repertory cinema-going and attendances steadily dropped. With limited leisure cash, audiences were going to the must-see first-run blockbusters and little else. The West End's Prince Charles became a successful second run 'dollar house', both exhausting the films' currency for other repertory cinemas in London and demonstrating that audiences were no longer interested in double bills. More independent film distributors turned their hands to video, working hard through their back catalogues and releasing films on sell-through just months after their first run theatrical release. New labels started dealing in the core Scala material of cult movies, rare horror and gay films. Retailing at £15, economics tipped the balance in favour of seeing films on video.

Although few would deny the superior pleasure of seeing films on the big screen, the Scala was becoming increasingly run-down. While multiplexes set new standards in presentation and comfort, the Scala got colder, and the combination of worn out prints and ancient, temperamental projectors (*not to mention projectionists. Ed.*) became more erratic. The cinema's grand white exterior now looked as though someone had thrown a bag of soot over it, and the lost letters of the neon sign were too expensive to repair. We put together a £1,000,000 Scala redevelopment proposal that involved turning the auditorium into three screens, where the infamous repertory programme would show alongside first run movies. The architect's sympathetic designs played upon the eclectic history of the much altered building. The plans retained the beautiful floors and Victorian curves while adding a wiggly bar, leopard skin carpets, video projection for Richard Kern's Deathtrip films and an intimate preview theatre. The Scala would remain an off-beat, atmospheric cinema, but one with warm auditoria and state of the art presentation. We would employ nothing but two-headed transsexuals to tear the tickets and serve tequila slammers at the bar. It looked good, but it never happened; there could not have been a worse time to be seeking capital investment, particularly in King's Cross.

It seemed that the local area was being strategically dilapidated. The Channel Tunnel terminal development, first mooted in 1988 and vigorously opposed by the Scala, continued to threaten the cinema's site. Crack and smack dealers proliferated, and a spate of drug users' deaths hit the headlines. Shop fronts were boarded up by day and squatted buildings burned. Homeless people slept in the Scala doorways. There was no doubt that those who could still afford to attend repertory cinema were being put off by King's Cross, while crucially the Scala was unable to capture the new early twenties age group. The music press had stopped covering any film other than national release, first-run American movies, while cuts in student grants and unemployment benefits hit young people hard; but ultimately, repertory cinema was simply not on this generation's cultural agenda.

Helen De Witt took over the programming of a cinema fraught with difficulties in mid-'92. The Scala could no longer get an audience for the all-night shows, despite a short lived flurry of interest in dude culture and trip madness. Why sit in a cold barn of a cinema when you can programme your own choice of five videos in a row and drink at home all night with your mates? There were now more horror movies available on tape than for the big screen, as the genre took its dive in the early '90s and the few titles made tended to go straight to video. The New Year's day event and the marathon horror preview festivals disappeared through the paucity of new films. The precious commodity of our non-video repertory favourite *The Driller Killer* was permanently withdrawn from the programme when the Obscene Publications squad showed

The new 'get tough' policy ensures owners take responsibility for canine footway foulers... (**Salo**).

up threatening legal action.

And the Scala was no longer one of the rare after-hours venues; in recent years, entertainments licensing had been extended to 3am and some clubs were open twenty-four hours. The Scala's late night audience had been lost to video and Ecstasy. The cinema was hired out again to rave club promoters, but the old building could hardly stand it. The landlords complained that the dull thudding noise from the cinema above was making the snooker balls fly off their tables. The financially beleaguered local authority started to find new infringements to penalise entertainment venues. Losing money like a drain from the film shows, the famous Saturday all-nighters were finally discontinued when the Scala was no longer granted the Music and Dance licences necessary for clubs. These were desperate measures; the cinema needed to operate eight days a week in order to keep its head above water. It was a struggle to get a substantial audience for anything other than sex films. Nearly every day became Blue Monday, and as December is a traditionally disastrous month for repertory cinema, the 1992 programme featured the Scala's A to Z of Sex in a style that spoofed Madonna's attention grabbing new book. Invoking the wrath of Mary Whitehouse and the local press, the Scala scraped through another month.

And then there was *A Clockwork Orange*. Lost since Stanley Kubrick's self-imposed 'ban' on the film's UK exhibition twenty years ago, it was programmed in an unbilled matinee slot on 1 April 1992 as part of a double with *If....* Someone informed the film's distributor, who passed the case on to the Federation Against Copyright Theft. FACT prosecuted, starting an acrimonious year-long court case that financially drained and threatened to close the Scala. A public appeal for funds was launched after the conviction at the end of March '93. Coloured an audacious orange, the April campaign programme poster featured a season of repertory films that would not have reached the big screen in the UK without the Scala, plus an exclusive first run of Palace Pictures' final production, Richard Stanley's *Dust Devil*. The cinema sold oranges and Droog in the Dock t-shirts, Gallon Drunk played a benefit show and each day of the programme was sponsored by a different, like-minded company: Forbidden Planet, Mute Records, Murder One, Compendium Bookshop, *The Face*, Dennis Cockell Tattooist. On 1 April the Scala staff put their name to a matinee double bill of *If...* plus a surprise film: Billy Wilder's *Witness for the Prosecution*. The evening show was a preview of *Braindead...* Still unable to acquire a Music and Dance licence, the Scala hosted a fund raising Orange Ball at the Cafe de Paris. Mark Lamarr read passages from Burgess' novel while designer droogs vamped an audience of Scalaphiles. Stills from favourite Scala films were projected, as if moving pictures had returned to the age of Paul's Animatographe. The fund raising campaign worked. Messages of support came from John Waters and John McNaughton, while donations flooded in from the film industry, friends and patrons, meeting the legal fees of the Scala's defence and contribution towards the prosecution's costs.

The Scala was in the clear for just a few weeks when it became apparent that the cost of renewing its twelve year lease would put it out of business for good. Without the prospect of capital investment to address an enormous schedule of dilapidation and unable to meet the proposed rent increase at its current level of box-office income, the Scala's plugs were pulled. The

Being the adventures of a young man whose principal interests are rape, ultra-violence and Beethoven.

BEST FILM OF THE YEAR. BEST DIRECTOR OF THE YEAR. NEW YORK FILM CRITICS' AWARDS 1971

STANLEY KUBRICK'S CLOCKWORK ORANGE x

(Left) Scourge of the Scala...

last days of a cinema are a messy business; nothing works properly except for the telephone, which never stops ringing. Amongst the bills arrived a letter awarding the Scala the cost of a new heating system, applied for two years ago. Too bloody late. Every successful day of the last programme was a knife twisting in the heart of the cinema, whereas each slack show for the last decade had been a cause of anxiety. Thirty staff lost their jobs and the cats lost their home. Hundreds of movies are also homeless, although De Witt is guest programming Scala slots at other cinemas while looking for a new venue.

People always say that cinemas are haunted, but the eerie sounds and movements are usually caused by the drop in temperature after a full house leaves the auditorium or by the vast amount of static electricity generated through the projectors. During the Scala's tenure at the King's Cross Cinema, there had been one natural death in the auditorium (the film showing was *Looking for Mr Goodbar*) and one suicide (a flier from the bathroom windows as Dr and the Medics played a club night). While the Scala wasn't haunted, the strange sensation felt when sitting in the dark, empty auditorium out of hours seemed to be the spirit of the cinema reverberating with all of the different people and pictures that passed through it. As the doors were locked one last time and the film prints left the building, the Scala's spirit died. Perhaps the King's Cross Cinema will be reincarnated as another species of picture palace, or maybe the developers will have their way and flatten the site to build a terminal facilitating the escape to Paris, where there is still a healthy repertory scene supported by French government tax relief for cinema exhibition.

On Monday 7 June 1993 at a midnight wake, the Scala showed its last film at the King's Cross Cinema: Cooper and Schoedsack's *King Kong*, a tribute to the death of our lovable giant. ■

ANTI-EVERYTHING

THE RISE, THE FALL AND THE NERVE OF GROVE PRESS

BY DAMON WISE

*"**** you and **** your ****ing cup of ****ing tea, you ****ing ****."*
Domestic bliss in the expurgated version of **Tropic of Cancer.**

Forty years back, the written word was king. Hemmed in and tamed by crippling moral strictures, the visual arts were fighting from a corner: censor boards trimmed spice from the skimpiest foreign skinflicks, acts of Parliament made sure West End stages scrubbed up clean and TV kept itself to itself, vying with the cocktail cabinet for precious house space.

The word, however, had the field to itself, simmering in tatty personal manuscripts, kept under wraps like mutant royalty until the distant day when this aberrant ink could spill out onto pristine pages, wrapped and bound in perfect parody of 'respectable' novels.

Some hope. Most writers scrawled away oblivious to the oblivion that faced their work. Scratching out *Our Lady of the Flowers* on prison-issue brown paper bags, Genet knew nothing of advances, royalties and PR — and when some philistine warden burnt the finished product on a whim, Genet just took another bag and started over. And who knew *Naked Lunch* was ever written until it wrote itself? Certainly not Burroughs, that's for sure.

Such novels break the rules and redraw the boundaries. Novels written with scant regard for the smug face on the dust jacket, the glib notice in the weekly press and a safe seat on the Booker shortlist — novels written because they had to be — not just because they could.

These two novels in particular share something else in common: both slipped out to the American public under the watchful eye of Grove Press. Part publishing priesthood, part literary wrecking crew, Grove Press did a demolition job on the nation's phony moral codes, printing scandalous new works by untested authors and welcoming the notoriety with open arms. If Grove Press believed in your work, they'd back it all the way to the Supreme Court if the need arose.

And it did. Often.

Grove's origins were humble enough. At the age of twenty-nine, founder Barney Rossett bought the company as an ailing concern in 1951. Output was sparse (a whole three novels) and esoteric, but this was irrelevant to Rossett. For $3,000 dollars, the entire Grove catalogue was shifted to his apartment, where Rossett could plan his next move.

A maverick since high school, Rossett began his publishing career with a short-run newsletter in eighth grade, first known as *The Sommunist* (a telling compression of communist and surrealist) and later *The Anti-Everything*. Unsurprisingly, his education was rather liberal: in 1938, at the age of sixteen, Rossett and friends staged a coup at his Chicago school as a (semi-ironic) statement against the burgeoning climate of war.

Four years later, Rossett enrolled at UCLA, though his hopes of dabbling with film-making were somewhat thwarted since the college had yet to establish its legendary film course. Disappointed, Rossett drifted into the armed forces, where he found the opportunity he was looking for.

"I was head of an army film unit during World War Two," he recalls. "Afterwards I had a film company, Target Films, and produced one feature film — *Strange Victory*, directed by Leo Hurwitz. It basically concerned racism in the US, although it had a very comprehensive account of the Second World War as fought in Europe, using American, German, Soviet, Czech, French and Canadian footage."

Leaving the army after the war ended, Rossett managed a two-year college course in Chicago and a spell in Paris with his painter girlfriend Joan Mitchell, before embarking on what was to be his career. With little to hand, Rossett must have been only too aware of his limitations, sniffing out the relevant gaps in the market place to avoid competition with the heavy-weights.

To begin with, Rossett's main forte was the overlooked classic, the least-known moments from otherwise loudly lauded careers, or obscure continental wonders, dusted off and prefaced with carefully chosen words of recommendation. But the changes evident in the output of his European counterparts, specifically Maurice Girodias' Paris-based Olympia Press, suggested that the chance was here to break free from the classics and head into unexplored territory.

Giving work to jobbing Brits and American ex-pat chancers, Girodias was busy exploiting the export market with dirty books to order. Cranking out twenty a year to 2,000 lusty readers, Girodias pre-sold his wares with titillating titles, then set his 'erotic armada' to work, bringing *White Thighs* and *Roman Orgy* joyously to life.

'Enough has been said about the influence of the printed word,' Girodias wrote in his introduction to *The Olympia Reader*, 'but never enough about the liberating influence of the printed four-letter word. Those literary orgies, those torrents of systematic bad taste were quite certainly instrumental in clearing the air, and clearing out a few mental cobwebs.'

As sales grew, Girodias began slipping in more and more avant-garde material, alienating his one-handed public but exciting the legions of the unpublished, whose unsolicited manuscripts flooded the Olympia offices. Rossett was quick to see the parallels between his and Girodias' fledgling companies (though, as founder of the Obelisk Press, Girodias' father had given him a rather more solid schooling in the trade) and moved swiftly, as did UK publisher John Calder, to take advantage of the new material.

But Rossett's first major blow was struck in 1957 with the publication of *Lady Chatterley's Lover* in a complete and unexpurgated volume (boldly proclaimed 'the edition that made history') that quietly boasted the full approval of Lawrence's widow, Frieda Lawrence-Ravagli.

Since the original edition had since fallen out of copyright, many eyes were on Grove to see how they would fare against the Postmaster-General, whose well-known antipathy to the novel had stalled its publication. After Allen Ginsberg's recent vindication over the literary values of *Howl*, Grove knew their obstacles were not insurmountable. Braving the storm, Grove took to the courts to uphold their constitutional

rights to mail the novel to whomsoever they liked, wherever they liked, whenever they liked. Faced with the evidence, the courts backed down — and pirate editions appeared within weeks.

Success came at a price, but at $35,000 the Lawrence verdict was a bargain compared to Rossett's next venture. Following up one red-hot read with another, Rossett delivered Henry Miller's controversial *Tropic of Cancer* and walked into another lawsuit that sucked nearly ten times the previous amount from the defence kitty. Miller had been a tough nut to crack, and even a cash incentive could not force him to sign. His was a double bind: he truly believed that *Tropic of Cancer* could not be published in its original form, but would never sanction a bleached-out compromise (a fill-in-the blanks version was rightly scotched).

'Part of my reluctance to wage open combat with our American authorities,' he wrote to explain at the time, 'arises from the fact that I see no evidence of genuine revolt in the people themselves. We have no real radicals, no body of men who have the desire, the courage and the power to initiate a fundamental change in our outlook or in our way of life.'

Assuring Miller that he wasn't out to exploit the novel's notoriety (or have him crowned, as Miller feared, 'the King of Smut'), Rossett finally talked the deal into existence. Handing over a $40,000 advance, Rossett extended his generosity to wary booksellers by offering full support for any dealers involved in local lawsuits. As a result, instead of facing one court case, Grove fought sixty all over America, finally winning

Another arousing scene from **Tropic of Cancer.**

MIRACLE FILMS present "I AM CURIOUS – YELLOW" 'x'
ENGLISH SUB-TITLES

(Top) 'Even its pornographic pleasures are non-existent, having vanished with the eleven censored minutes.' (**Monthly Film Bulletin.**) *This must be one of the 'uninteresting revelations about Sjöman's private life' then...*

(Above) Jennifer Jason Leigh searches for a baby's arm to hold the apple in **Last Exit to Brooklyn**.

out in the summer of '64. Success was not cheap: the company soon found itself experiencing the first of several serious cash-flow crises.

In the meantime, Grove had established itself as something of an *agent provocateur*, bringing in fresh and searingly original new talent. Rossett eventually laid his hands on Beckett, Genet and Ionesco, but he *always* jumped at American writers who bucked the system. Snapping up *The Subterraneans*, Kerouac's editor at Grove reshuffled the bebop prose into something more closely resembling an American — or at least Kerouac's previous — novel. After a quiet word from the author, Grove apologised, and the novel hit the bookstands with each beat nuance intact. Even Hubert Selby Jnr gained the leverage to insist on a literary 'final cut' clause in his contract. At Grove, even punctuation came at the writer's discretion.

Like Girodias, Rossett too grew bored and began to diversify. A bar materialised for a short time (though nothing to rival Girodias' own personal money-pit, the Grande Severine nightclub/restaurant), and even a theatre. But in 1964, Rossett transferred some of his attentions to film, having commissioned screenplays from five of his writers: Marguerite Duras, Alain Robbe-Grillet, Harold Pinter, Beckett and Ionesco. Though Pinter's script was later filmed by the BBC, only one of these came to fruition under Rossett.

Beckett's contribution, a twenty minute near-silent movie by the name of *Film*, began inauspiciously when it became clear that Beckett's ideal leading man, Charlie Chaplin, would have no interest in any projects other than his own. Coming in after Patrick Magee at slightly second-best (and facing death square in the mouth), Buster Keaton turned in a suitably bewildered performance. "Poor Buster," said Rossett in an interview with John Oakes in *The Review of Contemporary Fiction*, "I didn't get the feeling he understood anything he was doing."

Still, Keaton remembered his lines (not hard, the only sound in the movie is the word "shhh!").

Rossett remains impressed by Beckett's stoicism during *Film*'s filming, his only visit to the United States. The initial shot, a complicated set-up that took

a day to shoot and cost around a third of the entire film's budget, proved a complete and irretrievable flop when the rushes came in. Unable to reshoot, Beckett promptly rewrote the scenario, no doubt fighting the urge to stomp back to his trailer and sulk.

Thinking, perhaps, that production was somehow not well-starred for Grove, Rossett sidelined into distribution, picking up avant-garde shorts (buying Amos Vogel's entire 'Cinema 16' avant-garde film library, for example) and feature length cult oddities. The most famous acquisition, Vilgot Sjöman's explicitly sexual *I Am Curious, Yellow*, again brought Grove to the courts.

After two major successes, Grove had followed through with a triple when Burroughs' *Naked Lunch* finally beat an obscenity rap in the Supreme Court in 1965. It was a close shave, requiring two appeals, but victory was definitely Grove's. '*Naked Lunch*,' wrote Ted Morgan in *Literary Outlaw*, 'would be the last work of literature to be censored by the post office, the customs service, and by a state government.'

But something had to give, and that something was *I Am Curious, Yellow*. Rossett didn't mind too much. After all, the film had already grossed over $10,000,000 (not bad for a $100,000 investment), but what really rankled was that the court's eventual obscenity ruling against the film would soon be made redundant by the new wave of hardcore, from *Deep Throat* to *The Devil in Miss Jones*, that swamped US screens as the '60s gave way to the '70s.

It had happened again: Grove were just paving the way for the freeloaders and scamsters. And as the permissive society jumped moral America's rails, so Grove found itself more and more beleaguered. Cash was something of a problem — but then it always was. The real threat was coming from the Grove generation itself, those newly-PC liberals who tutted at Grove's supposed descent into softcore and sexual exploitation. Grove soon found itself in an unenviable position, being (literally) bombarded by the Right for publishing, amongst other things, *The Autobiography of Malcolm X* and a collection of Che Guevara's speeches, and pilloried by the Left for sexism and exploitation of sexual material. Matters came to a head when a union representing publishing employees attempted to unionise the workforce and pushed Rossett into a humiliating defeat. Needless to say, the authorities (particularly the CIA, it was rumoured) were wildly happy with the turn of events, and perhaps not a little proud of themselves.

Grove stood firm into the '70s, but somehow its resolve had been broken. After all, its reputation as a cutting edge publishing house began to seem somehow quainter with every passing year, and as taboos began to topple, Rossett would see every last one of his 'problem' novels — from *Lady Chatterley* and *Tropic of Cancer* to *Last Exit to Brooklyn* and *Naked Lunch* — make the transition from page to screen.

Rossett had always had plenty to contend with, even from his own stable. Fighting the Right was one problem, the Left quite another, and the middle was certainly not a healthy place for Grove to be. Bailing out, Rossett moved on to a new firm and a new set of ideals, leaving the past firmly in the past before its weight became too burdensome.

So as the '70s slid into the '80s, the home of free speech finally went on the market for a sum allegedly in the region of $2,000,000.

A small price to pay... ∎

WHO?

JEAN YARBROUGH...

BY KIM NEWMAN

'If there is enough time and space and printers ink,' wrote Andrew Sarris, 'eventually we must talk of everything.' The time has come to talk of Jean Yarbrough.

Though the Sarris who said of Edgar Ulmer that 'anyone who loves the cinema must be moved by *Daughter of Dr. Jekyll*, a film with a scenario so atrocious that it takes forty minutes to establish that the daughter of Dr Jekyll is indeed the daughter

(Previous page) "Feets, get to movin'!" The inimitable Mantan Moreland steals the show in **King of the Zombies.**

(Right) "Hey mac, there's a giant fake bat wrapped around your neck." **The Devil Bat** strikes...

of Dr Jekyll' could obviously come to terms with him, *The American Cinema* has no Yarbrough entry. Ironically, *Daughter of Dr. Jekyll* is almost a remake of Yarbrough's *She-Wolf of London*. In the auteur game, Ulmer survives but Yarbrough fades. Dying in 1975, Yarbrough wasn't around to be interviewed by Tom Weaver for *Fangoria* or *Filmfax*, and so is eclipsed in ink and space even by Reginald Le Borg or Edward Bernds.

If remembered at all, Yarbrough is a footnote to cult careers: Bela Lugosi, Rondo Hatton, Abbott and Costello, Lon Chaney Jnr, Basil Rathbone and John Carradine, not to mention Mantan Moreland, the Bowery Boys, Martin Kosleck, Glenn Strange and Joi Lansing. Horror critics are often keener on stars than movies: in his excellent *Poverty Row Horrors*, Weaver lists *The Devil Bat* among Yarbrough's best but dismisses the superior, Lugosi-less *The Creeper*. Definitive essays by Fred Olen Ray (on Hatton, *Midnight Marquee*) and David Wilt (on Dwight Babcock, *Hardboiled in Hollywood*) discuss the 'Creeper' films in depth but fail even to mention their director. Received wisdom is nebulous: W. Wheeler Dixon (*The 'B' Directors: A Biographical Directory*) praises *King of the Zombies* but mentions 'a nice performance from John Carradine', confusing it with Steve Sekely's semi-remake *Revenge of the Zombies*. The blurring extends to primary sources: *The Devil Bat* and at least two other early films credit 'Jean Yarborough.'

Dennis Fischer (*Horror Film Directors, 1931-1990*) makes a rare stab at defining Yarbrough, tagging him 'another of those faceless men who crank out one undistinguished B picture after another.' He concludes by labelling *Hillbillys in a Haunted House* 'a fittingly undistinguished finale to (a) consummately undistinguished career.' However, the piece repeats errors: contrary to many references, Hatton is *not* disfigured by acid in *The Brute Man* and Onslow Stevens *is* the monster in *The Creeper*. Dissecting the films purely as (mainly absurd) plots, Fischer ignores visual qualities, level of performance or downbeat worldview. Even a writer in tune with genre oddly echoes a mainstream sensibility (rooted in story, character and realism) that hinders attempts to take horror seriously, if not solemnly. As narrative, much horror is absurd: to distinguish interesting from dreary, we must often look rather than listen, feel rather than think.

But to set our hero against others of his fighting weight, Yarbrough's horrors are consistently above average for their studios and budget, and his Abbott and Costello are arguably better than Charles Barton's (*Meet Frankenstein, Meet the Killer*) or Charles Lamont's (*...Meet the Invisible Man, Abbott and Costello Meet Dr. Jekyll and Mr. Hyde*). The 'meet' movies, with dearly-loved guest stars, are better remembered but less *funny* than Yarbrough's *In Society* or *Here Come the Co-Eds* and could use his *mysterioso* touch. Lugosi gets more laughs, by no means unintentionally, in *The Devil Bat* than in *Meet Frankenstein* and Lou's 'oo-oo a monster' double-takes don't match Mantan Moreland in *King of the Zombies*.

Paying attention to the minutiae of '40s B auteurs, Yarbrough deserves to rank with Roy William Neill and John Larkin if not Jacques Tourneur and Robert Siodmak. Never given a prestige show like *The Wolf Man* or *Phantom of the Opera*, his films are more consistently watchable than those of George Waggner or Arthur Lubin. In William Beaudine or Sam Newfield movies, no director seems home: but Yarbrough, even with the same makeshift scripts, has atmospherics (cramped Monogram-PRC sets imaginatively lit), performances (no Yarbrough villain is as boring as the Great Karloff in Waggner's *The Climax*) and the odd genuine invention. Without characterising a modest talent as an innovator, it's worth noting he sets precedents: *The Devil Bat*, elaborating a sub-plot from Rowland Lee's *Son of Frankenstein*, pioneers the structuring of a film around 'body count' deaths and is the only PRC horror to have remakes (Newfield's *The Mad Monster* and *The Flying Serpent*) *and* a sequel (Frank Wisbar's *Devil Bat's Daughter*); *King of the Zombies*, influenced by George Marshall's *The Ghost Breakers*, is among the first horrors to play for knowing laughs without outright spoof and is *the* first to use an Axis heavy (the un-Germanic sounding 'Mikael Sangre' claims to be Austrian but his Teuton bark is unmistakably Nazi); *The Brute Man* may be the first prequel; *The Creeper* is an evolutionary junction, looking back to Lewton and the Mad Doctors as it anticipates '50s SF; even *She-Wolf of London*, Yarbrough's weakest, was instantly and cheekily copied as *Devil Bat's Daughter*, before mutating into *Son of Dr Jekyll*, *Daughter of Dr. Jekyll* and *Frankenstein's Daughter*.

Biographical details are sketchy: a Century Baby, Jean W. Yarbrough (or Yarborough — who knows?) was born in Marianna, Arkansas, on 22 August 1900 and educated at the University of the South at Sewanee, Tennessee. Entering movies in 1922 as prop man for Hal Roach, he made twenty-nine short subjects, two-reel comedies or music featurettes between *Don't Be Like That* in 1936 and *Molly Cures a Cowboy* in 1940, most notably an RKO run with comedian Leon Errol (*A Rented Riot*, *Dummy Owner*, *Berth Quakes*, *Crime Rave*). Billed as 'Yarborough', his first feature was *Rebellious Daughters*, one of the moralistic-exploitive grindhouse items now found hilarious by *kitsch*-consumers. Toplining Marjorie Reynolds and Verna Hill, it was made in 1938 for Progressive, an outfit so obscure that PRC and Monogram were a step up. In *Variety*, 'Hobe' mused 'maybe there's something to be said for censorship after all' and described the film as 'a hybrid meller-sexer... (a) penny dreadful shocker about how unsympathetic parents drive tender young girls down the primrose path from home to lives of sin in the big wicked city.'

The filmography tells the rest of the parabola. From 1940 to 1942, he was at PRC and Monogram, making sixty-minute Bs, then he transferred to Universal, a shaky major, and toiled in musicals and comedies, before a heyday when he sometimes produced his films and was entrusted with the studio's biggest assets, Abbott and Costello. He precipitately slid (why?) to Universal Bs and disappeared from the payroll when *The Brute Man* was sold to PRC in 1946; after freelancing for semi-majors, it was back to Monogram and cornpone comedies, a return to Universal for lesser Abbott and

Costello movies (he also worked on their '50s TV show), assignments at a Monogram renamed Allied Artists (unthinkably, AA would win the 1972 Best Picture Oscar for *Cabaret*), and lowly jobs for Fox and United Artists as gigs petered out. The single 1967 credit is for Woolner Brothers, who could easily be Progressive thirty years on; then it was a TV movie and fade to black. Look Upon My Works, Ye Mighty, And Despair.

The Devil Bat, Yarbrough's first major(ish) film, still plays, mainly to Lugosi-philes. Not quite as flamboyant as Richard Vollin (*The Raven*), Dr Paul Carruthers is more fun than most of Lugosi's red herrings or whinging maniacs: this 'kindly village doctor' oozes unctuous smarm and fake geniality, yet the dependable sneer always lurks. Yarbrough and PRC's (tiny?) art and lighting staff do their best Universal Frankenstein imitation as Lugosi broods over a ludicrous experiment (as someone says in the sequel, "what man would *want* to know the secret of enlarging bats?") and a stuffed rodent intercuts with close-ups of a live one (the trick also fails in *Murders in the Rue Morgue*). In the first scene, Lugosi delivers a vintage mad doctor speech *to the bat*: "my friend, our theory of glandular stimulation through electrical impulses was correct!" The big laugh line comes after another glandular jolt makes the bat even bigger, when Lugosi returns from the dungeon-cum-batcave and ducks out of a social occasion because "I am very busy working on a formula for a new shaving lotion." The juxtaposition of crackling arcs, devil bats and shadowy cellars with shaving lotion is absurd, but turns out to be the literal truth: the plot of *The Devil Bat* revolves around a cosmetics company which has exploited Lugosi. He murders the owners with his bats, which have been trained to slash throats smeared with that "new shaving lotion." There's an EC Comics feel to the perfume industry background, a jarring touch in an era when movie scientists resurrected the dead or transplanted gorilla brains rather than drew salary concocting scents.

PRC advertised *The Devil Bat* with topical vigour as 'more terrifying than bombing by night'; it moves snappily, with little of the padding that makes endurance tests of Bs like Newfield's *Dead Men Walk*. Formula ele-

The extremely convincing garden implement-wielding 'she-wolf' from **She-Wolf of London**...

Thrilling stuff from **King of the Zombies**, *the best Mantan Moreland film we've ever seen at 4am.*

shrill and irritating as he makes whiny excuses for the murders rather than, as here, revelling in the deaths of his enemies. *The Devil Bat* has the usual dud supporting actors in stock roles (the only memorable face is Yolande Donlan, the French maid, later a touch of Yank glamour in British crime movies) and the outright comedy relief (Donald Kerr) can't match Lugosi's thin-sliced ham. But it's the work of a comparatively fresh director with possibilities ahead, rather than an oldtimer like Beaudine (or the Yarbrough of *Hillbillys in a Haunted House*) at the fag-end of a once promising career.

It was showy enough, combined with *Caught in the Act* (with Italian ethnic joke Henry Armetta) and *South of Panama* (tongue-in-cheek spying co-written by Sidney Sheldon), to wing a marginal step up to Monogram, where Yarbrough shot *fourteen* movies in 1941 and 1942. Most are lost, but Yarbrough's first for Monogram, *King of the Zombies*, survives and is one of his (and the studio's) finest films, although it remains less-seen than many undeserving Bs that happen to topline Karloff or Lugosi. An early genre-bender, it combines Nazi perfidy, ethnic comedy, tropical temptation, haunted house creeping, two-fisted action, a song (well, a chant), in-jokes and the screen's first Bermuda Triangle plot. Dick Purcell, John Archer and Mantan Moreland (as valet Jefferson Jackson) crash on an island where an Admiral's plane has also gone down and come across the mansion of Dr Sangre (Henry Victor, in a role slated for Lugosi). The white heroes slowly catch on that Sangre is creating zombies through hypnotism, but Moreland is told the whole plot early by 'sepia sweetie' Marguerite Whitten and his patronising bosses refuse to listen whenever he tries to explain. 'Secret agents' Purcell and Archer don't recognise "a strange language" as German and, with astonishing insouciance, sleep together, suggesting either premature tolerance or an unwillingness to build

ments are given a slight spin: montages of newspaper headlines are overlaid with a bat-signal shadow which is more striking than the kite-prop that flutters in suspense scenes. Least effective are the supposed horror highlights: footage of the bat wobbling towards victims is repeated and the actual murders are mainly hurried offscreen. There are neat lines (hero Dave O'Brien sics the bat on Lugosi with "not so funny when it's your own jugular vein that's in danger, is it doc?") and Lugosi seems unusually aware of the comic silliness of the charade. By comparison, in Beaudine's *The Ape Man*, he is

two bedroom sets.

Most commentary on *King of the Zombies* has centred on Moreland: less offensively stereotyped than Willie Best in *The Ghost Breakers* if as fond of 'scared' business and odd colloquialisms ("eyes, if you look, I ain't responsible for what you see"). Comparing a gaunt butler to Slim Gaillard and voodoo drums to Gene Krupa, Moreland alone realises there's a world beyond the B through which he runs shrieking; almost all the felicitous business (referring to zombies as "perishables" or "has-beens", joining the undead with "gang way for Big Zom") belongs to him. The script is by Ed(mund) Kelso, who worked on the Darro-Moreland films, but the comic seems to improvise. Top-billed in black neighbourhoods, he gives a star performance, with hep jokes and sharp digs at stupid white folks. Though Victor is surprising as the restrained villain and the other blacks (Madame Sul-Te-Wan as a voodoo queen, Leigh Whipper as the butler, Whitten as the sassy cook) play for wry laughs, Moreland steals every scene that isn't nailed down, even with lame lines ("I thought I was a little off-colour to be a ghost"). Anyone who doubts the director's contribution, however, should consider *Revenge of the Zombies*: co-written by Kelso (reusing much of the earlier script), it shares cinematographer Mack Stengler with Yarbrough's film, recalls Moreland (again as Jeff, a character also in *Freckles Comes Home*) and Sul-Te-Wan, and benefits from starrier Nazis (John Carradine, Veda Ann Borg) and scrawnier zombies, but it's still a sixty-one minute bore, while *King of the Zombies* is a pacy treat.

Without overdoing it and despite Moreland's cut-ups in scenes involving zombies, Yarbrough still works in atmosphere: *King of the Zombies* has a dark, late-at-night feel not untouched by dread. The tinny heroics of the white cast suggest neo-existential claustrophobia as the action is trapped not only by the isolated island and the old dark house but by cramped shadowed sets. There is so much going on — a voodoo soul-transference rite, Sangre's zombified wife wandering by night, an attempt to get the Admiral to disclose Panama Canal secrets (macguffin also of *South of Panama*) — that we're never stuck with dreary police investigations or romances. Through a unique, unfathomable quirk, *King of the Zombies* got a 1941 Academy Award nomination for composer Edward Kay (Bernard Herrmann won for *All That Money Can Buy*). It's hard to hear anything in the scant drum themes or stock music cuts to differentiate the score from a hundred other done-in-the-afternoon jobs; the anonymous music 'supervised' by David Chudnow for *The Devil Bat* is more immediately memorable.

Maybe it was the Oscar nod, but when he moved to Universal, Yarbrough found himself a musical specialist, with an endless string of *Follow the Band*, *Twilight on the Prairie*, *Hi Ya, Sailor* (his first as a producer-director), *Weekend Pass*, *Moon Over Las Vegas*, *South of Dixie* and so on... According to David Quinlan in *The Illustrated Guide to Film Directors*, the best of this batch is *Weekend Pass*, 'a little film of considerable charm.' These time capsules of popular taste rarely surface, even as afternoon TV time-filler: hectoring wartime Americanism has gone beyond grating to become offensive and Universal's brassy cheer dates less well than MGM glamour, Paramount sophistication or Warners grit. Without the groundswell of *Hi Ya, Sailor*s and *Cuban Pete*s, Gene Kelly and Stanley Donen would have had nothing to rebel against when they reinvented the movie musical with *On the Town*.

Similar in feel to the musicals (in fact, stuffed with specialty numbers) are Yarbrough's biggest commercial hits, a 1944-5 trio with Abbott and Costello. All have points of interest: *Here Come the Co-Eds* has Lon Chaney Jr's Masked Marvel wrestled to a standstill by Lou; *The Naughty Nineties* films the famous "Who's on first?" ("and Watt's on second?") vaudeville act; and *In Society* features Abbott and Costello's most sustained and disturbing routine (excerpted in Milton Subotsky's *The World of Abbott and Costello*) as they try to deliver a consignment of straw hats to the 'Susquehana Hat Company' only to have every passerby fly into an irrational and destructive rage at the mention of Susquehana Hats. *In Society* climaxes with a breakneck fire engine chase that would be funnier if it weren't an exact copy of a scene in W.C. Fields' *The Bank Dick*. *Lost in Alaska* and *Jack and the Beanstalk*, Yarbrough's 1952 reunion with the team, show how soon they ran out of ideas: never as canny or interesting as Laurel and Hardy (or Hope and Crosby), Abbott and Costello swiftly turned into a middle-aged crybaby and a sour-tempered stooge with half the panache of Zeppo Marx. *Jack and the Beanstalk*, with Buddy (*Giant from the Unknown*) Baer, tries a *Wizard of Oz* trick by segueing from sepia to colour as the beanstalk is climbed, but is a tiresome, unmagical fairy tale skit. *Lost in Alaska*, a frozen North parody, is essentially a feeble retread of *Road to Utopia*; its bright spot is Tom Ewell as a cracked prospector whose antics show up the tired stars.

Middle-aged crybaby and sour-tempered stooge meet Buddy Baer. Hilarity ensues.

In his last year at the studio, Yarbrough switched from frothy to downbeat, moving to the lowest of Universal's B units to turn out a single *noir* (*Inside Job*, from a '30s story left behind by Garrett Fort and Tod Browning, in which ex-con Preston Foster is blackmailed into a heist) and three threadbare horror-monster-mystery items. British producer Ben Pivar, Universal's '40s horror supremo, was charged with developing characters to succeed the studio's Frankenstein and Dracula moneyspinners. With series openers like Christy Cabanne's *The Mummy's Hand* and Edward Dmytryk's *Captive Wild Woman*, Pivar demonstrates that the franchise horror craze has an exact parallel in the fright factories of the '40s. By 1946, the monster cycles (and frontline stars Karloff, Lugosi and Chaney Jr) were played out. Pivar

looked through the backlist for properties which could be adapted (ie: coarsened) into series, as he had done in mauling Karl Freund's *The Mummy* into the lumbering Kharis movies. He lit upon the mainly outstanding run of Sherlock Holmes pictures, starring Basil Rathbone and Nigel Bruce, produced and directed between 1942 and 1946 by Roy William Neill. These shared sets and effects with the monsters (Neill also got *Frankenstein Meets the Wolf Man*) and were pitched as much at horror fans as mystery devotees, with villainous players (Lionel Atwill, George Zucco, Henry Daniell) allowed to shine as they matched wits with the Great Detective.

Pivar's first spin-off was Arthur Lubin's *The Spider Woman Strikes Back*, which recalls Gale Sondergaard from *The Spider Woman* and partners her with Rondo Hatton, the acromegalic who'd made an impression as 'the Creeper' in Neill's *The Pearl of Death*. Though Sondergaard delivers more acting power than Veda Ann Borg or Evelyn Ankers, her fifty-nine minute vehicle is a stately plod through a ludicrous plot which is never as much fun as it might be. At the Pivar unit, Yarbrough was reunited with George Bricker, who'd provided the story for *The Devil Bat*, and would script all three films, though the stories came from Dwight V. Babcock. A *Black Mask* contributor, Babcock can be seen in the famous 1936 group photograph of the only recorded meeting of Raymond Chandler and Dashiell Hammett: with screenwriters Eric Taylor (*The Spider Woman Strikes Back*) and John K. Butler (*The Vampire's Ghost*), unashamed hack Babcock (whose Universal credits include *The Mummy's Curse* and *The Jungle Captive*) looks at the camera like a happy idiot while the haunted alcoholic geniuses try to avoid each other's eyelines.

Yarbrough's *She-Wolf of London* is better than *The Spider Woman Strikes Back*, but only just. Though, in tune with Pivar's pillaging, half the title is poached from *Werewolf of London*, it's another borrowing from the Holmes films, casting Dennis Hoey (Neill's Lestrade) as another dim-wit inspector and passing off familiar sets as fogbound London. With murderess Sara Haden using a garden weeder to seem like a werething, *She-Wolf of London* imitates *The Scarlet Claw*, the best of Neill's series, but the plot (influenced by *The Hound of the Baskervilles* and John Brahm's *The Undying Monster*) has heiress June Lockhart driven out of her mind when she thinks she has inherited a lycanthropic curse. Martin Kosleck is unbelievably cast as sympathetic love interest and there are moments of creepiness, but the comedic edge of *The Devil Bat* and *King of the Zombies* is sorely missed among tediously bumbling policemen and stodgy attempts at doom-haunted misery. Though imitated several times, *She-Wolf of London* did not fulfil Pivar's hopes and trigger a series, at least not until the late '80s when Universal revived the title for a little-seen werewolf TV show (aka *Love and Curses*). The best anyone (the authors of *Universal Horrors*) ever said of *She-Wolf of London* is 'Yarbrough makes the most of his limited resources and manages some real atmosphere in the prowling wolf-woman scenes.'

The other Yarbrough-Pivar-Bricker-Babcock films are more interesting as they try to make a horror star of Rondo Hatton and a continuing monster of the Creeper. The faintly patronising 'Mondo Rondo' attention paid *House of Horrors* and *The Brute Man* has focused on the bad taste of using real-life malformation in trashy horror, with a mocking emphasis on the gravel-voiced player's obvious discomfort with basic dialogue. Neither makes as good use of Hatton as *The Pearl of Death* (in which he is in shadows and has nothing to say), but Yarbrough certainly gets more from the unique performer than Lubin in *The Spider Woman Strikes Back* or Harold Young in *The Jungle Captive*. In earlier roles, Hatton is a stooge, lumbering off to do some mad scientist's spine-snapping, otherwise loitering in laboratories or alleyways (like the Hatton imitation in *The Rocketeer*). The Creeper movies try to build him as a character, borrowing from Humphrey Bogart's Roy Earle in *High Sierra* — in *The Brute Man* he commits crimes to fund an operation for an ungrateful handicapped girl — and Mike Mazurki's Moose Malloy in *Murder, My Sweet*. Like Moose, the Creeper is an outsized grotesque with unreasonable affection for irredeemable people. Hatton's croaked dialogue sounds like Mazurki's delivery; and Mazurki even took Hatton-type roles in *Dick Tracy* and *Night and the City*.

Much the better of the two is *House of Horrors*, which shares with later Universals (*The Jungle Captive*, *The Mummy's Curse*, *House of Dracula*) a shudder-pulp feel unlike anything until the *Kolchak: The Night Stalker* TV series. Set in a *noir*-ish urban jungle, this is an America where tabloid headlines harp on Creeper killings or escaped ape women and individual monsters have complex public histories. To take the acting weight off Hatton, the film has the Creeper hook up with sculptor Marcel DeLange, a swish fascist played by Martin Kosleck. A specialist in perverse bizarros, Kosleck delightedly seizes the opportunity to overcome fourth billing and take a rare lead. About to throw himself in the Hudson because unfair criticism has made him "the laughing stock of New York's art circles", DeLange finds the deformed Creeper in the river. Inspired to live, he uses his new friend as a model for a bust of Neanderthal Man. Because DeLange shows the thuggish psycho some kindness, the Creeper is happy to avenge him by breaking the backs of supercilious art critics. The funniest moment, nicely judged by Kosleck if not Hatton, is DeLange's lengthy fulmination against the tasteless malice and low intelligence of F. Holmes Harmon (Alan Napier), whereupon the Creeper groans "so you don't like the guy, huh?"

House of Horrors is remarkably sick, as if the ridiculousness of Universal's horror output gulled the Breen Office into ignoring the seamier side. "The Creeper's still alive," gasps a morgue attendant, "looks like I'll be putting in some overtime." The cynical tone is maintained, almost all the characters lifted from the B stereotype rut by viciousness. Hero Robert Lowery is a cheesecake artist who comes under suspicion because he throws a party when he hears about Napier's death. Cop Bill Goodwin is more interested in making time with girlie model Joan Shawlee than catching the killer. Heroine Joan Medford (Virginia Grey) is on DeLange's shitlist for being a nasty bitch (her hat is supposed to evoke gossip Hedda Hopper) and becomes less sympathetic in the finale by changing from career girl to marriage-happy geek ("I don't want to be an art critic any more, darling"). The scribblers who get their spines snapped, like critics in movies from *Laura* to *Theatre of Blood*, are snide and malicious parasites who delight in ruining hard-working, if insane, artists.

For a B, the film is quite ambitious: its Greenwich Village milieu is caricatured, but (like the perfume business of *The Devil Bat*) was unusual for a horror movie at the time, and DeLange's studio, dominated by strange artworks, is an eerie setting for his rants. Again, there is an attempt to dispense with the dull padding of too many Bs (*She-Wolf of London* included) by giving familiar situations an unfamiliar spin: typical is Yarbrough's effective stalker variant as Hatton pursues blonde Virginia Christine through waterfront shadows, only to have the victim react to the monster not with a scream but by trying to pick him up.

The Brute Man, made months later, is a step down: when Universal decided to discontinue B production, it was palmed off on PRC for distribution. Yarbrough tries to cover up with lighting, but the film is as threadbare as anything from Poverty Row and even features archetypal PRC 'star' Tom Neal (of Ulmer's *Detour*) as an unsympathetic and casually-killed 'hero.' Oddly, despite much prowling around the waterfront, the film doesn't end with the Creeper thrown into the river to cue the opening of *House of Horrors*, but simply and dramatically has him arrested and marched away. Aside from the fact that no mention is made of the Creeper having been killed at the end of *House of Horrors*, nothing suggests *The Brute Man* takes place earlier than the other film (or that this Creeper is indeed the same Creeper, any more than he is the British-based Creeper of *The Pearl of Death*), but it counts as a prequel thanks to it's 'origin' story flashback.

Continuing the misanthropy, *The Brute Man* reveals the Creeper is football star Hal Moffat (Fred Coby), Hampton University, class of '30, who can only get through chemistry by having brainy Clifford Scott (Neal) do his work for him. The lady-killing Moffat brags of the 'hot-date' he has set with Scott's own girlfriend (Jan Wiley) for the evening after an exam, so Scott gives him the wrong answers, whereupon the jock has to work late in the lab. When Scott and gal peek in to gloat, Moffat throws down a beaker of chemicals which explodes in his face. "The doctors told us the chemicals might affect certain glands and nerves," Scott explains, "and if they did his features would never be normal again." The now-married couple insensitively muse about their old friend, "one of them (*the doctors*) did say he was pretty bitter when he left...a thing like that could affect his mind." While one can almost sympathise with the Claude Rains Phantom of the Opera, disfigured with flung acid while making a scene in the office of a publisher he thinks is stealing his music, or Lionel Atwill in *Mystery of the Wax Museum*, trapped as a crooked business partner tries to

destroy his life's work, it's hard to feel much for this gorilla-brained chump. No matter how mushy the Creeper might get over blind piano teacher Helen Paige (Jane Adams) whose eyesight he tries to save by extorting money from his old university pals, he's still a self-centred clod who has apparently been killing people all these years for the lack of anything better to do.

While drabber and less entertaining than *House of Horrors*, *The Brute Man* isn't quite the atrocity its reputation suggests. The interesting and unconventional nastiness continues: the cops are time-serving dullards under pressure from buck-passing politicians ('MAYOR CHARGES POLICE LAXITY IN CREEPER KILLINGS' shrieks a headline), capable of "sitting here playing gin rummy with another Creeper murder on the front pages"; the Scotts, stuffy preppies who don't bother to notice their old varsity friends have been murdered, are the nearest thing to romantic leads; and the criminally naive blind girl blathers about how sightless people can see the true souls of ugly people but radically misjudges a murderer who was a bastard even before he got disfigured. Even more than in *House of Horrors*, Yarbrough focuses on Hatton's shadowed face: we can see his disease (which killed him before either film was released) accelerating, the grooves in his face deepening and his impeded, raspy voice unsuited to the unreasonable number of lines he is given. Perhaps the most pathetic thing about the film, also its nastiest touch, is the human monster is so incapable of exciting sympathy that the plot has to take account of it: the saintly Helen is happy without hesitation to let him go (presumably) to the chair. "That was a fine thing you did, helping us to trap the killer," the cops say after she has betrayed a man willing to commit major crimes for her; she muses cheerfully, "I wonder how he feels about it?"

After leaving Universal (nineteen films in three years) Yarbrough had no credits in 1947, but turned out four 1948 Bs at minors (the films released through 20th Century-Fox were produced by low-esteem subsidiary

Hot Shots — *Huntz Hall in search of the perfect suppository.*

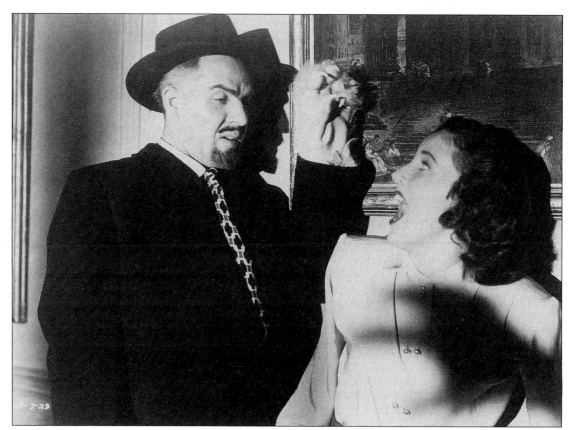

(Right) Onslow Stevens threatens Janis Wilson with death by glove puppet in **The Creeper.**

(Next page — top) **Master Minds** *— Glenn Strange (in a Jack Pierce make-up) ponders a bleak future with Huntz Hall's brain...*

(Bottom) Glenn Strange hangs around with more middle-aged crybabies...

Reliance). *The Challenge* is the first of a 1948 pair (the other is Frank McDonald's *13 Lead Soldiers*) with Tom Conway as Bulldog Drummond. The suave detective (by now so removed from his literary origins to be no different from the Saint, the Lone Wolf or the Falcon) solves murders connected with the search for a casket of gold. John Newland, originator of the *One Step Beyond* TV series and director of *The Legend of Hillbilly John*, plays silly-ass sidekick Algy. Jon Tuska, in his *In Manors and Alleys: A Casebook on the American Detective Film* comments that an 'interesting aspect of *The Challenge* was the variation on Agatha Christie's *Murder on the Orient Express* in which Drummond finds everyone guilty except the heroine played by June Vincent.'

The most interesting late Yarbrough (maybe his *chef d'oeuvre*) is *The Creeper*, produced by Ben Pivar and doubtless entitled to recall the Hatton movies. Here, Creeper is the name of a pet cat who unaccountably terrifies the heroine. Concerning claw murders in a medical research centre, the film is unique: the only serious American horror made between 1946 and 1951, it fuses the apparently antithetical B strains of the Karloff-Lugosi Mad Doctor cycle with the Val Lewton mysterioso-psycho *noir* series, but also looks forward from the shadows of the '40s to the antiseptic '50s and mutations like *The Fly* and *The Alligator People*. Maurice Tombragel's script (from a story by Don Martin, who wrote the novel on which *Shed No Tears* is based) is yet another rescramble of *She-Wolf of London*. Nora (Janis Wilson), daughter of philosophical scientist Dr Cavegny (Ralph Morgan), is tormented by nightmares that may be the after-effect of a fever picked up on a tropical expedition, and suspects she may herself be responsible for the clawings. Suffering Lewtonesque neuroses and dreams, Nora has visions of a giant, somewhat too fluffy, cats paw creeping over a windowsill or (in a primal scene) from under her bed. She is also engaged in a singularly bitchy

tussle with secondary female lead Gwen (the inevitable June Vincent) over handsome but weedy hero John Reed (John Baragrey), the type who says, "come now, give us a smile, in the interests of science of course." Gwen, a hard-faced Veronica Lake-alike, reassures her pop-eyed rival with speeches like "you've always been a rather neurotic type and a trip to the West Indies doesn't seem to have helped you... Tell me, don't you ever awaken from a horribly realistic dream in which you're not a person?"

The institute is staffed by suspicious characters: Dr Bordon (Onslow Stevens) is too helpful and decent not to turn out to be the guilty goatee, but there is a concerted attempt to make a red herring of Dr Van Glock (Eduardo Ciannelli), forever loitering outside doors claiming to be looking for the cat. Andrei, a mute lab attendant, is lit to present a Rondo Hatton-like appearance; the actor is David Hoffman, the little man with the distorted face who narrates *Flesh and Fantasy* and appears as a head in a crystal ball to introduce Universal's *Inner Sanctum* series. The team are supposedly developing 'symbiotic luminous bacteria' with the intention of making organs glow (to make it easier to perform surgery with the lights out?), but Bordon has discovered an apparently addictive serum which turns his hand into the paw. No reasonable explanation for the purpose of this experiment is ever advanced, and the film winds up with Nora going along with her boyfriend's suggestion that she not mention it to the police, making us wonder just what exactly has been going on for the previous, delirious sixty-five minutes.

The Creeper shows how much more sophisticated Bs had grown since *The Devil Bat*: the mad scientist is just as lunatic, but the working conditions of the average scientist are far more 'realistic.' Back-biting, jealous researchers pursue cracked projects in underlit but credible facilities: early on, we find Reed among the bubbling retorts and Bunsen burners Lugosi was overfond of, but this turns out to be his way of making coffee while he gets on with proper work. As usual, Yarbrough plays the B game only so far, then pulls a switch: the 'stalker' finale, as the villain closes in on the heroine, is conventionally set up, only to have Gwen shoot the shadowy figure invading her home and wound her own love interest just when she needs to be protected from the monster. It has elements from earlier Pivar-Yarbrough films (an unpleasant and useless police investigator, an oppressive atmosphere of dread and desire), but it's an all-out attempt to get high style into the genre. It is so thoroughly wrought it could almost be a lost episode of *The Outer Limits*: never did Yarbrough — abetted by cinematographer George Robinson (who worked on virtually every Universal horror) — try harder. A visit to a Chinese restaurant (exotic to the point of decadence in 1948) is scored with eerie oriental music and lit as if it were an opium den, though proprietor Philip Ahn is not a racial stereotype. In this unforced use of minority characters, *The Creeper* also follows Lewton: the standard thinking is that the RKO cycle was too cerebral and arty for the mummy's curses and mad laboratories of '40s horror, but this is only one of several (*The Soul of a Monster*, *Cry of the Werewolf*, *The Woman Who Came Back*) attempts to co-opt Lewton's innovations back into the mainstream monster movie.

The Creeper has so many dreams, montages, flashbacks, sleepwalkings (Nora is the sort of girl who gets out of bed and grabs a gun without noticing) and drug-induced frenzies that there seems to be no normal scenes connecting them. Among the devices Yarbrough uses are brief, pre-Peckinpah flashes of slow motion; images that ripple like disturbed ponds; hypnotic circles of fog around terrified faces; out-of-focus scenes of corpses surrounded by prowling cats; and overlapping dissolves that turn hand into claw. With high-flown dialogue ("Just then my life became a rather horrible round of squirming cats and hypodermic needles and serums bubbling in bottles"; "We'd be releasing energies that would result only in mutations, monstrosities and death. We can't benefit mankind, we can only do immeasurable harm") and frequent hallucinations (the influence, again, of *Murder, My Sweet*?), *The Creeper* tries for an oneiric feel that makes it an ideal four in the morning film. "Dreams are always strange, at least that's the way they seem," Cavegny muses in a keynote speech, "in their own peculiar way though, they have their own kind of logic."

After that, Yarbrough lost direction and backslid to Monogram. The bulk of his work was on series comedies, including the Bowery Boys' horror spoof *Master Minds* with Glenn Strange as Atlas, a man monster who receives Huntz Hall's brain, Alan Napier of *House of Horrors* as a mad scientist, and Jane Adams of *The Brute Man* as the girl. Hardly a plum assignment, it perhaps seemed worthier than his other quickies of the period.

After 1957, the career was essentially over, though Yarbrough had fluke credits in 1962 (*Saintly Sinners*, a small-town drama with Don Beddoe as a kindly priest who reforms crooks), 1967 and 1969. *Hillbillys in a Haunted House* is familiar in reference books because it features Basil Rathbone, Lon Chaney Jr and John Carradine, plus a gorilla and an Iron Maiden prop from the Corman Poe movies, in an old dark house. Though in the line of descent from *King of the Zombies* (atom spies pretend to haunt the house, though a real Confederate ghost shows up to see them off) and *Master Minds* (lots of creeping-about, with the horror stars peer-

Ace the Wonder Dog becomes spiritual advisor to Pat Robertson. Would you admit to having seen **Silent Witness?**

ing into the camera as if that alone were scary), this sequel to Arthur C. Pierce's *Las Vegas Hillbillys* has more in common with *Moon Over Las Vegas* and *Casa Mañana*: the slim plot pauses every so often for country music (from Sonny James, Merle Haggard, Molly Bee or ever-smiling stars Ferlin Husky and Joi Lansing), the most memorable excuse being the gunpoint exchange "what proof do you have that you're an entertainer?"/"My guitar?"/"Play!" The bad guys, commanded by a Dragon Lady (Linda Ho) who can barely pronounce difficult words, are rounded up fifteen minutes before the finish so the hillbillies (sorry *hillbillys*) can get out of the haunted house and hit a Nashville jamboree for numbers shot from a locked-down camera by a director who might not even have been in the room.

If not for references to/rip-offs of *The Beverly Hillbillies* (from which the appealing Lansing was borrowed) and *The Man From U.N.C.L.E.* (a good guy secret agency is called Master Organisation To Halt Enemy Resistance — MOTHER), you'd swear this highly-coloured but drab item was made ten years earlier. The haunted house episodes of *The Monkees* are funnier and only the embarrassingly enthusiastic Chaney delivers anything like the old spirit, while the bad tempered Rathbone and Carradine trudge through in search of a pay cheque. The songs include Lansing's syrupy but eerie 'Gowns, Gowns, Beautiful Gowns', an attempt at atmosphere, although the creepiest is a cheery rendition of 'The Cat Came Back', a children's song about an unkillable cat who survives abandonment, dismemberment, train wreck, etc. Compared to that serving of bone-freezing horror with a face-freezing grin, sliding panels, a shambling gorilla, rattling skeletons and secret

laboratories are mock turtle soup. Wheeler Dixon says the film 'manages to retain an ersatz dignity' but he's being unaccountably generous. That said, after the third or fourth viewing, it becomes compulsive in a Michael Snow sort of way: especially Lansing's moulded hair and the hillbilly who pronounces 'werewolf' as 'weirdwoof.'

After this lacklustre big screen exit, Yarbrough's last feature, a TV movie, was surprisingly high-profile: *The Over-the-Hill Gang*, a western comedy similar to *The Good Guys and the Bad Guys*, with Pat O'Brien as a retired Texas Ranger who sees off whippersnapping young badmen. Produced by Aaron Spelling, the lightweight picture nostalgically stars Chill Wills, Walter Brennan, Edgar Buchanan, Andy Devine and Jack Elam, plus a once-in-a-lifetime teaming of Ricky Nelson and Gypsy Rose Lee. It was successful enough to warrant a sequel: George McCowan's *The Over the Hill Gang Rides Again*, with Fred Astaire in O'Brien's role. Yarbrough died in 1975 and this is the most anyone has thought of him since. The lost continent of his filmography deserves to be raised from the sea-bed and he should at least get credit for the intriguing aspects of his horror films. He never won a major commission (anyone whose career highlights are Abbott and Costello hardly had a shot at the pantheon) but was consistently interesting, at least in the '40s. The purpose of this piece has not been to rank him with James Whale or Mario Bava, but to single him out from the anonymous masses. Struggling through Desi Arnaz musicals and Bowery Boys comedies and unimaginable losses like *Silent Witness* and *According to Mrs Hoyle* was genuine talent, and maybe even cinematic sensibility.

Jean Yarbrough, hail and farewell! ∎

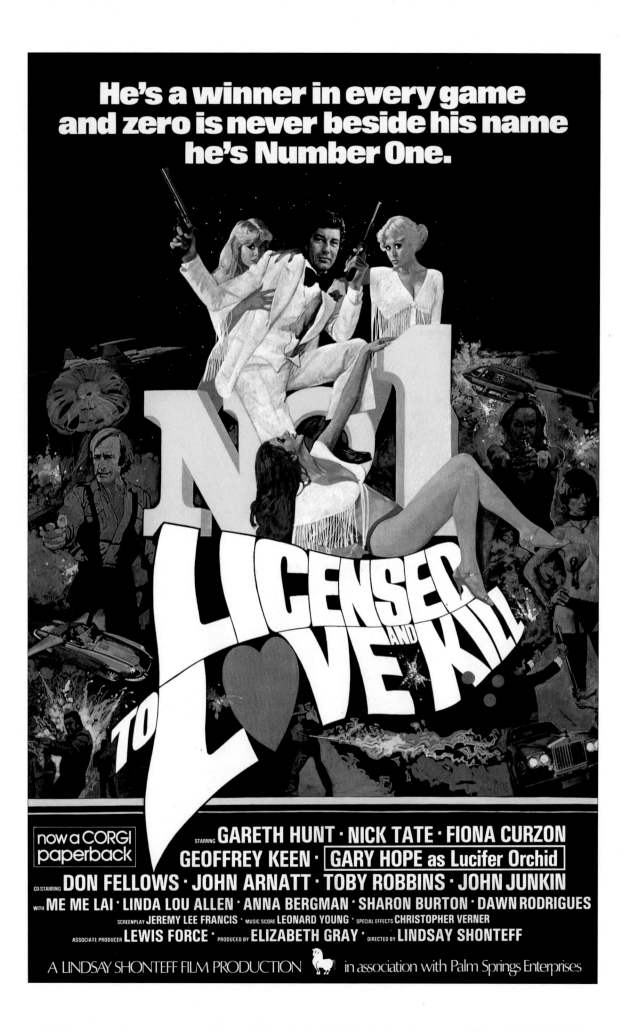

(Above) Mariangela Giordano contemplates her career in Gabriele Crisanti trash...

(Left) Two typical 'video nasty' viewers refute claims they've been depraved and corrupted. (**Braindead**.)

HILLBILLYS IN A HAUNTED HOUSE

FERLIN **HUSKY**
JOI **LANSING**
DON **BOWMAN**

They'll scare your pants off

...and give you a chill for life!

ALSO STARRING
JOHN **CARRADINE**
LON **CHANEY**
BASIL **RATHBONE**

You'll have to read the entire book to figure out why these lobby cards are here...

(Left) Franco Nero in Fulci's **Tempo di Massacro,** *a film that is not very good.*

(Below) Django gets his weapon out.

THIS WOMAN HAS JUST...

CUT, CHOPPED, BROKEN AND BURNED FOUR MEN BEYOND RECOGNITION... BUT NO JURY IN AMERICA WOULD EVER CONVICT HER!

I SPIT on your GRAVE

AN ACT OF REVENGE!

Starring CAMILLE KEATON ERON TABOR RICHARD PACE ANTHONY NICHOLS
produced by JOSEPH ZBEDA
written and directed by MEIR ZARCHI
RUNNING TIME 98 MIN

Yarbroughaphy

1936: DON'T BE LIKE THAT*
FIGHT IS RIGHT*
LALAPALOOSA*
ALL BUSINESS*
AND SO TO WED*
BAD MEDICINE*
DOG BLIGHT*
SO AND SEW*
1937: A RENTED RIOT*
HORSE PLAY*
INLAWFULL*
RHYTHM ON THE RAMPAGE*
SINGING IN THE AIR*
SWING FEVER*
TRAILING ALONG*
WISE INSURANCE*
1938: DUMMY OWNER*
A BUCKEROO BROADCAST*
BERTH QUAKES*
HECTIC HONEYMOON*
MUSIC WILL TELL*
THE PHOTOGRAPHER*
REBELLIOUS DAUGHTERS (PROGRESSIVE)
PICKETING FOR LOVE*
RUSSIAN DRESSING*
1939: CRIME RAVE*
PLUMB CRAZY*
START THE MUSIC*
SWING VACATION*
1940: MOLLY CURES A COWBOY*
1941: THE DEVIL BAT/KILLER BATS
KING OF THE ZOMBIES (M)

THE GANG'S ALL HERE/IN THE NIGHT (M)
scrappy Frankie Darro and the estimable Mantan
Moreland drive trucks
FATHER STEPS OUT/CITY LIMITS (M) a remake
of *City Limits*
CAUGHT IN THE ACT (PRC)
LET'S GO COLLEGIATE/FAREWELL TO FAME (M)
scrappy Frankie Darro and the estimable Mantan
Moreland crash the campus scene
TOP SERGEANT MULLIGAN (M) an imitation of
Abbott and Costello's *Buck Privates*, with Frank
Faylen and Charles Hall as comic bums
SOUTH OF PANAMA/PANAMA MENACE (PRC)
1942: FRECKLES COMES HOME (M) comedy for the
sticks with bumpkin Johnny Downs outwitting
cityslicking gangsters
MAN FROM HEADQUARTERS (M) light-hearted
mix of hardboiled reporters and gangsters
LAW OF THE JUNGLE (M) studio-bound exotica
with Arline Judge, John King and Arthur
O'Connell 'pursued by a marauding gorilla'
SO'S YOUR AUNT EMMA/MEET THE MOB (M)
comedy for the sticks with spinster Zasu Pitts
outwitting cityslicking gangsters
SHE'S IN THE ARMY (M) the *Private Benjamin* of
1942, with snotty WAC Veda Ann Borg discovering patriotism and Lyle Talbot
LURE OF THE ISLANDS (M) more studio-bound
exotica, with he-man G-Men Robert 'Big Boy'
Lowery and Guinn Williams after tropical Nazis
(sample banter; Lowery: "Pick your man and fire at
will"; Williams: "Which one is Will?"), while stripper Margie Hart and starlet Gale Storm fill sarongs
POLICE BULLETS (M) another light-hearted mix
of hardboiled reporters and gangsters
CRIMINAL INVESTIGATOR (M) 'cheapest of the
wartime Monograms' (pace Don Miller, *"B"
Movies*). With Robert Lowery
1943: SILENT WITNESS/THE ATTORNEY FOR THE
DEFENSE (M) with Ace the Wonder Dog taking
the stand to bust a crime ring.
FOLLOW THE BAND (U) with an early, tiny
Robert Mitchum performance and hayseed Eddie
Quillan singing 'What Do You Want to Make
Those Eyes at Me For?'

So's Your Aunt Emma.
I'll say she is.

GET GOING (U)
GOOD MORNING, JUDGE (U)
HI YA, SAILOR (&P; U) with seaman-songwriter Donald Woods supposedly composing 'The More I Go Out With Somebody Else'.
SO'S YOUR UNCLE (&P; U)

1944: **IN SOCIETY/ABBOTT AND COSTELLO IN SOCIETY** (U)
MOON OVER LAS VEGAS (&P; U) reunites Anne Gwynne and David Bruce (of *The Mad Ghoul*)
SOUTH OF DIXIE (U) does the same!
TWILIGHT ON THE PRAIRIE (U) with hayseed Eddie Quillan singing 'I Got Mellow in the Yellow of the Moon'
WEEKEND PASS (U) an attempt to make a romantic item of Martha O'Driscoll (of *House of Dracula*) and Noah Beery Jr with a WAC background.

1945: **HERE COME THE CO-EDS** (U)
THE NAUGHTY NINETIES (U)
ON STAGE EVERYBODY (U) with Jack Oakie and Peggy Ryan plus the screen début of Julie London and 'Stuff Like That There' (revived in *For the Boys*)
UNDER WESTERN SKIES (U) another attempt to make a romantic item of Martha O'Driscoll and Noah Beery Jr, this time with an Old West background.

1946: **CUBAN PETE/DOWN CUBA WAY** (U) mixes Desi Arnaz with 'Rhumba Matumba'...
HOUSE OF HORRORS/JOAN MEDFORD IS MISSING (U)
INSIDE JOB (&P; U)
SHE-WOLF OF LONDON/THE CURSE OF THE ALLENBYS (U)
THE BRUTE MAN (U/PRC)

1948: **THE CHALLENGE** (Fox)
SHED NO TEARS (Eagle Lion) a domestic noir, with Wallace Ford faking his own death to collect insurance, then learning that his wife plans a double-cross; the female lead is June Vincent

"I'll never end my career by appearing in an Al Adamson movie!" boasts J. Carrol Naish in **Yaqui Drums.** *Wrong.*

THE CREEPER (Fox)
TRIPLE THREAT (C) a pigskin drama produced by Charles H. Schneer, Ray Harryhausen's partner, with Richard Crane as a swellhead football player who reforms after personal troubles which don't involve a beaker of chemicals or spine-snapping...

1949: **HOLIDAY IN HAVANA** (M) a reunion with Desi Arnaz
THE MUTINEERS (M) a Jon Hall-Adele Jergens-George Reeves gun-running adventure
LEAVE IT TO HENRY (M) with Raymond Walburn as a henpecked husband-cum-inventor, as are *Henry, the Rainmaker* and *Father Makes Good*
HENRY, THE RAINMAKER (M) 'Man uses science to make rain, can't stop it when it starts.' (*Horror and Science Fiction Films*, Donald C. Willis)
MASTER MINDS (M)
ANGELS IN DISGUISE (M) yet more Bowery Boys larks

1950: **BIG TIMBER** (M) a Roddy McDowell Northwoods logging drama
JOE PALOOKA MEETS HUMPHREY (M) dim-witted boxing comedy with old associate Leon Errol
JOE PALOOKA IN HUMPHREY TAKES A CHANCE/HUMPHREY TAKES A CHANCE (M) another dim-witted boxing comedy with Leon Errol
TRIPLE TROUBLE (M) further Bowery Boys larks
SIDESHOW (M) an undercover thriller with T-Man Don McGuire posing as a carny to trap jewel smugglers
SQUARE DANCE KATY (M) a Vera Vague musical

1951: **FATHER MAKES GOOD** (M)
CASA MAÑANA (M) a Robert Clarke musical
ACCORDING TO MRS HOYLE (M) a Spring Byington-Anthony Caruso remake of *So's Your Aunt Emma*

1952: **LOST IN ALASKA** (U)
JACK AND THE BEANSTALK (U)

1954: **NIGHT FREIGHT** (AA) a Forrest Tucker truck-driving melodrama

1956: **CRASHING LAS VEGAS** (AA)
HOT SHOTS (AA) even more Bowery Boys
THE WOMEN OF PITCAIRN ISLAND (Fox) with James Craig and Lynn Bari, set among the mutineers' descendants in the historical aftermath of *Mutiny on the Bounty*. 'Low-budget garbage' (*Leonard Maltin's Movie and Video Guide*)
YAQUI DRUMS (AA) a Rod Cameron-Robert Hutton-J. Carroll Naish western. 'Soggy' (*Leonard Maltin's Movie and Video Guide*)

1957: **FOOTSTEPS IN THE NIGHT** (AA) an Albert Band-scripted crime movie with Bill Elliott and Don Haggerty.

1962: **SAINTLY SINNERS** (UA)

1967: **HILLBILLYS IN A HAUNTED HOUSE** (Woolner Brothers) the timeless songs include 'We're On Our Way to Nashville, Tennessee', 'Livin' in a Trance', 'Someone Told My Story in a Song', 'Tell Me Shoes, Was She Walking Out on Me?', 'Swinging Doors, a Jukebox and a Barstool', 'Heartbreak USA' and 'I Got Into the Wrong House Again Last Night'

1969: **THE OVER-THE-HILL GANG** (Thomas-Spelling)

* = short. AA = Allied Artists. C = Columbia.
M = Monogram. PRC = Producers Releasing Corporation.
Fox = 20th Century Fox. UA = United Artists.
U = Universal.

SPAWN OF TARANTULA!

PART 2

BY DAVID McGILLIVRAY

The author discovers the surviving print of **The Hot Girls**...

THE STORY SO FAR:

David is a strange little boy. He shows no interest in westerns and instead develops an unhealthy obsession with horror films — particularly *Tarantula* — and other morbid subjects. When he grows up, he makes feeble attempts to break into show business. Eventually he is asked to write screenplays — *White Cargo* for Ray Selfe and *House of Whipcord* and *Frightmare* for Pete Walker.

(Right) Anthony Sharp learns of women's admission to the priesthood...

(Bottom) The result...

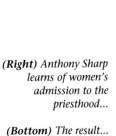
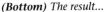

NOW READ ON!

In the '70s, in case you'd forgotten, Britain had a film industry. Of course, it was a pale shadow of the mass production of the pre-television era. But it was by no means inconsiderable. In the summer of 1974, fifteen British films were in production. And even the independent sector, making low budget exploitation movies mainly for the home market, was busy enough to keep hundreds of people, myself included, in full-time employment.

It took only a few months for the word to get round that I was knocking out fast scripts for peanuts — £100 for three days work on *White Cargo*, £200 for a fortnight on *House of Whipcord*. The next director to solicit my low-rent services was Norman J. Warren.

Everyone who meets Warren thinks he's the nicest guy in the business. One of the world's greatest unsolved mysteries is how anyone so inoffensive can have survived the movie jungle for thirty-five years. Perhaps he sold his soul to the Virgin Mary.

Like every director for whom I worked, Warren was potty about movies. In the back of his West London flat he had his own cinema, complete with tip-up seats and a curtained screen. Made when he was only twenty-three, his short film *Fragment* was shown at the old Paris-Pullman cinema in Kensington, where it was seen by Bachoo Sen, an art house distributor with ambitions to expand his horizons and his bank balance. He hired Warren to direct a sex drama with interminable nude bedroom scenes called *Her Private Hell*.

My path first crossed with Warren's in 1967, when I was working as a gopher for the cutting room in which he was editing this pioneering piece of limp porn. I was so star struck that I failed to notice for at

least a year that Warren had only one functional arm. The other had been paralysed by polio.

We kept in touch, a shared interest being Warren's unfulfilled ambition to direct horror films. In 1973 it looked as though he was going to get his chance. He had a script called *The Naked Eye* and wanted me to rewrite it. Considering I laboured on multiple drafts of the doomed screenplay, it's remarkable that I can no longer remember a thing about the plot. But that's the case.

I do know that the lead was to be played first by James Mason, then Joss Ackland and finally Vincent Price. American International were putting up the money and I had no cause to doubt that the film would start shooting as planned on 11 March 1974.

A few weeks prior to this date I flew to America in another of my capacities, film buyer for a no-hope distributor called Paladin, destined to be wound up in 1975 with debts of £58,000. In New York I met the now legendary producer Sam Sherman, who ran me a print of his incomprehensible salvage job, *Blood of Ghastly Horror*. I felt that Britain wasn't ready for this unique work and, even twenty years later, its time still may not have arrived.

On the last Saturday of my trip, Vincent Price's biographer told me that the horror *maestro* had just embarked on an American lecture tour, an odd thing for him to do as he was due in Britain on the following Monday to start work on *The Naked Eye*.

Back in London, Warren, grey with worry, told me the money hadn't come through. He said he'd avoided asking his doctor for sleeping pills because the temptation to take an overdose would have been too great. I was stunned, because, up until this point, my movie career had been coasting along so well. Writing Vincent Price's new horror film seemed the next logical step on my swift journey to the Dorothy Chandler Pavilion on Oscar night.

Nowadays, of course, it would take a whole lot more than a two-timing distributor to send us in despair to the barbiturate bottle. Even if international stars are begging to work on deferments, even if the financiers are asking to whom the million dollar cheque should be made payable, we know only too well that the film tends not to start shooting. Why? That's harder to say. One could just as easily ask why an eventual handful of movies survives every production obstacle to reach the screen. Would you have even opened a script called *Memed My Hawk*?

The Naked Eye, however, was to rise again in a new form. Bits were taken from the script and fashioned into a new story. I developed this into *Satan's Slave*, Warren's first complete horror film, shot over a long period from 1975 to 1976. We shall return to this in the next exciting instalment.

But first let me mention an artful little dodger called Laurie Barnett, who roped me into a whole slew of dubious projects. I believe I'm right in saying that he earned his living as a boom swinger, but whenever I met him he'd had another idea (for anything from a TV quiz show to marketing the pictures on the sides of orange crates) and was looking for a sucker to finance/develop/package it.

To my regular employer Pete Walker, a toff who worked in Mayfair and lunched at Wheeler's, Barnett was a jumped-up barrow boy who epitomised the Wardour Street vulgarity from which Walker longed to escape. But I found Barnett very hard to resist. He had an impish sense of humour and wore a perpetual grin, even when I was screaming at him to pay me my fucking money.

In 1973 he wanted to produce a film about a blackmailer who extorts a million pounds from the British government by bombing London landmarks. He mentioned the idea to Ray Selfe, who thought I was the man to script it. I did the job in a fortnight and was paid £25.

Bomber! was my one and only attempt at a mainstream action adventure. Barnett's original intention was to stage the climactic chase round Marble Arch, Hyde Park Corner and on the London Underground without permission and grab shots *ciné vérité*-style with hidden 16mm cameras. This is the version I would have paid to see.

Unfortunately, things soon got out of control. Within months the script was reputedly on the desk of every studio head in Hollywood and names like Sean Connery and Dustin Hoffman were being bandied about. Unbelievably, this top level bandying continued for the next decade.

In 1980, the trade press announced that *The Bomber* had started shooting in London locations under Douglas Hickox's direction. It hadn't because a bunch of Swiss gnomes hadn't come up with the cash. As late as 1983, the film was still on the brink of production, this time with Alex Grasshof directing James Garner. It wouldn't surprise me if my battered old script is still being hawked around right now.

The films that Barnett managed to get in front of the cameras tended to have lower aspirations (just below the belt, actually). The most remarkable of these was *The Hot Girls*, one of the seediest British sex films ever made, which he co-directed with the notorious John Lindsay. I left it off my CV for twenty years. But the older you get, the less you care.

Throughout the '70s, Lindsay was Britain's leading producer and exhibitor of hardcore porn. He and Barnett had already made two softcore movies and *The Hot Girls* was to be their third. The budget was £6,000 and the money was right up there on the screen.

I created the script, all twenty pages of it, from virtually nothing, and completed this task plus the umpteenth draft of *The Naked Eye* in five days at the beginning of 1974. Barnett didn't think much of my efforts. At a memorable script conference, he told me that his producers had taken particular exception to one scene in a sauna because it lowered the tone of the film. It wasn't one of his jokes.

Barnett threw my script away and made the film up as he went along. For one of the scenes he wanted Tony Crawley to interview a Danish popsy called Helli Louise. Tony wisely declined, leaving muggins to fill the bill. After we'd finished shooting, the set was cleared and we went down the pub while Lindsay captured some unsimulated humping for the foreign version.

The Hot Girls opened in the spring of 1974 at the Jacey, Trafalgar Square. I went along for the opening night and was dumbfounded. The film appeared to consist almost entirely of naked dolly birds cavorting in a variety of locations while the camera crash zoomed into their pubes. Then there was me looking ridiculous in a pair of Mungo Jerry sideboards, before we returned to zooming into pubes. The minute I hear that a print of this junk has survived, I shall break into the laboratory with a jar of acid.

There was little time to ponder the maxim that you're only as good as your last picture. Barely had my embarrassment subsided when Barnett and Lindsay hired me to pen another skinflick, this time a veritable paradigm of the British sex comedy, *I'm Not Feeling Myself Tonight!* But the lads had to wait their turn. The great Pete Walker had now completed the shooting of *Frightmare* and was anxious to embark on our third collaboration.

This time I was no use in supplying a word, like 'cannibalism', that would set his showman's mind rac-

(Below) Sheila Keith triumphs again in **House of Mortal Sin.**

(Bottom) "Never mind Father, maybe you can get a bit part in **The Hot Girls.**"

ing. He went in search of inspiration himself and found it in a piece of pulp fiction about a killer vicar. Seated with him by the swimming pool of his Esher mansion, I expressed reservations about having a loopy Reverend bumping off his parishioners. It sounded too much like Ealing comedy. "More tea, vicar?" asked Mrs Wilberforce before being bludgeoned to death with a rock cake...

It was probably Walker, a lapsed Catholic, who suggested changing the vicar to a priest. An evil priest was not at all risible and we could introduce lots more unorthodox murder weapons. I think that at that first meeting, during which we thrashed out most of the story of *House of Mortal Sin* aka *The Confessional*, we planned the poisoned communion wafer and the strangulation by rosary beads.

Walker was as gleeful as he always was in the early stages of a project's development, but especially so on this occasion because he thought he'd found a theme so controversial that it would top the skull-drilling cannibalism of *Frightmare*. I was quite happy to go along with him. 'It should give me the opportunity to write some more barnstorming dialogue,' I wrote in my diary that night.

The rough synopsis was completed, all but the ending, in just over a week. I wanted to iron out some illogicalities, but Walker was delighted with what we'd got and wanted me to get on with the screenplay. Again it's thanks to a diary entry that I'm reminded of ploys I used. On 6 June 1974, I wrote: 'I shall keep up my sleeve certain thoughts I have. Walker normally rejects ideas if we talk about them, accepts them if he sees them on paper.'

House of Mortal Sin is about the dreadful exploits of Father Meldrum, accurately described by one critic as 'a sexually repressed drooling madman.' Walker wanted Richard Greene, TV's Robin Hood, for the role, but ended up with a now sadly forgotten actor, Anthony Sharp. He has a sinister housekeeper, a part always intended for, and indeed played by, Walker's favourite villainess, Sheila Keith. Meldrum gets the hots for young girls, especially Jenny Welsh (Susan Penhaligon), whose forbidden allure sends him completely off the rails.

Despite living in an area of North London largely populated by Irish Catholics (it's known as County Kilburn), I was so ignorant of the Catholic religion that I didn't know the difference between mortal and venial sin. I had to research almost from scratch, but without ever revealing to my informants the real reason I needed the facts. I felt so guilty quizzing dear Sister Edna of the National Catechetical Society that I almost blurted out the truth and asked her to forgive me.

At Mass at my local church, I stood and sat and knelt when everyone else did, and simultaneously scribbled notes. When the censer was produced, I got the idea of hitting somebody over the head with it. Afterwards, a stern old priest named Father Bagnall curtly answered most of my remaining questions. Needless to say, I left without daring to bring up the subject of celibacy.

I worked on the screenplay for several days without knowing how the story was going to end and without knowing how one character was going to figure in the plot. There were even more contrivances than in *Frightmare*, but I tried to make them plausible. Walker was diffident about the pages as I delivered them to him, saying they read like a *"Play For Today* with mur-

Suburban witchcraft! Nudity! Human sacrifice! You read about it in the Sunday tabloids! Channel 4 will probably do a fundamentalist exposé now! It must be true! (A still from **Satan's Slave**.)

ders." When he'd read the whole script, he said it hadn't turned out the way he'd intended. He said he wanted to work on it himself and would call me when it was ready for me to polish.

While I was waiting for this summons, Laurie Barnett and John Lindsay persuaded a distributor called New Realm to back their next sex film and dragged me in as the writer. Like Walker, Barnett had found a trash novelette, in this instance *The Sex Ray*, about a gizmo that stimulates the libido, and wanted to plagiarise it.

On 15th July, Barnett paid me £100 upfront and we set about writing the synopsis. We started in Grodzinski's patisserie, continued on a bench in Oxford Street and finished in a pub. I then auditioned for a film called *Hennessy* and got three days work playing a rioter. My days were very full.

I'm Not Feeling Myself Tonight! (my title, completely irrelevant to the story of an odd job man at a sex research institute, who develops a sound wave that turns people on) was written in just under a fortnight. When people asked me what I was working on, I told them I was writing the first British sex comedy that would be both sexy and funny. I really believed it.

Although my natural inclination is towards horror, I'm a member of the last generation who grew up listening to radio comedy. *The Goon Show* and *Hancock's Half Hour* were major influences, and from childhood I tried to emulate Spike Milligan's anarchy and Galton and Simpson's use of language. I never came close, but comedy gave me something to fall back on when the British horror film disappeared at the end of the '70s.

In 1974, however, the world — or, at any rate, director Joe McGrath — was not ready for McGillivray's sense of humour. McGrath was to rewrite virtually the whole of *I'm Not Feeling Myself Tonight!*, which turned out as funny as *On the Buses* on a duff night and as sexy as a seaside postcard. Consequently, it was just what the public wanted and in 1975 it ran in London's West End for month after month. The whole ghastly story of its production will also have to wait for the next episode of this chronicle.

Back at Pete Walker's Mayfair office, I agreed to implement his changes to *House of Mortal Sin*. I ended up rewriting more than half the script, but to no avail. Walker still didn't like it. He thought it was too wordy and that not enough happened. I daresay he was right. I was too fond of dialogue. On 4 September he told me he was going to hire another writer. "You're the boss," I replied.

I thought it unlikely that Walker would find another writer in my price range. In 1974, the Writers' Guild minimum for a screenplay was £2,500. The same year I wrote five screenplays and received £2,575 *in toto*. But I could afford to be extremely nonchalant about being fired. In the days when Britain had a film industry there was always another script to write. On the day Walker dispensed with my services, I had lunch with Norman J. Warren, who gave me £100 and a synopsis of something that was then called *Evil Heritage*, but would later become *Satan's Slave*.

As always, the screenplay had to be delivered pronto. I surpassed myself by completing it in nine days. I have *Satan's Slave* on video, but I've never had the courage to play it. My memory is that the thin story of devil worship had to be padded on almost every page, mostly with unspeakable dialogue.

Just now I had to check the *Monthly Film Bulletin* to reacquaint myself with the plot, in which wicked Uncle Alexander (Michael Gough) wants to use the body of his niece to resurrect an ancestral witch. Everyone knew the script was no great shakes, but Warren was not going to be thwarted a second time and drove the production on with grim determination.

It took years. It was 1978 before the film premièred in London on the second half of a double bill. But up until that time we had a great laugh. It was an archetypal shoestring production in which everyone did everything. The producer's wife took on the continuity and I went down to the set one day to find the co-producer digging graves.

This kind of resourcefulness was actually prohibited in the days when the all-powerful ACTT could have a movie shut down if the requisite number of chippies weren't employed to play cards behind the set. *Satan's Slave* got away with murder by being shot in secrecy. By rights, now that the unions have lost control of the film industry, there should be cheapjack horror movies being shot in every English country house. Why aren't there?

I'd barely begun the *Satan's Slave* script when Walker telephoned me. He'd had an idea how *House of Mortal Sin* could be improved. Would I like to come back on board? Hmmmm... Our first meeting on 24 September did not, according to my diary, augur well:

'I found to my grave disappointment that he hadn't had any ideas about what he wanted to do with the script despite his complaints. All he had done was to type out a new pre-credits sequence. He handed it to me saying that the rest would follow much as before except that there had to be less chat and more ingredients. I didn't know what he meant and there followed a heated discussion.

'Finally he started getting dramatic and said *he* hadn't got time to think up ideas, that was the scriptwriter's job. Hadn't he sparked anything off? I said no. So he sat down on his sofa and looked dejected and said he didn't know what to do.

'I said that the only thing I could do to enliven the script was to start over again with a new plot. I suggested an idea. He didn't know how to react and started bringing the discussion to a conclusion. Yes, he admitted that all along I said it was contrived. Yes, all right, the sub-plot *is* useless. But starting again...? We left it. He said he'd ring me. I mentioned my time was

Peter Walker back in the good old days of safari jackets and big collars...

The author (centre) contemplates further 'unspeakable' dialogue for **Satan's Slave** *while moping around a heath disguised as a priest.*

precious.'

My time, as it happened, wasn't precious at all. I was taking a brief respite, and on 22 October I was able to accompany Laurie Barnett to Birmingham Crown Court, where John Lindsay was on trial for conspiring to publish obscene films.

In a sensational case Lindsay was accused of shooting *Juvenile Sex* and *Classroom Lover* at weekends in Birmingham's Aston Manor secondary school. The star was the school's head boy. When Lindsay was found not guilty, Barnett and I excitedly made plans to screen the films at Ray Selfe's new cinema, the Pigalle, near Piccadilly Circus. The plans came to nothing, but from 1975 Lindsay showed hardcore porn at cinema clubs all over the country. He claims the police falsified evidence in order to ensure his arrest and imprisonment in 1983.

In twelve days in November 1974, I bashed out a complete rewrite of *House of Mortal Sin*. Walker suggested the addition of two minor scenes, which I agreed to. He then sent the script to the printer. Virtually every line in every shot of every scene was

filmed exactly as I wrote it. I kept no copies of my scripts and therefore can't say why this version was perfect while the others were unacceptable. Probably I got rid of the 'useless' sub-plot, whatever that was, and added even more murders.

By December, all animosity between Walker and myself was forgotten. He invited me to his Christmas party. In all the years I worked for Walker, it was the only time we met socially. He got drunk on champagne and told me to get working on a fourth horror movie, preferably set in a sunny climate.

Although I'd been a professional screenwriter for only two years, my attitude to the movie business had altered. I'd matured from a hanger-on who gladly would have dropped his trousers to see his name on the screen to a hack who earned a living churning out screenplays to order. I considered the possibility of a fourth film for Britain's greatest exploitation movie director, then wrote in my diary: 'Unless I really need the money badly, I doubt whether I'll do it.'

Blasé was not the word.

(To be continued.) ■

FLOUNDERING ON THE BOTTOM

BY RAMSEY CAMPBELL

Is there any more convincing evidence of the decline of standards than that Michael Medved is taken seriously in some circles as a commentator on film? Nothing about him has changed since *The Golden Turkey Awards*: the same unwillingness to let facts get in the way of his opinions, the same leaden humour, the same petulant tone of a child who has found that the world and other people's views of it aren't exactly as he wants them to be. Indeed, the prevailing tone of his recent colour-supplement attack on Demi Moore might lead people to speculate exactly what kind of grudge he harbours against her. I remember, less with affection than with a wince at the appropriateness of it, how in the early days of

EXCLUSIVE FILMS *presents*

GEORGE NADER · CLAUDIA BARRETT

in

ROBOT MONSTER Ⓤ

with SELENA ROYLE · GREGORY MOFFETT · PAMELA DAWSON

Channel 4 he dressed up as an ape with a tin head in order to introduce *Robot Monster*, to which film he'd added subtitles intended to nudge the audience into laughing but whose stupidity outdid that of the film. The film was innocent: Medved is not. The turkey, that creature which gobbles incessantly and which continues to be active even when it has nothing above its shoulders, is his appropriate emblem. What I most disliked about his first book, *The Fifty Worst Movies Ever Made*, was the sense that he and presumably his fraternal co-author felt entitled to resent having had to watch allegedly bad movies in order to make a lot of money out of them.

Yet I believe there's nothing wrong with deriving as

Michael Medved makes off with Demi Moore...

(Above) *Grade zero smut from a man who has sex with his glasses on...*

(Right) *Imbeciles in search of direction. 'Worst Films Ever Made!' proclaims the director. Let's hear it for honesty in advertising...*

much fun as you can from inept movies. If I thought otherwise I would have walked out of *Def by Temptation* and *Traces of Red* and *Damage* and *Stay Tuned* and the remake of *A Kiss Before Dying* and *Wild West*, the recent Film on Four production, and *Shining Through*, surely the funniest Hollywood melodrama for many years. And I'll happily — well, maybe that's an exaggeration — watch on behalf of *Shock Xpress* films that only its contributors and readers might brave. Maybe I'm acquiring a reputation for this activity, and that's why Douglas E. Winter sent me *Penpal Murders*, one of many films by Steve Postal of Florida (to be precise, P.O. Box 428, Bostwick, FL 32007, phone 904-325-5254). I shall endeavour to convey at least some of the experience of watching this film.

The cassette is inserted. The machine emits a mechanical retching but fails to eject it. An FBI warning appears on the screen with a buzzing as of an enraged wasp woman, and gives way to the sight of a man in a Puritan hat screaming a great deal while being pursued by two people with mops over their faces. He wakes in bed with his hat on and screams some more. "Steve, you're having a nightmare," says his wife Karen several times, establishing the Postal approach to dialogue and making the audience suspect she is addressing them. Steve goes out with his hat on to walk the dog, then comes home to feed the cat while someone switches a tape of Vivaldi's *Four Seasons* on and off with an audible click to provide

soundtrack music. "Jenny's coming," his wife says. All this has taken four minutes, and then:

STEVE POSTAL PRODUCTIONS PRESENTS
PENPAL MURDERS
STARRING JAY BROCKMAN, JENNY TUCK,
ANGELA SHEPARD
DIRECTOR OF PHOTOGRAPHY STEVE POSTAL
SCENARIO BY STEVE J. POSTAL AND GAIL A.
POSTAL
WRITTEN AND PRODUCED BY STEVE POSTAL
AND GAIL POSTAL
DIRECTED BY STEVE POSTAL

And then Steve, who we can deduce is played by Jay Brockman, screams a great deal while being pursued by two people with mops over their faces who now poke him with extra mops. All of the stuff before the credits has been a — surely not a selection of highlights from the film? Steve wakes in bed and screams "No" and "Get away" for thirty-six seconds until his hat falls off. After some more of this he declares his intention of taking a walk.

STEVE POSTAL PRODUCTIONS PRESENTS
PENPAL MURDERS

What's happening? Has the audience ingested some previously unknown psychoactive substance, or would that have been an advisable approach? Steve walks the dog, dragging Vivaldi after him. Perhaps it's unfair, even though I intend to continue doing it, to draw attention to the borrowed score: after all, the recent Aikman Archive video of Murnau's *Nosferatu* sounds as though someone has grabbed the first couple of discs that came to hand, an organ recital and the latter half of Saint-Saens' Third Symphony. But I digress. Steve feeds the cats again...

STARRING JAY BROCKMAN, JENNY TUCK,
ANGELA SHEPARD

Presumably they're happy for their names to be repeated, since both Angela Shepard and Jennifer Tuck were vampires from outer space in the 1990 Steve Postal production of that title. Steve goes back to bed with that wretched hat on and argues with Karen about his penpal who is coming from California, and the audience wonders if they're making up the dialogue as they go along, and whether the mass marketing of the video camera has given rise to a new form of sadism. Not only does Steve Postal film the mugging of his performers in merciless closeup, but he tends to begin each shot before they've started acting and hold it after they've given up.

DIRECTOR OF PHOTOGRAPHY STEVE POSTAL
SCENARIO BY STEVE J. POSTAL AND GAIL A.
POSTAL
WRITTEN AND PRODUCED BY STEVE POSTAL
AND GAIL POSTAL
DIRECTED BY STEVE POSTAL

So perish nearly fifteen minutes of my life. The cassette box threatens a running time of 110 minutes, and the fact that Jay Brockman affects the most unconvincing stammer of all time makes each of his scenes feel not much shorter than that. Can the appeal of such a film be that, as with a good deal of contemporary horror writing and poetry written for performance, every member of the audience can feel they could produce something at least as good — and be right? Did Woody Allen film *Husbands and Wives* in the style of an unwatchable home video to prove to all of us with a video camera that film-making isn't that simple? *Husbands and Wives* made me physically ill, and I kept my eyes shut for the last half-hour of it — indeed, after the press show half a dozen green-faced members of the Merseyside press gazed with dismay at the buffet. I'm not quite sure what effect watching *Penpal Murders* has on me, but I think it's time to read a book.

Here is *Science Fiction Stories* by Mark David Tingay (£8.50 from Aurora Books, a division of the Book Guild Ltd). The first story is 'The Spore'. I quote.

'The remains of a body skin was laid out on the grass, covered in blood, then as Anne ran up she screamed and pointed.

'Then as John looked up a mass of flesh was pulsating. When he saw this his first reaction was to run, but he was glued to the spot. Then, in a split second, the organism flew at John. He tried getting out of the way, but it was no good, the thing had latched on to him. As he stood there in total panic watching this thing start to crawl up his body, the thing expanded then leapt into the air. As the organism dropped down, its body at this stage was twice as large.

'(...) He shouted "Help me Anne!" She fainted on the lawn, and when a couple of seconds had passed the organism had finished devouring John and now was crawling along the floor to Anne.

'When Anne awoke, she saw the thing crawling up her legs. She screamed, the thing started to devour her legs in a frenzied way. When she felt this, she died of heart failure. When the organism got no response, her structure was pulped and devoured in one mouthful as the thing was gobbling and chewing.'

Let nobody say that some prose can't convey the same experience as some films. Just now I have the sense of a different kind of consciousness attempting to communicate with me. I must say I feel a little odd. Maybe the best place is bed. But *Penpal Murders* awaits, in my dreams and next day when I stumble, feet dragging and head lolling, into the room where the video is.

Steve and Karen eat another meal — maybe that's their fee — and argue some more. If Steve Postal's use of music seems to owe something to Godard, perhaps Warhol can be blamed for his apparent determination to leave every take in the finished film. But who is to blame for the dialogue? Here are, I assure you, the very opening lines of yet another argument:

Karen: "Here we are again — the big brain talking so profoundly and so early in the morning at that."
Steve: "Tough crap to you! It took you so long to say these things but it's not like you said them before. I could be sitting at the beach now with some curvy curvy-shaped brown-skinned girl who would talk to me with respect." (*The reader is reminded to imagine all Steve's dialogue being spoken with a stutter.*)
Karen: "Yeah, sure, you piece of I don't know what."
Steve: "Why do you say that? You ever hear the saying 'the road less travelled was the better road'? Maybe I'll just travel down that road."

Alas, he stays where he is. Perhaps people really talk like that, and we're witnessing a new kind of hyper-realism. Perhaps people in Bostwick do, and Steve Postal's work will eventually spread the style as Bill and Ted popularised Valleyspeak.

We are now twenty-five minutes into the film. Jenny the penpal arrives, accompanied by Vivaldi. Perhaps the presence of three people in the film will improve matters.

Jenny: "Steve, it's me, Jenny."
Steve: "Jenny, is that you?"
Jenny: "Steve, Steve."
Steve: "Jenny, don't move, I'll be right there."
Steve walks ten yards.
Jenny: "Steve..."
Karen: "Jenny, is that you?"

Eventually all three somehow manage to get into the house. Jenny is shown her room. Steve immediately has a birthday and holds onto his hat while he blows out the candles on his cake. Jenny acts by staring away from the camera and her co-stars, and who can blame her? The three make conversation. Was New York crowded? Did Jenny get lost in Penn Station? Did she have trouble finding the train? How did she get from JFK airport to the station? Was it easy for her to take a vacation? How did she get from the house to the station? Why is a neighbour chainsawing trees outside? Why is the house suddenly next to a railway? "With the sawing of the wood and those trains a person could go crazy here," says Jenny. I know how she feels. The birthday scene lasts ten minutes. Is the dialogue supposed to be awkward? I'm reminded of the problem Ed Wood set himself in *Night of the Ghouls* of trying to make a sham seance look more inept than the rest of the film. Are the Postal players making it up as they go along? Are they going along? In ten-minute bursts the film is hideously funny, but after ten minutes... Karen sits in bed and brushes her hair. Jenny gets out of bed and brushes her hair, and I find Mark David Tingay lying on the floor — not the young test technician from south-east London himself, you understand, just his book. Surely this will help me clarify my thoughts.

'Then after a couple of seconds, the block of ice was sinking beyond belief, then it fell deep down into the mountain's core. When the block of ice was falling very fast down this form of rounded tunnel, its presence was magnetic...

'Then the block of ice came to a stop. It had landed in a marsh, and the temperature was cold at the start, now at boiling point as the ice floated around in the marsh. The temperature was increasing with every second, then as the block lay there, it started to melt until John finally was floating on his own.

'After a couple of seconds, John came to out of his ice cabin, then as he opened his eyes to see where he was, he had the shock of his life... He tripped and went under the water as he submerged again...'

Maybe the end of the story makes everything clear.

'Then, as the ship came into dock, it roared then turned into a golden shade, with John as the top figure.'

Are we present at the birth of a new use of the language? Are Tingay and Postal similar in seeing things they struggle to communicate? It occurs to me to wonder what Tingay tests as a technician. I think I'll go and lie down.

I dream of analysing *Penpal Murders* in terms of its sexual politics, but when I emerge from the toilet next morning I seem to have left my ideas behind. I climb back onto my cross and restart the tape. Karen takes the dog for a walk. Jenny sprawls on top of Steve on the couch and demands to know why he didn't sleep with her last night. She threatens to check into a motel because he doesn't love her but goes back to bed instead. Steve follows her into the room and, unless my mind is finally crumbling, they repeat the same dialogue. Karen comes home and falls asleep. Steve and Jenny go to bed together. He says "I'm not ready" four times, and "I can't do it because I've got the flu." Jenny takes a shower from the waist up. Karen brushes her hair and goes out, leaving them in bed together. God be praised, the film is half over.

Steve types a script. Karen asks if he always stutters. She fails to find the cooking oil and eggs which are in the refrigerator and complains at, my God, length about it. Karen feeds Steve breakfast. He says "Leave my hat alone. Don't touch my hat. Leave it alone. Don't touch my hat." I begin to feel that Michael Medved and Steve Postal deserve each other. The dialogue then, well, it sort of.

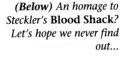

Steve: "Trees are more important than this house."
Jenny: "Why do you talk so slowly?"
Steve: "Trees help me write."
Jenny: "What am I in your house? A slave? A toy? Let's get married."

Karen rings up to demand what they had for breakfast. Steve explains to Jenny how to call him on a pay phone — how... to... call... him... on... — when she goes shopping. He types a lot and screws up each page of his script, but alas, this is only fiction. Karen comes home and throws the pages about. Jenny rings up and invites him to dinner. "Where are you?" Steve says, and without waiting for an answer, "I'll be there in thirty minutes. That's half an hour." Perhaps we are to see the actors on location and with other people, but no, after a fade to black all we see are the same three buggers returning to the same wretched bungalow. Steve complains to Karen that Jenny was flirting with a cop and loses his temper, which involves breathing hard and holding onto his hat with both hands. Steve tells Karen to get in bed with Jenny so she won't go home. Karen does. Steve appears and tells her to get out of bed. He gets in the bed. Karen goes out. There are several shots of cows. Has Steve Postal been watching Eisenstein? Do I need my head examining? Let me turn to Mark David Tingay for relief.

'While they were looking around in the town they saw a 'for sale' sign up one of the town's streets, so they knocked on the door, and asked for the guide.'

Perhaps relief is not the word.

'Dr Samuals rushed over to the guide, in a frantic effort to stop him from hitting the ground. But it was all in vain because the guide passed out and smashed on to the ground with a thump. As Dr Samuals and Mr Harding saw this, their first reaction was to hurry to his aid.'

The Book Guild Ltd, of which Aurora Books is a subsidiary, advertises in the *Sunday Times* book section: 'Have you written a book that deserves to be published?'

'While they were walking, they got twenty feet down the preserved fossilised corridor, when they came across a stone wedged in the sand. They couldn't believe their eyes, then as Mr Harding got close to it, the stone started to sink.'

I know the feeling. Jenny takes a shower from the waist up and goes shopping while Steve writes. The cast take turns to open the squeaky front door. Karen comes home and tells Steve that Jenny was making out with someone. Steve holds onto his hat and rages, followed by six seconds of him not acting. He strangles Karen

while the dog wanders into the shot. Karen escapes into the bedroom. He tries to strangle her by holding her shoulders. They switch to having sex. Jenny comes home and accuses Steve of being poor. He slaps her face. "You hurt my little nose," she wails. They have sex. Jenny kills Karen with a carving knife. Steve removes his hat and his stutter and laughs at immoderate length at Jenny and says "So you love me" several times. Steve strangles Jenny and drops his hat on top of the corpses. And wakes up. I wish I could. He gets a phone call from Jenny and laughs a lot.

THE END

Steve types the end credits. German Shepherd Dog was played by Lady. Cats were played by Rusty, Susie, Whitey, Tiger and Teddy Postal. The story was based on the book *Penpal Murders* by Stephen J. Postal and Gail Postal. The British edition could be published by Aurora Books. The credits are followed by the last five minutes of a Florida movie set in a casino and starring Miles O'Keeffe and Dedee Pfeiffer.

Is Steve Postal entitled to look down on any other film-maker? Well, actually, yes, and Doug Winter is to be [deleted] for proving it by sending me *Street Soldier*. This is the work of Tim Anthony, who can be contacted for 'the best in muscle movies' at P.O. Box 14738, Dayton, Ohio 45413. He should sell Steve Postal his camcorder.

The film stars Tina Plakinger and her muscles — a zoom staggers at her wearing a leopard-skin and wanders out of focus — and Tony Anthony, who poses for the camera and seems unaware that the videotape has rendered him as green as the Hulk. His back view is flesh-coloured, but when he turns round again he becomes an interesting mixture of green and pink. Various other actors are listed — Debbie Dayo, Roger Revlon, Amber Rhoads, Otis Scales but unfortunately whoever has typed out the names on the screen hasn't grasped that longer names have to be split between two lines. We can only speculate about how those performers reacted to being listed as Phyllispadur, or Felix Niclsn, or Marshawalon, or Chucstewart. Maybe muscled people think of themselves that way. At last the credits tell us that the film is written, produced and directed by Tim Anthony. They have lasted six minutes while a synthesizer wails on the audience's behalf. Before long we may be sorry they came to an end.

Tony Anthony flexes his muscles for forty seconds in slow motion. Ninety seconds of stock shots of New York are accompanied by a rap in which a synthesised voice keeps saying "boogie." The film begins. A car with cartons perched on the luggage rack draws up and the driver exchanges some dialogue with a woman. I should like to tell you what they said, but despite several rewinds I've been unable to make out a word. The woman tells a man in a beret something incomprehensible and he gets in the car. Some people walk along 42nd Street and stare at the camera. A man with a microphone announces a fight by a river. A woman in a leopard-skin who I take to be Tina Plakinger fights another woman while they try not to laugh. There's an interminable slow motion shot, complete with noise bars, of the leopard-skinned woman pushing the other. She gets her down on the concrete and brandishes a knife. The other says something incomprehensible. She's dead. Listen, you only have to read about this, I had to watch it. The survivor joins some bikers and dunks a python in the river while the music, if that's the word, drowns out their dialogue. A girl in a house talks incomprehensibly on the phone and then goes along the hall to tell a man with a green face something. Some men in a room say something about state's evidence. "You stick your nose into my business and I stick your nose in a turtle's shell," one tells another, and recommends fishing as a cure for nerves. He takes a turtle out of a box. "Learn to relax like him," he says, and his henchmen hold the man addressed down on top of the turtle. The turtle walks away. Good idea.

'All his arms and legs were paralysed.' (Tingay, p25)
'As he spoke his face was disjointed and out of sequence.' (Tingay, p26)
'His friend had gone from his midst.' (Tingay, p31)

You know, I'm beginning to wonder if Mark David Tingay could be a late surrealist. But back to *Street Soldier*. I tell myself that it's only a film. Some people with machine guns and other weapons hang around in a Manhattan street and discuss kidnapping before eventually kidnapping a young woman who tries to look impressed. The owner of the turtle turns out to own a nightclub too, and talks to a woman about finding a contender for a fight while she does her best to look interested and to stay in focus. Did whoever developed autofocus for the camcorder ever dream what horrors they were bringing into the world? Tony Anthony walks about in a street and eventually enters the nightclub, where he throws various people about in a dark corner in order to get to the owner, who says he'll match him with the champion. "My name is Rodolfo Inaudible and don't you forget it," he says.

The kidnappers gaze at their victim somewhere in the open and discuss something while the camera totters about in search of them. One of them uses a gun to poke the victim, who smiles. A plane arrives at an airport. A taxi driver picks up Tina Plakinger and drives her round some unidentifiably dull city areas for several minutes. She goes to a gym and works out with much use of the facial muscles, to a song which several rewinds have convinced me includes the line "The energy of a eunuch is the only way." Tony Anthony arrives and sweats a lot while he works out. Both performers acquire a greenish tint and tell each other, though not the audience, the names of the characters they're playing. The gym scene, in which they brandish their muscles for ten minutes, is presumably the hard core of the film, the kind of thing people send Tim Anthony money for.

Rodolfo Incomprehensible phones in search of a female challenger while one of his men hangs around in the background with a machine-gun looking for someone to shoot. "So a couple of girls got killed," Rodolfo says into the phone. "That makes it more inviting." Tina and Tony run out of a lake in slow motion. Wind on the microphone carries away most of their dialogue, but not enough. We learn that someone called Mama Dog killed Tina's sister in the arena.

People in a nightclub dance. Fights are announced. Tony fights an opponent, mostly out of focus or off-screen or in slow motion with noise bars. The onlookers shout "Come on" except for those trying not to laugh. The fight comes to some sort of end which Tony walks away from. The master of ceremonies makes an incomprehensible announcement. Tina and Mama Dog jump about a bit and pat each other. Tina kills Mama Dog. Onlookers attempt not to look amused.

'Then suddenly his legs gave way underneath him, as he was resting on the floor.' (Tingay, page 36)

A man wearing glasses who says he watched the fight phones Tony to ask him to rescue his kidnapped daughter. Tony and Tina turn green and discuss their relationship. They go out of focus and walk along a street in the company of some bits of rock songs. They visit a clairvoyant who tells them something. Tony meets a man with a horse and they discuss the kidnapping while the camera falls about. Tony calls someone, perhaps Tina, on the phone and drones at length about not needing their help. Tony and two men creep up on the kidnappers who are standing about under a river bridge. A kidnapper pretends not to notice that Tony is about to mime hitting him on the head with a length of pipe. Another kidnapper tries not to laugh. The kidnapped girl is told to escape. The man on the horse shows up. Shots are fired. People fall down. Tony and a kidnapper fight, taking care not to hurt each other. Tony tries not to laugh.

Tony phones the girl's father and goes out of focus. There are shots of New York streets. Tony wanders into one. The camera wobbles about inside a subway train. The camera staggers along some streets. Tony does something on a train. Tony walks up a stairway to a train and pretends not to see the camera. Tony gets on a train and reads something. It rains. Tina stands in a doorway to the sound of carnival music. Tony approaches and says something. Tina says "Can you handle a woman like me? I am the ultimate female, you know." Tony says something. The end. The credits all over again. An FBI warning, out of focus. Can I stop now?

Mark David Tingay's book will cost you less than either of these videos, and I'd say it was money better spent. I haven't even begun to quote from the second half of the book ('When the sun's heat touched the outer skin of the beacon, the heat caused the beacon to change appearance. This change was relative to a tower, this tower became known as a spirit of evil because of its resemblance to Satan's hell, and the mysterious unknown') but I hope I've quoted enough to persuade all of my readers to invest in a copy. It certainly has more personality than many a best seller, and I think we should do our best to put it up there with them. Home video is becoming a new form of vanity publishing, but call me a Luddite if you will, or a pickled earwig if you prefer, or an edible maggot, or a dancing slug, or a mouldering pair of earmuffs for that matter — it is rather less fun. Have I ranted long enough for this year's *Shock*? What's this the postman has brought me? My God, another package from Doug Winter... ∎

(After numerous complaints and investigations the Sunday Times *ceased to accept adverts from vanity publishers in October 1993. Ed.)*

(Above and left) More imbeciles from Florida's world of 'entertainment'...

INSIDIOUS LITTLE GLOBS

BY ANNE BILLSON

You know where you are with the horror genre. Once you've been primed by advance knowledge of director or title (the words 'zombie', 'gut-cruncher' and 'cannibal' are fairly reliable signifiers), you can sit without flinching through a gore-storm of exploding heads and erupting entrails.

But it's the rogue elements, ones you weren't expecting, that can haunt your dreams and turn them into nightmares. The insidious little glob can hold its own among a plurality of gore. Take a screening of *Hellraiser* I once attended: the audience were old hands at this sort of thing. They lapped up the flayed corpses, the claw hammers-to-the-cranium, the sado-masochistic thrill-seekers from hell. But the detail that *really* got to them, the insidious little glob that provoked the noisiest reaction of the evening, was when one of the characters gashed his thumb on a nail. That was the bit that *really* hurt.

It's not often you get the opportunity of spotting a glob like this in a horror movie, which is so concerned with a superabundance of splatter that lesser injuries tend to blend into the scenery. But it's not the horror genre that concerns us here. What I'm trying to get to grips with are those squibs of unpleasantness that intrude without warning into what you had been thinking was good, clean, boring fun — in other words, a film that sneaked past one's guard disguised as mainstream entertainment.

The most insidious thing about insidious little globs is that they occur outside their natural habitat. They crop up in the most innocuous surroundings, and they are so frequently subjective that it makes a mockery of attempts to restrict access to certain types of films to certain age groups. One man's glob is another man's amusing visual conceit, slice of raw realism, or missed-it-completely.

When I was a child I used to hide, terror-stricken, beneath the dining room table every time I heard Elvis singing 'Rock-a-Hula Baby'. I have never been able to work out what it was about that song that scared me, but my reaction to films was — like that of other children — every bit as primal and mysterious. My parents were strict but fair, and the only time I remember them actively forbidding me to watch something was when I was packed off to bed shortly after Janet Leigh arrived at the Bates Motel. What my parents didn't realise was that it didn't take a shower murder to give me nightmares.

I was haunted for years by the scene from *The Lost Weekend* in which Ray Milland goes into *delirium tremens* and sees a mouse having its head bitten off by a bat, and this was several aeons before I'd sipped my first shandy. Blood trickles down the wall, but blood was not a *sine qua non* for a scene to acquire glob status. I was equally freaked by Edward G. Robinson's bug-eyed expression as he sank into the mire at the end of *The Red House* or by the scorched face of the Arab blinded by an exploding rock in *Sammy Going South* — a film to which my parents had happily escorted me in the belief that it would be a jolly African variation on *The Incredible Journey*. Even now I feel rather proud that one of my earliest, most upsetting memories — of a scene in which dozens of unemployed girls are crushed to death by a collapsing staircase — turned out to be part of an Italian neo-realist film (*Roma Ore 11*) by Giuseppe De Santis. God only knows what I was doing watching stuff like that in the first place.

For me, the most impressive globs of the '60s arrived *en masse* at the end of *The Charge of the Light Brigade*. My father had taken me to it in the belief that it would be educational, and he was right, though not in the way he imagined. Having already seen clips of Richard Williams' *Punch*-inspired animations on TV, I had the vague idea I was in for some sort of comedy, only to end up thoroughly traumatised by the final charge into the Valley of Death, though admittedly

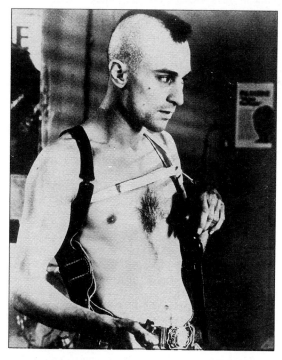

(Previous page and above) **The Wild Bunch** — *Peckinpah disinters the western.*

(Left) **Taxi Driver** — *'If you were honest, you would rather (it was) not watched by certain types.' Brian Appleyard,* **The Independent.**

one might nowadays feel hugely cheered by the spectacle of hooray-Henry types having their faces blown off and David Hemmings bleeding from the mouth.

One can see that in retrospect 1968 was the watershed, not just with regard to the Hollywood studio system and a new generation of cineliterate film-makers, but also in terms of escalating glob factor. *Night of the Living Dead* was a harbinger of a zillion zombie

Piper Laurie goes bonkers with a big knife in **Carrie**.

being sheared off by a pane of glass in *The Omen* raised one's eyebrows, it was only because it was unusual for decapitation to be depicted so graphically in such a big budget, star-packed production. *The Possession of Joel Delaney*, on the other hand, caught me unawares simply because one could never have predicted in a million years that a film starring Shirley MacLaine would also have severed heads in it. Roman Polanski's deceptively low-key approach at the beginning of *Chinatown* (nice detective story in period costumes) suckered me into forgetting this was a director who had previously gone splatter-mad in *Repulsion* and *Macbeth*. Jack Nicholson having his nostril slit by his own director left this viewer whimpering in proboscis-sensitive shock.

By the time I had sat through the '70s — otherwise known as the Last Great Golden Era of Cinema — I was able to take things like the chest-bursting scene from *Alien* in my stride. But by then I was expecting the unexpected. By the end of the '80s, mainstream movies had been well and truly permeated by casual violence, sudden death and oodles of gloop. You could hardly sit through a chiller, thriller or run-of-the-mill cop-opera without encountering some element of splatter. It's not that I think this is bad, exactly, it's just that when so much of the mainstream consists of souped-up B-movies with psychos in them, there's not a lot of left-field left.

There is a line of thought which maintains that viewers are apt to be desensitised by constant exposure to violence. Of course we are! It's a defence mechanism; if I weren't desensitised to a certain degree, I would miss most of the films I go to see because half the time I would have my head between my knees. I used to get upset when characters bled from the mouth (and I bet there's an interesting cod-Freudian explanation to that), but nowadays, characters only have to get biffed across the face and they're dribbling gallons of red drool and I don't even blink.

Try me on real-life footage of death and disaster though, and it's another matter. I have absolutely no problem in distinguishing fact from fiction. And this is not a plea for moderation. I do not believe that less necessarily means more, and I have no objection to film-makers piling on the excess if they possess a suitably warped and fantastic imagination — like David Cronenberg, say, or Abel Ferrara or John Woo. I just think it a shame that, with the current tendency for every run-of-the-mill bullet hole to erupt into a crimson parabola, the small and singular glob has lost much of its capacity to impress.

But the glob is not a thing of the past — far from it. Glob-spotters can always hit paydirt if they know where to look. Or rather — because this is the whole point of the glob — if they *don't* know where to look. *The Silence of the Lambs* and *Cape Fear* are pre-sold as scare-machines and rarely deliver the goods where it really counts — on the creep-up-and-bite-your-ankle front. Such is the nature of the glob that mediocre movies, in which mediocre film-makers suddenly and inexplicably exercise a modicum of imagination (or steal it from their special effects department), often provide the happiest hunting grounds.

Not many people I know were impressed by *FX 2*, yet it contains a quintessentially glob-ular moment when a character gets shot in the stomach at the *exact same moment* she sinks her teeth into a hot dog. Sean Young landing on her head with a sickening crunch after

movies in which veins were drained and giblets flaunted. And, one year later, when *Easy Rider* ushered in the Era of Unhappy Endings, *The Wild Bunch* introduced the idea that bullet holes were not neat, round things but gaping wounds out of which spilled blood and guts. In this company, the odd mouse having its head bitten off didn't quite carry the same charge.

As the '70s got underway, genre and generic conventions began to leak into the mainstream. The movie brats took to splatter like ducks to water, and all bets were off. Characters began to bleed from the mouth left, right and centre. I didn't mind Robert Shaw being bitten in half by the shark in *Jaws*, especially since it stopped him wittering; it was the bleeding from the mouth that bothered me. Amid all the bucketfuls of blood on display in *Carrie*, a hardcore glob-watcher such as myself could still experience a passing *frisson* at the sight of sympathetic gym mistress Betty Buckley bleeding from the mouth in the prom scene, but by the time De Palma progressed to *The Fury*, sympathetic psychic researcher Fiona Lewis was bleeding out of every orifice, and then some, which might have been a hundred times as gross but which sort of lessened the impact.

Francis Ford Coppola injected squibs aplenty into the first two parts of *The Godfather*, yet the most upsetting scene he ever filmed was the toilet regurgitating blood in *The Conversation*, primarily because until that point the film had been pristine and its violence latent. Having not seen Martin Scorsese's *Mean Streets*, I tootled along to *Taxi Driver* like a lamb to the slaughter, so utterly unprepared for the bloodbath at the end that I had to put my head between my knees in order to stop myself fainting — and this in the front row of the Leicester Square Theatre. Afterwards, I went through a protracted phase of cinemagoing uncertainty, in which I approached everything — even Mel Brooks films — with the expectation that anything could happen at any minute. And that, when it did, I would probably faint.

Nevertheless, there were still occasions when one would be caught off-guard. If David Warner's head

actress, I wouldn't like my head to hit the floor like that, not even in a movie. The plane crash in *Alive*, with its screaming passengers sucked out of the back of the disintegrating fuselage, is total glob-o-rama, because it taps into a fear that is universal.

And there you have it. The reason globs stick in your subconscious and give you nightmares is that *they remind you you're going to die*. Globs reflect real life — and death — in a way that can be strangely irrelevant to the rest of the film in which they have been implanted, but which make sense on a gut level. Unless we're in an unusually paranoid frame of mind, we don't go through the day in a state of readiness, expecting to encounter Tom Savini-esque special make-up effects at every turn. Life is not a horror film — *but horrible things do happen*. And when they do, it's usually out of a clear blue sky, without any dramatic signposting or narrative tip-off.

The classic glob-u-like moment of all time is one that has been so immortalised on the cusp between fact and fiction that it is now a vital part of our modern mythology. To experience the essence of the glob in action you need look no further than the world's most famous documentary footage, the Zapruder film of President Kennedy being shot. Blue skies and cheering crowds one minute, a mist of vaporised brain-tissue the next. No matter how many times you watch it, it still packs a punch. This is for real, and we're all going to die, so there. ■

(Above) **Easy Rider** — *No happy ending for hippies...*

(Left) **Cape Fear** — *Robert De Niro reminds you you're going to die...*

being pushed off the top of a tall building in *A Kiss Before Dying* had a certain glob appeal; if I were a film

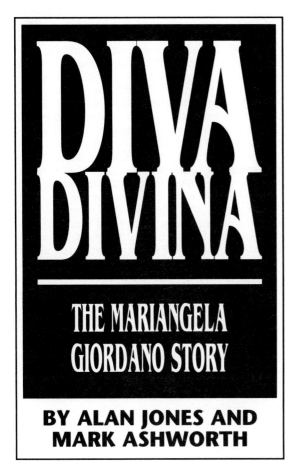

DIVA DIVINA

THE MARIANGELA GIORDANO STORY

BY ALAN JONES AND MARK ASHWORTH

There's an anecdote director Michele Soavi likes to tell about *The Sect*: "We knew we had a film that would be popular at film festivals. And it was. But festival organisers around Europe never wanted me to present it, or the star Kelly Curtis, or the writer Gianni Romoli, or even Dario Argento who produced it! No, they would always ask for an appearance by Mariangela Giordano who has roughly twelve minutes of screen time in the entire movie!"

Mariangela Giordano played Katryn in *The Sect*, the teacher doomed to die a far bloodier death than was eventually seen on screen. In common

with much of her recent work, a lot of her performance ended up on the cutting room floor.

But with that production, sultry Giordano clocked up her fifty-ninth role in a career spanning nearly forty years and every genre the Italian film industry has had to offer. Famous in her home country before Barbara Steele had even enrolled at Rank's charm school or Edwige Fenech wore her first mini skirt, she starred in the highest grossing *peplum* movie in Roman history. Destined for international stardom until hit by a devastating stroke of bad luck, she has worked with every major director from the sleazy (Sergio Garrone) to the classy (Ettore Scola). She has also become infamous to genre enthusiasts for a series of spaghetti shockers which remain as startling today as they were when first released at the gruesome height of the early '80s gore boom. Giordano will soon receive long overdue attention in Italy thanks to a reference book about Genoese actors currently in preparation. For Genoa, in the northern Italian region of Liguria, is where her extraordinary story begins and it's one she tells for the first time in the English language.

The greatest influence in Mariangela Giordano's life was her father, Angelo. "He was a Commander in the Italian navy during World War Two and I thought I'd lost him forever when his ship sank in the port at Genoa. I was five years old and can remember what a disaster it was for the family. We had no money and our life was a constant struggle. Imagine our shock when, eight years later, we found out he wasn't killed after all." Quite why he hadn't got back in touch with his family, Giordano professes never to have understood herself, "But in the interim he'd become a journalist and novelist and had written a book called *Chronos*." While her mother stayed in Genoa, she decided to live with her father in Imperia (near San Remo) where, at age thirteen, she was elected Miss Cinema of Imperia. It was a title which prophetically set the seal on the rest of her life.

"It was then I decided to drop out of school and become a dancer," she added. "I even took piano lessons! I was sure nothing would come out of this though and had more or less made up my mind to be a journalist like my father." But her smouldering Latin looks, even at this early age, were being noted and she suddenly found herself chosen as Miss Cinema of Genoa. A third beauty contest win followed — Miss Cinema of Liguria — "And while I was seeing people about a job in journalism, I was also getting lots of publicity in the very newspapers I was being interviewed by! After the Liguria win, offers poured in from impresarios saying I had all the right qualities to become a leading soubrette. But my father thought such glorified extra work was worse than walking the streets. That was a popular misconception at the time — acting equalled prostitution. So he said I could work with him as a fully fledged member of staff. Naturally, I was thrilled. Then one day we learnt a movie was being shot locally. I was desperate to go and watch and my father granted his permission as long as I was chaperoned."

The film being made on location was *Ultimo Addio* and, "Like everyone involved in the business learns quickly, it proved to be a very slow and boring process. The major disappointment was how unglamorous it was." But while hanging around the set she was introduced to the director, Roberto Bianchi Montero. (Montero went on to make the choice grunge items *Eye of the Spider* and *The Slasher is the Sex*

Maniac.) She continued, "I almost fainted when he asked me to play a small part in the movie. He had been expecting another actress to come from Rome to play the role but she had just called to say she'd taken another movie instead. He gave me two hours to reach a decision or he'd get someone else. I quickly called my father and managed to talk him into giving his consent. I could twist him around my finger at the time. I was a very spoilt child." So Giordano stepped in front of the cameras for the first time — "I enjoyed it. It was exciting." Yet there was something no one had thought important enough to tell her. She remarked, "I was then expected to immediately pack my bags and go to Rome to film my other scenes on a soundstage. I had no idea! I thought I'd done my bit. Because I was just fourteen, I could only travel with permission from the head of the Genoese police. When Montero said he'd become my official guardian that permission was granted."

Despite his misgivings about the film industry, Angelo sent his daughter off with reluctant blessings. She recalled, "I had been offered a film before this. However, the two Genoese backers were so slimy it coloured my father's view of the industry forever." Once in Rome, she moved into the Grand Hotel and, after completing her work on *Ultimo Addio*, decided she didn't want to go back home. "Rome was just entering the whole *la dolce vita* era. Who wouldn't want to be a part of that?" she laughed. But her expensive hotel lifestyle had to go, "So I moved into a little *pensione* where they didn't ask for documents, something rare for the time. It was a 'Boarding House for Young Ladies' and only after my father called to check I was alright did we realise it was a brothel!" Naturally outraged, Angelo insisted guardian Montero personally

Mariangela models slave girl chic in a couple of Ursus movies...

put his precious daughter on a train home to Genoa. "But on that train I met the national Olympic swimming team. One of the group was gold medalist Carlo Pedersoli who told me to follow my dreams if I truly wanted to be an actress. I got off at the next station and took the first train back." Pedersoli was to become one of Giordano's best friends and, when he changed his name to Bud Spencer and became half of the world famous cowboy duo with Terence Hill, he helped launch her later spaghetti western career.

Now calling Rome her base, Giordano needed to find work. She returned to the *Ultimo Addio* production office for casting information and advice. "But they'd shut up shop and there was no one there apart from a lawyer, who asked me why I wanted to enter such a hard profession. What I told him must have impressed him because he said, 'If I'm able to find you a movie tonight, stay. If I can't, I want you to promise me you'll be on the 10.30 train back to Liguria.' I had nothing to lose so I accepted his bet." Two hours before the deadline, he called to say they needed a girl for a new Riccardo Freda film. (Freda was a year away from changing the Italian horror scene forever with *The Devil's Commandment*.)

She continued, "I rushed to the Jolly Film offices (*Jolly would later co-produce Mario Bava's* Black Sunday *and Antonio Margheriti's* Castle of Blood) and waited for the production assistant to turn up. And I waited and waited. Then this man came in and asked me who I was and what was I doing there. When I told him, he asked me to come into this enormous office. That's when I found out it was Freda himself and he was furious no one had told him I was there. He'd only come in to see why the lights were still on! Literally an hour before, he'd signed up an actress for the lead role in *Da Qui All'Eredita* who he knew was all wrong for the part. He thought I was perfect for it but there was nothing he could do. Except he fired the production assistant for not doing his job properly and gave me a smaller role as a newly wed girl." Giordano only worked for six days on this comedy, which starred Domenico Modugno, the singer/actor who would have a huge worldwide pop hit with 'Volare' in 1958. But she won the bet with the lawyer, who turned out to be Carlo Caino, director Mario's father and Gianna Maria Canale's agent. (Canale starred in Freda's *The Devil's Commandment* and *Theodora, Slave Empress*.) Giordano signed a contract with him for three years.

However, during this time, Giordano never seriously thought of what she was doing as a proper career. She said, "Everything was just for fun. I was having a good time. All the parts I got were purely decorative but it didn't bother me." Then she was cast in Goffredo Allessandri's *Gli Amanti del Deserto* with Anna Magnani and Ricardo Montalban. "It was my first important part. We shot on location in Spain for four months and, because it was a Spanish/French co-production, I started being offered leading roles in films being made in those countries." *El Reflejo del Ama* was the first to put her name above the title and was one of five Spanish movies she made that same year. These productions opened Giordano's eyes to what was actually possible in the film industry and were directly responsible for spreading her fame throughout Europe.

But in order to work in Spain she had to have a passport. "Which meant I also had to lie about my age," she added. "A sixteen year-old would not have been allowed employment abroad in those days. So I faked my passport, which means no one will ever know how old I really am! My year in Spain was a mixture of great joy and sadness. I was up for an award at the San Sebastian Festival. However, while making the last film, *Cara de Goma*, my father died, and because I was working every day, I couldn't go home for the funeral. I still get upset thinking about that. At the time I became very thin. I didn't eat and got depressed. I stopped working for a while too." Not for long though. Italy was entering the *peplum* golden age and Giordano's sensual beauty was a perfect complement to all the superheroes flexing their muscles in such small scale epics as *Colossus and the Amazons*, *Ursus*, *The Rape of the Sabine Women* (with Roger Moore!) and *Ursus in the Valley of the Lions*. In fact, Carlo Campogalliani's *Ursus* was the most successful *peplum* ever on home release, beating both Steve Reeves vehicles *Hercules* and *Hercules Unchained*.

When the *peplum* trend abated, Giordano hung up her seven veils and slave girl costume to genre hop through the next five years. She played five different roles in the pop musical *Canzoni a Tempo di Twist* ('Songs with a Twist Beat'), directed by Camillo Mastrocinque, who would later helm *Crypt of Horror* and *An Angel for Satan*. Her co-star was teen heartthrob Pino Donnagio, who gave up his pop idol/song-writing career to concentrate on composing soundtracks. She then starred in Marcello Andrei's *In the Eye of the Needle*, the second watershed movie of her career. She explained, "My co-star was Vittorio Gassman, the gentlest, kindest actor I've ever met. I played a girl who thought she was ugly, and I was later surprised to win lots of prizes for my performance at many film festivals. Up until *In the Eye of the Needle*, I was messing around. I viewed my early career as a joke, an enormous laugh. I took it seriously from here on and threw myself into every part. From this point on, I can honestly say I made every movie with love."

While appearing in some spaghetti westerns at the tail end of the vogue (with her credit often Anglicised to Mary Jordan), Giordano met a producer who was to play an important part in her later career. Gabriele Crisanti had successfully produced the Superargo-style adventure *The Devil's Man* and was about to make two Sergio Garrone westerns back to back. *No Graves on Boot Hill* and *No Room to Die* both starred Giordano for one main reason — Crisanti fell in love with her. Their stormy relationship was to last twelve years, fifteen movies and encompass the most depressing period of her life, the seeds of which were sown in 1971. That was the year director John Sturges (*The Magnificent Seven*, *The Great Escape* and so on) arrived in Rome to cast his new picture *Le Mans*. Steve McQueen was already signed for the starring role of American racing driver Michael Delaney and Sturges needed someone to play his girlfriend. Giordano was Sturges' choice and, after she successfully screen tested with McQueen, the director told her to pack her bags and wait for a summons to the French locations.

The call never came. Sturges was fired from the picture, Lee H. Katzin took over and the William Morris Agency swiftly stepped in and offered their client Elga Andersen for the role instead. Giordano was oblivious to all this. She said, "I had a contract, I wasn't worried. I only found out what had happened when I met a friend one day who said, 'What are you doing in town? I thought you'd be in France. They've nearly finished *Le Mans*.' I knew nothing about it. Steve McQueen felt so badly about the whole situation, he promised me a part in another movie he'd be making." Sadly, when

One of Mariangela's many screen cat fights. This one's in **Ursus**.

McQueen made good his offer seven years later, it led to the most devastating disappointment of Giordano's career. *Le Mans* wasn't a box-office success and it's doubtful Giordano would have gained any benefit from it on an international level. (Whatever happened to Elga Andersen?) But *Jimmy Angel's Story* might have been a different proposition altogether had it ever been released.

Jimmy Angel's Story was a simple western transplanted to the Amazon jungle. It starred McQueen and was directed by his buddy Sam Peckinpah, with whom he'd made *Junior Bonner* and *The Getaway*. Giordano continued, "We were in the Amazon for six months and it was a very dangerous film to make. I was always being chased under waterfalls! Steve knew he was ill while we were making the picture and I don't think the punishing schedule helped." McQueen died of cancer soon after principle shooting was completed and the project died with him. Because McQueen was also the sole producer, there was no money available to complete it. Peckinpah never edited the footage, nor was it ever shown, and Giordano remains convinced she would have had a stab at international stardom had things worked out differently. Yet this aborted project does answer one major question. From this point on she would often bill herself as Maria Angela Giordan. She revealed, "Peckinpah was a very superstitious person. He was into numerology and didn't like my name. It didn't scan numerically according to him. So he did my charts and worked out that I should change it to Maria Angela Giordan for luck. It didn't work did it? It wasn't lucky at all! But I still use it on occasion in remembrance of them both."

After this depressing setback, Giordano was desperate to return to any sort of work at all. Thanks to Crisanti, she went from the sublime to the ridiculous and over the next two years made a series of horror movies for him that arguably rank as the grossest made

in Italy. In many ways, the writing was on the wall when Crisanti had earlier asked her to star in *Quant'e' Bella La Bernarda, Tutta Nera Tutta Calda* and *Le Impiegate Stradali — Batton Story*. The former translates as 'How Beautiful is Bernarda, All Black All Hot.' When you learn the name Bernarda is also slang for vagina, the deliberate *double entendre* becomes obvious. As for the latter, 'batton' is a vulgarisation of the already crude word *batonne*, meaning whore. Reflecting on her accidental scream queen career, Giordano pondered, "Looking back I shouldn't have done them. But I was in love with Gabriele, I would have done anything for him. Now I can see how the increasingly gruesome ways he had me killed in them was a reflection of the breakdown in our own relationship."

The first movie Giordano made for Crisanti in 1979 set the tone for the whole bizarre series. *Malabimba* was directed by sexploitation auteur Andrea Bianchi, the man responsible for *Strip Nude for Your Killer* and the Carroll Baker vehicle *Confessions of a Frustrated*

Housewife. Written by terminal hack Piero Regnoli, director of *The Playgirls and the Vampire*, it was a *Sexorcist* variant about the evil spirit of nymphomaniac Countess Lucrezia possessing innocent Bimba (Katell Leannec) and forcing her to commit lewd sexual acts in an old castle. Giordano played Sister Sofia, the castle's live-in nun, who allows Lucrezia into her own body and then jumps over the battlements in an act of ultimate self-sacrifice. After an impressive start — the sex-mad spook, unleashed by medium Elisa Mainardi during a seance, unzips trousers and exposes breasts — repetitive stretches of softcore writhing gradually slacken the pace to a virtual halt, though the revival of Berto Pisano's exquisite *Death Smiles at Murder* score papers over many of the cracks in its bargain basement plot.

Giordano recalled, "We made the movie in twelve days working day and night and through the weekends. The location was an abandoned castle that hadn't been lived in for fifty-five years and was now used solely by film companies. (*Massimo Pupillo set* Bloody Pit of Horror *there and Bianchi was to return in 1985 for* Game of Seduction.) We shot the movie in March 1979 and it was freezing. I remember when we came to shoot the scene where the ghost enters Sofia's room. Wind was howling through the corridors and it was cold, mouldy and damp. I got very ill that day what with all the dust and filth flying everywhere. And I wasn't wearing any underwear! But Gabriele hadn't taken out any insurance policies on the film and was scared I wouldn't be able to complete it. So I couldn't go to hospital until after everything was finished. That's why I'm leaning on walls a lot of the time. I was so sick, I literally couldn't stand up! My make-up artist got ill too and he almost died. That evil spirit infested the whole production! Anyway, when the movie was finally in the can, I went to hospital and discovered I'd caught a rare virus that couldn't be cured. It had something to do with my thyroid gland

(Above right) Cowboy stuff from **Djurado**.

(Below) "Oh well, at least I don't have to do a sex scene with him..." Mariangela contemplates a particularly convincing **Zombie 3** *make-up.*

(Below right) Guess who's coming to dinner? Mariangela becomes the Antipasto in the notorious **Giallo a Venezia**...

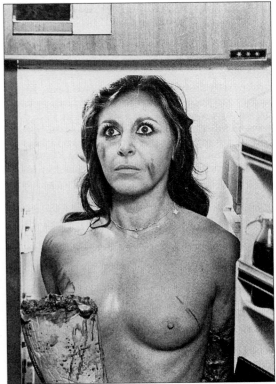

exploding. Despite all that, there's something I quite like about Sister Sofia. She's one of the 'nicest' characters I've ever played."

But something Crisanti did on *Malabimba* was completely unknown to Giordano at the time. A version including hardcore porn close-ups was prepared for more liberal markets. Surprisingly, the tamer version still contains a brief shot of an erect penis during the comically perverse scene in which Leannec fellates her crippled grandfather to death. Even if Giordano had known about this, it's doubtful she would have cared as she was put on a ninety day cortisone treatment to ease her illness. Crisanti had also just signed a deal with ELEA Cinematografica to produce *Giallo a Venezia* and needed Giordano as his leading lady once more. Banned in practically every major territory throughout the world, *Giallo a Venezia* is a shocking, sleazy chiller, with suspects connected to an illicit sex and drugs ring being murdered in various brutal ways.

Directed by *Batton Story*'s Mario Landi, who helmed numerous Inspector Maigret episodes for Italian TV, *Giallo a Venezia* shares with them an ordinary televisual flatness, as well as the plodding detective angle. However, the grubby nastiness of the explicit slayings has rarely been duplicated, even if the usually picturesque Venice location looked more like seedy Swindon! The demises include a man doused in petrol and set alight, scissors being thrust into a prostitute's crotch and Giordano being chased naked around her apartment, tied to a kitchen table, having her leg messily sawn off and being stuck in the fridge. If anything, *Giallo a Venezia* proved Giordano was a real professional, a trouper. She recalled, "Frankly the movie is a haze in my memory. I was still very sick and had a constant fever throughout all my scenes. For some reason I was always on a kitchen table in Gabriele's movies. Hmmm! In this one I remember being tied down on it with telephone cords. The actor tied them so tight, they cut into my flesh, and I had marks around my wrists and ankles for three months afterwards."

There was worse to come. *Zombie 3* was a crude but reasonably effective *Dawn of the Dead* cash-in about a professor (Renato Barbieri) researching the magical rites of the ancient Etruscans. He unwittingly releases the living dead from a burial site in the grounds of an isolated country mansion where weekending guests soon find themselves on the menu. *Zombie 3* may not be the best zombie movie ever, but Andrea Bianchi's action-packed, grotesquely gory comic strip features the cinema's favourite flesheaters in all their full-blown, maggot-eaten glory. The bad taste highlight belongs to Giordano: one of her breasts is bitten off by her incestuous, zombiefied son (played by the creepily repellent Peter Bark). She shrugged, "That scene was so ridiculous, I could hardly keep a straight face. I had a rubber breast fitted over my own which looked so fake I can't believe anyone took it seriously!" Hopelessly directed by Bianchi (the cast look more at risk from the wayward camera moving to peculiar angles than the shuffling, sack-cloth clad Etruscans!), there's enough glistening offal on display to satisfy the most jaded gorehound even though Giordano feels it's the shoddiest movie she's made. That's something reflected by the ending — a doom-laden quote from 'The Prophecy of the Black Spider' rendered laughable in the English version by conspicuous misspellings.

But there was far worse to come! Of all the rip-off sequels the Italians have quickly rushed into production, Mario Landi's follow-up to Richard Franklin's

Patrick remains the oddest. Sleazier, and more enjoyable, than its Australian model, *Patrick Still Lives* finds Patrick Herschell (Gianni Dei) in an irreversible coma after being hit by a bottle thrown from a speeding van. Lying in a special ward at a plush country clinic run by his father (Sacha Pitoeff), he's affected by negative vibrations and telekinetically engineers the violent deaths of other guests with shady pasts. While not as pathologically violent as *Giallo a Venezia*, the late Landi's final work for the big screen has no shortage of grisly moments, each prefaced by a pair of staring eyes tackily superimposed on screen. Paolo Giusti's throat is impaled on a hook. There's a vicious dog attack. And there's Giordano's violation by a floating poker...

She sighed, "When I'm filming, I throw myself into the role and I don't think about the ramifications of what I'm doing. It's like I have an alter-ego. While I never have a problem over what actions I'm doing at the time, sometimes I have looked back in astonishment and thought, 'Did I really do that? Did it look that vulgar?' *Patrick Still Lives* is the worst instance of how shocked I was in retrospect by something I'd done on film. That poker scene is so disgusting, so terrible, only Gabriele could have sweet-talked me into actually doing it! I played an old maid who arrives in the kitchen (again!) and is attacked by a possessed poker. It took two days to film that scene, and because the poker had to keep thrusting between my legs before it came out of the top of my head, it got more and more painful as we kept going. And it was cold and freezing. I don't know why Gabriele always insisted on making these movies during winter." One sequence Giordano did remember with affection in this claustrophobic carnage classic (which reused the electronic beeps from *Zombie 3* soundtrack) is the drunken cat-fight she has with busty glamour-puss Carmen Russo. She smiled, "That was fun. All my pent up rage at Gabriele is in that brawl."

But her relationship, both personal and working, with Crisanti was coming to a close. The movie that finally ended it was *Satan's Baby Doll*, directed by Mario Bianchi under the pseudonym Alan W. Cools. (Bianchi was Mario Bava's assistant director on *Five Dolls for an August Moon*.) Obviously at a loss over what to rip-off next, Crisanti and scripter Piero Regnoli decided to cannibalise their own back cata-

Incestuous rubber breast-eating from **Zombie 3** — *a favourite of cinema-going liberals everywhere.*

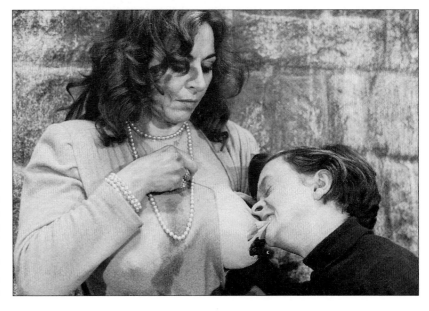

Satan's Baby Doll. *What we always suspected about nuns... Consider: it's probably more 'fun' seeing these stills than sitting through the whole movie...*

logue for this minimalist replay of *Malabimba*. This time, during a black magic ritual in the crypt of a remote castle, the ghost of a murdered Countess (Marina Hedmann) rises from the grave to use her daughter (Jacqueline Dupre) as an instrument of revenge against her killer husband (Aldo Sanbrell). Originally conceived as a porno project — hence the presence of hardcore heroine Hedmann (aka Marina Frajese) — it was eventually released in 1982 in a cut down soft version.

Giordano reprises her role as a self-sacrificing nun, climactically crushed to death in the embrace of Hedmann's reanimated corpse, with the addition of some discreet masturbation padding. She said, "Enough was enough. Remaking *Malabimba* was a stupid move. I didn't want to do the sex scenes. I felt used, abused and exploited. I wanted to get back to quality, mainstream pictures. So I finished with Gabriele and my horror career was over." Even so, *Satan's Baby Doll* is probably the artiest Crisanti production of them all. Arcangelo Lanutti's effective lighting manages to purvey a shadowy and unsettling atmosphere, while touches of mystery are provided by Nico Catanese's score, combining electronic effects with heavy metal and chanting voices. It's undoubtedly the not over-talented Bianchi's

most interesting work.

Giordano was to have one further brush with horror. But it was to come after she had reestablished herself in the A-movie arena with *Io e Mia Sorella* ('My Sister and I') and *Stasera in Casa di Alice* ('Tonight at Alice's House'), two big budget hits from director/comedian Carlo Verdone. She said, "Verdone was brilliant. More than any other director I've worked with, I had the most collaborative relationship with him. I've never found it with anyone else. He taught me to believe in every single detail of the script and now I can't work in any other way."

Her experiences working with maestro Ettore Scola on *Il Viaggio di Capitan Fracassa* were a different matter. She explained, "I had my entire part cut from the final film! Happily the movie wasn't a success or I'd have been more annoyed. It made me realise how much the Italian industry has changed since I began all those years ago. Everyone used to work for the sheer pleasure of making something entertaining. Now it's purely a business, a Cecchi Gori monopoly, and being an actor has become a sad job. There was one scene in the Scola movie he made me shoot fifty-two times. Why? The candle behind me never flickered correctly! That just about sums up the industry to me these days. It was during this trying scene that I said, 'Come back Crisanti, all is forgiven!' Well, nearly."

Nevertheless, it was Mario Cecchi Gori who insisted Giordano be cast in Michele Soavi's *The Sect*, produced by Dario Argento for Penta, the distribution company he owns with his son Vittorio. She enthused, "I loved the final picture even if a lot of my role was cut out. It was important because it gave me the chance to work with a young, dynamic crew. Michele and Rafaele (*Mertes, the lighting cameraman*) have so much love for movies, their enthusiasm was contagious. With such commitment on their part, it always made me want to try my best. Michele would take the time to explain clearly what he wanted me to do, which was very helpful as I had to learn the lines in English." The one scene Giordano regrets being cut the most was her very gory death in the hospital. People who've seen the unedited footage still shudder at the memory of Giordano's painful demise as blood spurted out of her many wounds like a fountain. "I didn't mind being naked in front of the crew. I didn't mind jumping around covered in blood. It was a real pleasure because Michele deserved that sort of obligation from me as a true artist."

Since *The Sect*, Giordano has made *Abbronzatissimi*, a seaside comedy in the *American Graffiti* tradition, and *Chi Hai Rotto Papa'*, which she called "A nice children's comedy where I play a witch. I modelled myself after the queen in *Snow White and the Seven Dwarfs*." Would she have had the career longevity she's achieved if she had become a world famous name after starring with Steve McQueen? Reflecting on that question in her Rome penthouse surrounded by vases of *giallo* (yellow) roses, her favourite flowers, she said, "I've often thought about that. I doubt it. I've lasted this long because I was never famous. I was always one of those faces people recognised but could never put a name to. Nor did I give enough attention to the publicity side of the business. I never gave interviews or did photo spreads. I was too busy having a fabulous time. I tend to look at my movies in terms of what country I was in, who I was meeting, where I was going and how great all that was. Certainly not in terms of my performance." ∎

MARIANGELA GIORDANO: Filmography

1955: ULTIMO ADDIO/DRAMMA NEL PORTO
(Roberto Montero Bianchi)
DA QUI ALL'EREDITA (Riccardo Freda)
IL CORTILE (Luigi Capuano)
IL FALCO D'ORO (Carlo Ludovico Bragaglia)
1956: LA BANDA DEGLI ONESTI (Camillo
Mastrocinque)
GLI AMANTI DEL DESERTO (Goffredo
Allessandri)
1957: EL REFLEJO DEL AMA
IL DIAVOLO NERO
BUON GIORNO PRIMO AMORE
MENSAJEROS DE PAZ
CARA DE GOMA
1958: QUANDO GLI ANGELI PIANGONO
1959: GLI SCONTENTI
1960: COLOSSUS AND THE AMAZONS/LA REGINA
DELLE AMAZZONI (Vittorio Sala)
1961: URSUS (Carlo Campogalliani)
IL RE DI POGGIOREALE (Dulio Coletti)
**THE RAPE OF THE SABINE WOMEN/IL RATTO
DELLE SABINE** (Richard Pottier)
1962: URSUS IN THE VALLEY OF THE LIONS/URSUS
NELLA VALLE DEI LEONI (Carlo Ludovico
Bragaglia)
CANZONI A TEMPO DI TWIST (Stefano Canzio)
1963: IN THE EYE OF THE NEEDLE/LA SMANIA
ADDOSSO (Marcello Andrei)
1964: SETTE A TEBE (Roy Ferguson)
1965: UNA VERGINE PER IL PRINCIPE (Pasquale
Festa Campanile)
TE LO LEGGO NEGLI OCCHI (Camillo
Mastrocinque)
1966: COME IMPARAI AD AMARE LE DONNE
(Luciano Salce)
1967: DJURADO (Gianni Narzisi)
1968: VENGEANCE/JOKO, INVOCO DIO...E MUORI
(Antonio Margheriti)
1969: NO GRAVES ON BOOT HILL/TRE CROCI PER
NON MORIRE (Sergio Garrone/Willy S. Regan)
**NO ROOM TO DIE/UNA LUNGA FILA DI
CROCI** (Sergio Garrone/Willy S. Regan)
LA STIRPE DI CAINO
I QUATTRO DEL PATER NOSTER (Ruggero
Deodato)
1970: THE REWARD'S YOURS...THE MAN'S MINE/
LA TAGLIA E' TUA...L'UOMO LO AMMAZZO
IO (Eduardo Mulargia/Edward G . Muller)
1972: DECAMERON NO. 2 — LE ALTRE NOVELLE
DEL BOCCACCIO (Mino Guerrini)
1973: DECAMERON NO. 4 (Paolo Bianchini/Paul
Maxwell)
1975: QUANT'E' BELLA LA BERNARDA, TUTTA
NERA TUTTA CALDA/QUANT'E' BELLA LA
BERNARDA CHI LA TOCCA CHI LA GUARDA
(Luigi Dandolo)
DON MILANI (Ivan Angeli)
L'ALTRO DIO (Elio Bartolini)
1976: LE IMPIEGATE STRADALI — BATTON STORY
(Mario Landi)
BIG POT/IL COLPACCIO (Bruno Paolinelli/
John Huxley)
IL CONTO E' CHIUSO (Stelvio Massi)
CHE DOTTORESSA RAGAZZI (Gianfranco
Baldinello)
1977: UN GIORNO ALLA FINE DI OTTOBRE (Paolo
Spinola)

DOVE VOLANO I CORVI S'ARGENTO (Piero Livi)
1978: LA MOGLIE SICILIANA/MOGLIE NUDA E
SICILIANA (Andrea Bianchi)
IL COMMISSARIO DI FERRO (Stelvio Massi)
JIMMY ANGEL'S STORY (Sam Peckinpah)
1979: GIALLO A VENEZIA/GORE IN VENICE/
THRILLER IN VENICE (Mario Landi)
MALABIMBA (Andrea Bianchi)
1980: ZOMBIE 3/LE NOTTI DEL TERRORE/NIGHTS
OF TERROR/BURIAL GROUND/ZOMBI
HORROR (Andrea Bianchi)
**PATRICK STILL LIVES/PATRICK VIVE
ANCORA/PATRICK 2** (Mario Landi)
SATAN'S BABY DOLL/LA BIMBA DI SATANA
(Mario Bianchi/Alan W. Cools)
1981: PAULA MUJER DE LA NOCHE (Alfred S. Brell/
Aldo Sanbrell)
EROTICON
THE MOTORCYCLE/IL MOTORINO (Nini
Grassia)
1987: NOI UOMINI DURI (Maurizio Ponzi)
IO E MIA SORELLA (Carlo Verdone)
1988: IL VOLPONE
1990: IL VIAGGIO DI CAPITAN FRACASSA (Ettore
Scola)
STASERA IN CASA DI ALICE (Carlo Verdone)
1991: THE SECT/LA SETTA/THE DEVIL'S DAUGHTER
(Michele Soavi)
1992: ABBRONZATISSIMI
CHI HAI ROTTO PAPA'

Television:

1985: SKIPPER (episode 3)
1988: POLIZZA INFERNO (episode 'Big Man')
1989: IL VIGILE (episodes 1, 10 and 13)
1990: DONNE ARMATE (mini series)

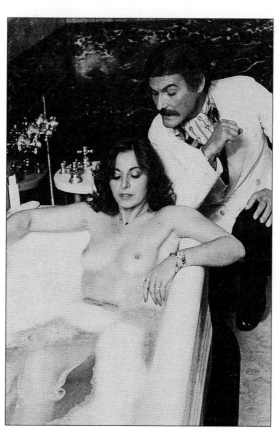

Patrick Still Lives.
*Mariangela wishes he
didn't.*

DJANGO THE BASTARD

ALWAYS DRAWS SECOND, SHOOTS FIRST, STRIKES AGAIN, DEFIES SARTANA, DOES NOT FORGIVE, AND SO ON...

FRANCO NERO INTERVIEWED

BY EDWIN POUNCEY

Franco Nero is probably one of the best known and most prolific Italian actors alive. Born in 1942, he achieved fame in 1966 with his titular role in *Django*, a brutal spaghetti western directed by Sergio Corbucci. Commencing with a mysterious stranger arriving in a pasteboard town dragging a coffin behind him, *Django* progresses through numerous scenes of Gothic sadism and outrageous carnage to an apocalyptic climax. Its graphic violence (including an ear severing, prefiguring *Reservoir Dogs* by some twenty-five years, and a scene where Django has his hands crushed

DJANGO

(Left) A scene from **Django**. *You have to wait for the next page for the 'funny' captions...*

(Previous page) *Franco Nero 'today'.*

and mutilated) proved too much for the British censors, who rejected the film in 1967. Contrary to popular belief, *Django* has not been permanently banned since its initial rejection — it was simply never formally submitted to the BBFC again until 1992. Potential distributors were told in the early '70s that, given the controversies arising from such films as *Straw Dogs* and *A Clockwork Orange*, it might be better left unreleased.

When the question of its release arose again in 1974 and the distributor was informed that a number of major cuts would be necessary, all plans for its release were shelved. Apart from a (presumably unofficial) video release by Inter-Ocean in the early '80s (a well-worn and washed out print, albeit with original Italian credits), it remained unseen in Britain until the Scala Cinema gave it its theatrical première in 1991. In 1993 *Django* finally appeared on British TV as a part of a 'Moviedrome' season, and both it and *Django Strikes Again*, its 1987 sequel, are available on video.

This interview with Nero took place in March 1993, prior to *Django's* video release. He proved to be charming, informative, knowledgeable and, with those unforgettable blue eyes shining like sapphires, impressive to say the least.

FN: *Django* and *A Fistful of Dollars* were two of the most successful Italian westerns in the world at the time. Even now they're considered classics. I was filming in Austria recently — making this movie about the super cannon that Saddam Hussein was trying to build with the complicity of many countries — and *Django* was shown on TV there twice in two weeks! I couldn't believe it. They told me that it was shown on TV all over the world for years. This was when Art House Productions contacted me and asked me to promote *Django* in London. I said, "What do you mean pro-

mote *Django*? That was over twenty-five years ago!" They said, "No, we are releasing it on video now." NOW!?! I couldn't believe that it had been banned in Britain for such a long time.

SX: Were you aware of the controversy that involved *Django* and caused it to become banned in Britain?

FN: I did not know about it at all, it came as a bit of a surprise. They asked me, "Why do think they banned *Django*?" I said, "I don't know, don't ask me." I think that maybe the British censors were very severe because, at the same time, they were showing *The Wild Bunch* and *A Clockwork Orange* and many other really violent movies.

SX: So, on reflection, why do think they came down so hard on *Django*? Was it because there was no real money to promote it?

FN: I think so. That was the main reason, because the western is pure fantasy. I don't think you should be so severe with a western. When you have gratuitous violence in modern movies, where you know things on the screen could have happened in real life, then that is something else. But when it is a fantasy, even sex, if it is in the right context...why not? That's part of life.

SX: And now Hollywood is being criticised by people like Michael Medved for promoting films that contain scenes of sex and violence. What are your feelings about the 'Hollywood vs America' debate?

FN: Listen. Everybody's against violence. If you are a civilised and responsible person you are against violence, especially if you have children. But all these Hollywood guys are talking this way because they happen to be very successful.

(Top) Tomas Milian gives Franco head in **Companeros**.

(Above) Of the many infantile photo captions in this volume, several refer to choppers — this time it's Tomas Milian's in **Companeros**.

SX: You recently, and rightly, criticised *The Silence of the Lambs* actor Anthony Hopkins for denouncing his role as Hannibal Lecter.

FN: Mr Hopkins is a great actor and I respect him, but why didn't he say these things when he was starving? It's easy for him to speak out now because he has so many choices before him. For me, so long as you're not violent inside that's the most important thing. I'd always be against gratuitous violence and sex, but if it's part of a fantasy or a fairy tale then I would do it. If you make a western, what do you want to talk about? Even *Dances with Wolves* was violent, it had some very heavy scenes in it. Why didn't they speak out about that movie? Have you seen *Last of the Mohicans*? *Unforgiven*? There is no violence in these movies?

SX: A western without violence would be like pasta without sauce, surely? Violence is part of that particular tradition.

FN: Yes, but that history was distorted by Hollywood. When I was a child I would look at American western movies and there would always be the cowboys as heroes and the Indians as bad guys. When I grew up I understood that this was not true. Indians were Americans, the pure Americans, and they were being slaughtered. When I was five the hero for me was the man on the horse, I was always dreaming about him. Then when I was a teenager I went to see so many westerns...*High Noon, Gunfight at the O.K. Corral*...I mean many, many westerns. I always loved them and this is why I need to make a western every once in a while. I've made more than one hundred movies, I've worked with some of the best directors in the world, but once in a while, like now, I need to do a western. My next project is a western that will be ecological and against racism. I will be on the side of the American Indian.

SX: That sounds rather, er, familiar...

FN: I scripted out my western four years ago, that's two years before *Dances with Wolves*. At the time nobody wanted to invest money in my western because they were not popular. But now, because of the success of *Dances with Wolves, Last of the Mohicans* and *Unforgiven*, now I can do it.

SX: To return to *Django*. Who deserves credit for creating the main character in that film — yourself or director Sergio Corbucci?

FN: I think Corbucci deserves all the credit for creating the Django character. He wanted an anti-hero, someone who was not like the usual clean American hero, someone who had a little bit of the devil in him and was a son-of-a-bitch. I was twenty-three when I made *Django* and I was not supposed to be the actor. The actor that was originally chosen for the part was Mark Damon — who later became a distributor — but he was busy doing something else. There were three producers involved. One said, "We must wait for

Mark." The second said, "I have someone else in mind." Corbucci said, "We should use this young guy Franco Nero." There was a fight between them, so they got hold of pictures of Mark Damon, me and this other guy and took them to the distributor. They said to the distributor, "Listen, we have a little problem here. You choose which actor you like from these faces." The distributor reached out and put his finger on my picture, so I got to make the movie. I remember being uncertain about making a western, very uncertain, until I was advised by a much respected Italian director to do it as I had nothing to lose. When a young actor has nothing to lose it means he's starving.

I got £200 for playing Django at the time. There are, of course, some funny stories about making that movie. We started shooting and then two days later we stopped because the story was not quite right. This was two days before Christmas, so this producer flew to Spain to get some more money and came back with a co-production deal. In the meantime Corbucci's brother, Bruno, had rewritten the screenplay during the Christmas holiday. After New Year's Eve we went to Spain for a week and then flew back to Italy to carry on filming.

SX: Tell me a little about the conditions you had to work in. Was that filthy, muddy set you had to wallow around in for real?

FN: It was very heavy. I'll never forget that opening scene where you see me dragging the coffin behind me for a long time in the credits sequence. I remember Corbucci instructing me, "When you are sure that you are at the end of the mountain, then you disappear and you can stop dragging the coffin." I did everything myself and I remember it took a long time to arrive there. Finally, when I was sure that I was out of sight of the camera, I collapsed on the floor. It was raining that day and the crew had played a joke on me by going home. I was stuck out in the rain for two or three hours. In Italy we like to play jokes like that, but that was a little bit heavy. In the scene where I am in the quicksand, that was the middle of winter, that was January and the water was ice! I remember Corbucci kept giving me cognac all the time to keep me going, but after that I had to spend two days in the hospital being massaged with alcohol because I had almost frozen to death. They were hard movies to make, very tough, physical movies.

SX: What do you think about the glut of Django movies that followed?

FN: Well, this is a typical Italian custom. You may remember in the late '50s and early '60s the Italians were making (*sword and sandal*) movies about Hercules. Because they made one with Steve Reeves that was so successful they then made about a 1,000 more in the space of two years. They died out when westerns like *A Fistful of Dollars* and *Django* came out. They made 3,000 westerns and, of course, that dies out as well. Then I made some movies about the police before *The French Connection* came out. I made one called *High Crime* that was so successful that they made 3,000 police movies. After about two or three years they totally disappeared. People get bored. That's the trouble with Italy, everything is fashion.

SX: How many of the *Django* spin-offs have you seen?

FN: They made so many. They were cheap movies and I was very upset about that. I made westerns after *Django*. One was called *A Professional Gun*, one was *Companeros*, and one was called *Keoma*. They were all very wonderful westerns.

SX: *Keoma* was billed as a *Django* movie in Germany.

FN: That's my problem with Germany, that is the country where most of my films were retitled *Django*. *Django* was so popular in Germany and Austria that the distributors kept calling everything I made after it Django movies. I made an underwater movie with sharks (*The Shark Hunter*) and they called it 'Django and the Sharks'. I made a mafia movie (*Il Giorno della Civetta*) and they called it 'Django in the Mafia'!

SX: Why did you take so long to follow up *Django* with *Django Strikes Again*?

FN: After *Django* I made two westerns in Europe the same year. One was *Tempo di Massacro* and the other was *Texas, Addio*. They were released one after the other, then I went to America to do *Camelot*. After that I came back to Europe and made movies with such great directors as Buñuel, Fassbinder, Chabrol and Zeffirelli. But once in a while I would return to making westerns.

SX: What do you think is the thing that appeals to people about the Django character?

FN: He's in the air, we don't know where he comes from and we don't know where he disappears to afterwards. He's like a ghost and that's the secret of his success. You shouldn't ask too many questions about Django, you should just watch him and that's it. I think I played him very cool, very simply, without moving the face too much. Don't think that it is easy being an actor, you have to be believable just with your face without using too many expressions. That's why in a western you need special faces, the eyes need something, a certain charisma. John Wayne once said a very funny thing. He said, "I have two expressions. One with the hat and one without the hat." That was a joke, but in a way it was true. He knew he had to be believable with or without the hat.

SX: Would you ever be tempted to play Django again?

FN: Yes, I would do it again, absolutely. Of course I would play him differently because I am now more mature, but I think I shall do it again. We say in Italy that you must never spit on the thing that brought you success. ∎

*More **Django** stuff.*

MAYBE THE EYE IS NOT IN THE HEAD

THE SEX PSYCHEDELIC

BY DAVID KEREKES

Hardcore pornography on screen is an agent, an impulse. It exists to promote a response. Everyone is happy and everything is beautiful, even potential nastiness is carefree and fun, because in hardcore pornography there is no consequence. Only sex. What goes on on that screen does so to make us, the viewer, feel good. Make us happy deep down.

Push most any hardcore porn movie into your VCR and chances are that, barely out of the opening credits, you'll be encountering the pulsing swings of fleshy throbs. The sex. The point. Needless to say, the swings of focus flow thick and fast hereafter. This, together with the estranged, stilted dialogue and nonsensical scenarios, makes it close to amazing that porn isn't deemed elitist cinema and appreciated by a mere handful of 'hardcore' enthusiasts.

A film. Opening credits roll. Stockinged legs. A foot squeezes down on the accelerator. The curly-haired blonde then wafts a red rose under her nose. Pulls the car out onto the freeway. Affords herself a casual smile in the rearview mirror. *Who's driving that car? Where is she driving it to? For what reason?* These are questions you need not ask yourself in the porn movie — this woman is DRIVING TO THE SEX. It's like in Harry Preston's *Honeymoon Horror*, that fight scene in the bedroom which results in fire, burning the place down. One of the protagonists gets his face disfigured in the blaze and spends the rest of the movie hunting down 'the others'. But it all hinges on that fire. And so, when the feuding couple hit a bedside cabinet and the oil lamp burning on top of it wobbles precariously but doesn't exactly topple, an unseen hand — evident nonetheless — is required to knock it from its perch. It's where the film's going. Irrespective of bumbling inconsistencies.

The next time we see the blonde, she will be pressing her breasts against the camera lens, wobbling. We know that.

INTERIOR. A PLUSH APARTMENT. A man, a woman, a drinks cabinet. The man pours a drink.
CHARLIE: Why didn't you bring your girlfriend along, Lulu?
LULU *[firmly]*: Oh Charlie. It's because she's a lesbian and you want to really *fuck.*
CHARLIE: Why, naturally.
LULU: And what about Timmy?
CHARLIE: Why Jim — he'll be along for a 'black and white'. You'll like that.
LULU: How's your pecker today, mm?
CHARLIE: It's grown up. It's big enough for me.
LULU: Ya. If it's up, you know! Ha ha ha.
CHARLIE: You know it's the gravity.
LULU: You need a super cunt.
CHARLIE: That may be the case. Do you like it? *[Meaning the drink.]*
LULU: The perfect can-opener for a girl who wants eager for more *(sic).*
CHARLIE: C'mon. Give the glass here.
LULU *[half-pleading]*: But why?
CHARLIE: Remember. You're here to fuck, not to get drunk.
[CHARLIE answers the door. Enter JIM, a black man wearing a necklace of sharks' teeth.] Hey, Jimmedy-baby! Lay it on me!
JIM *[jolly]*: How you doin', Charlie? Heh heh.
CHARLIE: Yeah. *[Both men go downstairs to the drinks cabinet.]* Have something for your ear *[?].*
JIM: Oh, but thanks. Heh heh heh.
?: Thanks momma. *[A squeaky voice; no one in the room says this.]*
JIM *[To LULU]*: Hey, baby, how ya doin'?
LULU *[low and sexy]*: Hell-o.
JIM: Hmm. Nice t –.

Explicit sex on screen. It's out there on the same sub-

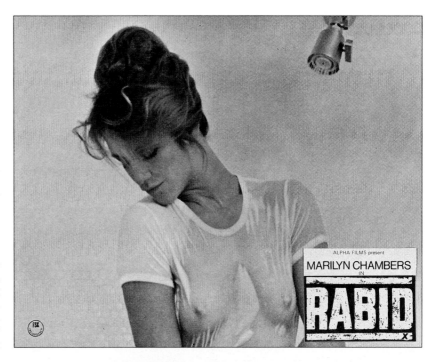

ALPHA FILMS present
MARILYN CHAMBERS in
RABID
X5

jective limb as *Death Bed The Bed That Eats.* Lulu keeps bouncing from foot to foot, hyper. *Why is she doing that? Is she acting?* The controls are set not for your super cunt Lulu, but our psyche. What's more, shifting constantly from left to right, she refers to Jim as 'Timmy' and talks funny too. Jim won't stop doing his big ol' black man laugh, while Charlie (John Holmes, who looks close to biting the big one and can't sustain an erection) will leave the set in a moment for several minutes. There and then deciding he has to go 'take a piss'. Can you do that in the movies, just get up and go?

Beyond the porn loop — the ten minute porn movie — most hardcore should, effectively, render itself redundant as pornography. I am reminded of a short strip the comic artist Liberatore (famous for *Ranxerox*) did for the Italian magazine *Il Male*. In it, an adolescent sits alone, stroking an erection while watching a porn movie on TV. When, on screen, a measure of Vaseline is brought into the frame, the lone viewer similarly applies a lubricant to his member. However, he ejaculates long before his TV counterpart does. Which is why the porn loop, short as it is, is so suited. It isn't *necessary* to go on any longer. What's the point? No one's watching. The loops quickly set their isolated characters — or rather, the PEOPLE WHO ARE GOING TO FUCK — into nice easy scenarios. Give them a little confection — have one knocking on a front door or something — and quickly get them naked, heated up and, yes, having the sex. This they do for some minutes, then they squirt their stuffs and the loop ends. Nice and efficient. No storyline. No bullshit. Perhaps when the next loop is played, it will be found to contain the same people who are going to fuck, but in a different room, but that's okay — so long as the fucking starts soon.

Pornography is its own stereotype. With few exceptions, it could be set anywhere, played by anyone. That is, everyone looks and behaves the same, in largely the same places. Which lends the whole thing a certain peculiarity. Any attempt to detract from this stereotype image diminishes the peculiarity not a jot, as we shall see later with *The Devil in Miss Jones* and

(Previous page and above) The only stills of Marilyn Chambers we could print in a family publication. Sorry, perverts.

Little Girls Blue. Pornography is locked in its own world. Hardcore porn cannot be any more or any less pornographic than the next movie. They are where they're at. And to get in we don't watch them like we might a regular movie.

A man lies in a hospital bed eating a banana. He hears a noise coming from behind the curtain circling the next bed. He gets up to investigate. Peering round, he spies two nurses engaged in a lesbian act. He watches unnoticed. Meanwhile, a third nurse arrives on the ward and tells the man to get back into his bed. There, they too engage in sex. The film switches between the two couples. He comes and it ends. Another encounter

The Erotic Adventures Of
Dickman & Throbbin
*They're Here
and Sex will never be the same...*

A JEROME TANNER FILM

STARRING JOHN HOLMES AS DICKMAN AND TOM BYRON AS THROBBIN
ALSO STARRING AMBER LYNN • JOANNA STORM AND KARI FOX
CO-STARRING PETER NORTH • KELI RICHARDS • REGINE BARDOT
STEVE DRAKE • MARC WALLICE • JESSICA WILDE AND PAT MANNING
PRODUCED AND DIRECTED BY JEROME TANNER
A WESTERN VISUALS VIDEO PRESENTATION

would be that in which a Customs officer at a busy airport (working from behind a wooden table), discovers a female wristwatch smuggler. She is taken into a private office and 'strip-searched' by Miss Durex, the female officer on duty. Their orgasms are large in coming. (Let us not forget the exquisite colloquy in the opening scenes here: asks the Customs officer, "Anything to declare?" Replies the woman, "I have a suitcase full of panties." "*Panties?!*" bleats the officer, as if that be just the craziest damn thing he has ever heard.)

These people are all driving to the sex. Irrespective of bumbling inconsistencies.

Analytiker, a German film from the early '70s, opens

with two men and one woman entering a room and sitting down together. Presumably they all work for the same construction company; each wears a gaudy bright yellow safety helmet. "I've never had it with two men before," says the girl, and they all disrobe for sex. Another, *Maximum Perversion*, circumnavigates its series of sexual set pieces with the monologues of a lady narrator. One sequence has a French gentleman — of "high esteem" — administer a champagne enema to a girl on a tabletop. From her chair in the corner, overlooking the scene, the madame tells the camera, "Hello friends — this is something you should all try at home", as a jet of bubbly escapes the girl's anus. In *Sexrauch*, a jailbird climbs a prison wall and makes good his escape in a stolen car. Having abandoned his conspicuous convict's uniform to walk around naked, he then breaks into a house and discovers a woman taking a shower. Covered in soap suds and eyes closed, the woman tells the stranger, "My, you're handsome." Opening her eyes she reels back in surprise.

The blonde woman driving the car is in trouble because of a double-booking at the exclusive health club she owns: a male party and a female party have arrived together. One guest opens a door and lodges her complaint directly with the camera, staring at the viewer. Off-screen, the proprietress offers her apologies. So the sex scenario of Jim Reynolds' *Insaziabili Voglie* is established, a picture starring Moana Pozzi as the proprietress and Cicciolina as Cicciolina (in her fixed Cheshire Cat grin and halo, a sex psychedelic unto herself). Five minutes into *Insaziabili*, Pozzi is pulling down her black negligee for a young jock. She rubs her globes together longingly (?) and helps him out of his Hawaiian shirt. When the couple kiss, they do so at a distance, tongues flicking together at the tips, the hum of sexual pleasure on the soundtrack clearly belonging to neither of them. Then a door opens slightly for the return of the woman who stares. Cut back to the sex. The couple are no longer there, replaced instead with thighs entwined and genitalia. The staring woman backs away from the door, a slight quizzical expression on her face as if that's not what she's looking at at all.

Sex is where the psychedelic is going. That hand unseen, evident nonetheless, has helped nudge the oil lamp from its perch and the fire has started. The characters have done their talking, swung their swinging. The sex has arrived. A man and woman undress. The camera zooms in on specifics. (Penetration takes place.) Gets closer. Zooms in. Sometimes slips in-and-out of focus. At its closest vantage point, the camera remains immobile, but wants to get closer still, so slips in-and-out of focus some more. Back to immobile. Those naked human forms have been relegated to colour. Not even phallic any longer, the penis colour goes forth and comes back. The vagina is a slightly darker umber. Fleshy throbs of focus, together. Back and forth.

Every hardcore picture grants extensive coverage of the sex. The screen becomes a blur of slowly shifting shapes like the billowing of *Blue Velvet* curtains. Cutaways might reveal impossibly ecstatic facial expressions as a direct result of the shifting taking place, but quickly, quickly, that camera locks in again on the PENETRATION. Moves in. The come shot will bring a momentary release from the shapes, but not even that is clear: the man, about to come, pulls his penis from the woman so that he may take hold of it

SATURDAY NIGHT Beaver

JOHN
HOLMES

ANGEL

VANESSA
D'ORO

Penguin
Productions ®

GEORGE COULOURIS · VERA DAY

in

The Woman Eater

A COLUMBIA PICTURES RELEASE

(Above) Giant weed wearing boxing gloves eats woman.

(Right) Cosmic monster at a bus stop.

COSMIC MONSTERS

FORREST TUCKER · GABY ANDRE · MARTIN BENSON

Produced by GEORGE MAYNARD · Directed by GILBERT DUNN   A DCA Release

(Above) Some **Slugs** at work.

(Left) A still from an art movie.

Two lobby cards from movies we're not going to pay Stephen Jones for reviewing.

in his own hand and jerk himself off. And the woman *appreciates* the orificial snub, the seminal fluid plopping onto her breasts, her ass cheeks, her face. Rarely her hair.

All of which, of course, is accompanied by a cacophony of groans, bass heavy. Constant, consistent moans of lovemaking pleasure. Things get louder and faster in anticipation of the big squirt. Sight and sound go round and round and they come out here. All over the place.

INTERIOR. A LIVING ROOM. Two men are seated, one woman stands.

CHARLIE: C'mon baby, let's undress a little. Show us a little skin.

JIM: Mmm, yeah. Heh heh.

LULU *[loosening her clothing, showing a stockinged leg]*: Oh, you like it, mm?

JIM: You're alright honey.

CHARLIE: Lulu! Take your time and make it hot! Wheel a little. Shake your booty.

[Incredible, wild guitar shunting commences.]

Hey, you should have been a stripper in Vegas.

LULU: I was one.

CHARLIE: Well, why'd you give it up?

LULU: Because I'd rather *fuck*.

JIM: Them show girls have it worse than nuns in a convent.

LULU: Yeah, that's why I'm here. *[LULU strips down to her underwear.]*

CHARLIE: Ah, Lulu *get it on. [CHARLIE has his pants round his ankles. LULU bends over and puts his penis in her mouth.]* Ahhh. I think you'll need to defy Newton's law of gravity. Ha ha. Show Jimmy your wet pussy, he needs to check if it's wet or not.

JIM: Oh, Charlie, she's got a wonderful cunt. I didn't realise when I was fucking her yesterday. But now that I can inspect it, I can see what a wonderful hole she has.

CHARLIE *[ecstatic]*: She's got it up! Now I don't care if I come prematurely. All this shit's got my beanstalk hard . . . Oh, ohh. Fantastic. Where have you been all my life? Ohhh, look how she uses her hand.

JIM: Hey man. Don't hog all of that chick. Let me have a little of it.

CHARLIE: Hey honey, see if you can swallow a bit more.

JIM: It's a miracle she can even get it in her mouth. When God gave out cocks, you must have thought He said socks and said 'I'll take two of 'em'. Heh heh heh heh.

CHARLIE: Hey, ball him for a while. I gotta go take a piss before I fuck you.

[CHARLIE gets up and walks out of shot.]

JIM: Shut up and take your piss.

Women in porno tend to keep their high heels on. Some of the sex scenes in *Insaziabili Voglie* are intercut with brief (split-second brief) shots of Las Vegas. Cicciolina's servicing of two men at once is capped rather abruptly when, upon reaching the vinegar stroke, the scene shoots suddenly to that of Hollywood Blvd. When the camera returns, Cicciolina and cohorts have been replaced by a lesbian 'black on white', whose sensitivity towards one another produces yelps of unadulterated joy when a tongue so much as flicks over a knee cap. Indeed, the arousal is so great that by the time the first pair of knickers are

Cicciolina

IN ACTION

THE FIRST LADY OF THE ITALIAN PARLIAMENT

being drawn down, with all the convulsing, squealing and contorting, one could almost expect some form of mutual hysterectomy to be taking place.

Moana Pozzi, about to bed another butt, bends over and flashes the great whiteness that is her own ass at the camera. At us. From a far corner, we jerk to attention and bound across the room towards the milky white mass, seemingly limitless as we approach. Are we trying to get in that crevice? Penetration is often so close that it becomes difficult to see who is doing what to whom.

A cutaway shot of Cicciolina seated in an armchair heralds the Moana Pozzi penetration about to take place. The man on the bed groans in anticipation.

In the trailer for *A Dirty Western*, a husky voice commands: *"A DIRTY WESTERN is set in the old West, 1880. [Shot of men on horseback.] A DIRTY WESTERN follows the relentless pursuit of three convicts and their terrified hostages. [Men on horseback; long-shot.] A DIRTY WESTERN is the beginning of a new era in quality adult film-making. It will satisfy your every emotional need."* [Cut to the full-screen visage of a hairy male butt. It swings up and out of shot, tailing an erect penis and leaving, screen-centre, the gaping blackness of a dilating vaginal hole.] *"Will satisfy your every emotional need..."* but looks silly and ugly too.

And it makes an *unk unk unk*ing noise as it goes.

The sex loops of the '70s are invariably cheap, one room affairs, with a mellow ricochet guitar sound set to a twelve-bar blues chord progression (you may need to lean in close to catch this, unobtrusive as it is). Occasionally, the score will crank into a wild guitar shunting, drowning everything else out — the sound

of wannabe guitar heroes suddenly making a break for it without so much as a segue or a fade-in.

The sex loops of the '80s and '90s are direct-to-video productions. Longer than the ten or fifteen minute maxim, and very much more sanitised, they lack the sense of fun of those coital encounters of yore. Their plots rarely facilitate settings such as an airport Customs lounge, or props like bright yellow bash hats. Gone too are the axe heroes, replaced by that technológical marvel: the tweaking bip bip synth. Whereas a company like Taboo in the '70s might churn out innumerable loops with podgy, motherly women and (hey girls!) fatherly, often balding and sinister-looking men, they at least had a character about them (and a keen sense of the grotesque). Direct-to-video porn, on the other hand, chooses as its role models men who wear headbands and Traci Lords. Unbelievable people, guilty of the over-climax. (In Lords' last appearance as a porn starlet, *Traci I Love You*, a voice over in a very bad French accent makes plain [kind of] his feelings for "Traci, Traci, Traci" as she rodeos around the set.)

Each release from Videorama, the Dutch porn giant, used to open to the company's masthead pounding backward and forward against a slowly rotating Bridget Riley swirl. Now, their logo is a pair of red lips and the words 'have fun'. A lot more fun was to be had with the swirling pattern thing.

In one Videorama release, *She's Got the Juice*, two guys chew the fat. The younger one appears to be 'method acting', but badly — pushing his hands into the air and rolling his eyes, slamming a beer can down on the table at every opportunity. His friend hits him with some motherfuckin' black-ass jive talk. Inexplicably so, seeing as he's Caucasian. Talking of

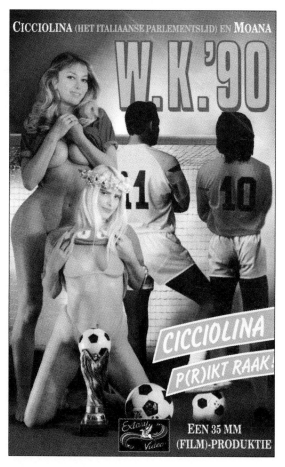

past conquests, the younger man hasn't had much luck. His buddy, however, fat and balding as he is, has "dem bitches" falling all over him. "Eazy ma-an, *eazy*. Relax. How many times 'at I tol' you, I knows white women. I *knows* white women..." He insists with numbing frequency, several vignettes going to illustrate his prowess.

The sleeve notes to *She's Got the Juice*, incidentally, though they refer to no one in the actual movie, describe 'a lass' whose 'solid tits are almost dancing to the rhythm of the fuck-beat, and her hands are caressing towards the orgasm.'

As a counterpoint to the happiness and beauty of most direct-to-video features, there now exists a DIY home-bedroom porn industry. Adult fairy tales continue to spawn an endless tirade of titles like *Battlestar Orgasmica*, *Waves of Passion* and *Sex Heist*, but recent years have seen a return of the porn loop. A man and a woman, pummelling lazily for the last fifteen minutes, discuss their groceries, speak of "Madge" and the decorating that needs doing in the hall. A homely encounter, starring a couple you have probably passed in the street. Such shorts are often made by, and for, married couples. Or couples that are into the swapping scene. A skinny, middle aged man, naked but for his socks, is having intercourse with — presumably — his wife on the living room carpet. They are going at it for an eternity (real-time) when the doorbell sounds. "That. Must. Be. Them. Now," says the man getting up with an erection. Through the frosted glass of the door behind them, naked forms can be seen. The man goes to the door, his erection bouncing before him, and opens it. A second couple stand naked in the hallway, smiling. (Did they ring the doorbell like that? How did they get in the house?) "Hello."

A suburban orgy takes place.

Elsewhere, a screen opens to purple/pink. Automatic focus causes the image to drift slowly away as the camera pulls back, revealing a grandmother in glasses, holding onto her garish sex. Tickling it with her free hand. She moans like she thinks they do in Traci Lords' films. Abstractedly.

The new porn loop has chiselled hardcore pornography into something distant — a kind of hardcore for softporn enthusiasts — with its nice clean settings, impossibly attractive individuals and sterile sex. It is little surprise that home-made camcorder porn should be proving increasingly popular. It harkens back to a more furtive and sordid pleasure, one a little tastier round the edges. A TV set goes blank. Bored, the woman watching from her couch flicks through a girlie magazine. She throws several hardly subtle glances behind the camera, clamps a hand between her legs, gets off the couch and does a little dance. The man with the camera is clearly reflected in the TV set, encouraging her. Later, that same man will come to repair the television, the camera suddenly very still as if it's on a tripod or something.

Hardcore on screen was pulled from the relative obscurity — and male exclusivity — of the sex loop almost single-handedly by director Gerard Damiano. Not only did Damiano push its running time up to feature-length, but he took it out of the frat houses, the bedrooms and the 'nature' evenings, and put it into real theatres. Theatres frequented by both men *and* women. This he did in 1972 with *Deep Throat*, a truly awful picture. That same year, Damiano also made *The Devil in Miss Jones*.

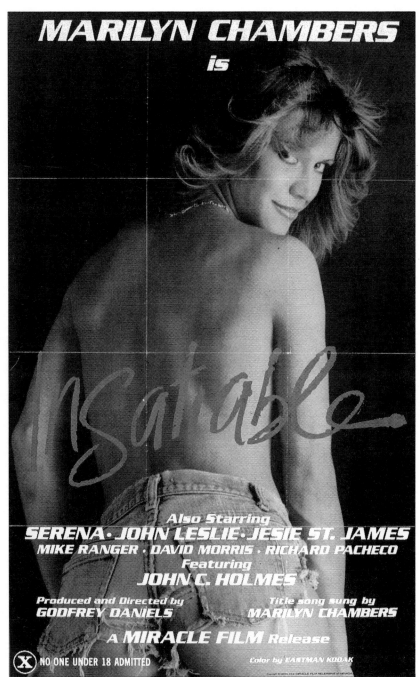

Porn, as we have seen, would seem to operate on a LIFE IS BEAUTIFUL, EVERYONE IS HAPPY premise. Not *The Devil in Miss Jones*; this is a porn movie with an incredibly dissolute atmosphere. It doesn't care to follow the standard hardcore motifs. The means by which this picture DRIVES TO THE SEX is totally alien to the likes of *Insaziabili Voglie*, *Insatiable* and *Debbie Does Dallas*; regular porn stuff. Neither is the plot a mere bumbling inconsistency by which the sex can be arrived at — the plot and the sex scenes are VERY IMPORTANT here. But still, *The Devil in Miss Jones* remains a hardcore porn picture. It promotes no less of a sexual response in the viewer than the most frivolous of porn loops.

Miss Jones (Georgina Spelvin), lonely middle-aged virgin, slips into a bath and slices her wrists. When she comes round, it isn't to the surrounds of her humble apartment or in a hospital bed, but in a stately room with a view outside of lush green fields, while she's seated at a table conversing with Abaca. Abaca tells Miss Jones that, because she has taken her own life, she is on her way to Hell. She pleads with him to allow her a little more time, to let her experience the pleasures she never had during her lifetime. After all, the spinster argues, she has nothing more to lose. This wish, Abaca grants, advising Miss Jones to "walk through that door."

A melancholic piano refrain (all black notes by the sound of it) permeates the movie, and Linda November singing the main theme, 'I'm Comin' Home', does little to raise the spirits.

Miss Jones' indoctrination commences with The Teacher (Harry Reems) — a man who gets the spinster to loosen up — and continues through to rolling in oils with another woman, masturbating with fruit and a snake, and taking on two men at once. These are isolated pleasures that have no bearing on one another, except as requisites in Miss Jones' hierarchy of experiences. The throbs still focus and the colours pulse, but here the sex *is* significant. It is going somewhere.

The sex vignettes are interspersed with Miss Jones' dialogues with Abaca, existential talk of Hell and eternal damnation. A punctuatory question throughout the movie, that of "How much time do I have?", is finally answered when Abaca tells his subject that it is, indeed, time for her to leave this purgatory. However, Hell, it transpires, is not a place of fire or devils, but a single unique white-washed cell. Miss Jones' private Hell is to be locked in with a halfwit who has no interest in satiating the now sexually frustrated woman. When Miss Jones pleads with the man to help get her off, he wants only to search the room for a non-existent fly. "Damn you! Touch me!" she pleads, while attempting to arouse herself. The man gazes, glassy-eyed around the cell as Miss Jones frigs herself forever short of an orgasm. "Help me!"

Hardcore pornography on screen is locked within the world of the PEOPLE WHO ARE GOING TO FUCK getting down to it at every available opportunity. Which tends not to leave much scope to go beyond the hackneyed dialogue or penetration shot. But what should happen if a film-maker decides to take a different approach? Gerard Damiano almost single-handedly cultivated XXX-rated films into a workable and accessible medium with *The Devil in Miss Jones* (and, to a lesser extent, *Deep Throat*). Yet the hardcore industry all but turned their backs on this incredible precedent, settling instead for getting to the penetration, fast.

Of course, *The Devil in Miss Jones* does have its contemporaries. A number of other Damiano features spring to mind. And, a decade later, Rinse Dream's *Café Flesh*. But it's a shaky legacy that has all but died out in the '90s, where sex is not only the point — it's all there is.

"Highly innovative . . . superb acting . . . fallout and see CAFÉ FLESH." — Hustler Magazine

THE TIME . . . Five Years After The Nuclear War.
THE SURVIVORS . . . Post-Nuke Thrill Freaks Lookin' For A Kick.

Café **FLESH**

The Creators of NIGHTDREAMS present a motion picture too hot for a world with a future.

Starring PIA SNOW MARIE SHARP and ANDREW NICHOLS as MAX

INTERIOR. A LIVING ROOM. *A black man, naked except for sharks' teeth, has his penis in a woman's mouth. She is naked but for her stockings and high heels. The blues is playing.*

JIM: Oh . . . ahh. Lulu, you've already got me ready for action. You're wild, you really are. Ow . . . oh yeah. Hold back. I don't wanna come yet. I could but — *damn you're good.*
[CHARLIE returns, naked.]
CHARLIE: Alright honey, I'm back. You need more than one, so why don't you try two? Mine's pretty limp so blow one up.
LULU: You mean you can get it up already?
JIM *[to LULU]*: With you everything's possible.
[LULU sucks on the two penises alternatively.]
CHARLIE: Ouch!
LULU: I took a bite out of it.

CHARLIE: You almost bit it off!
JIM: Hey Lulu, we're not masochists, honey.
CHARLIE: Yeah. We're just kiddin'.
JIM *[to CHARLIE]*: That's the trouble with honkies, they don't take sex seriously.
CHARLIE: Hey! I'm ready for fucking.
JIM: Heh heh.
[LULU is on all fours, sucking on JIM's penis. CHARLIE penetrates her vagina.]
LULU: Ooh . . . take it *slow.*
CHARLIE: At last I got a juicy cunt. It's so wet that at last my cock can slip in and out without any friction.
JIM: You're talkin' like my little brother, man. Like it's your first piece of ass.
CHARLIE: My elephant cock is up and it's staying up. The gravity usually pulls it down, you know. *[Guitar shunting commences.]* Oh dammit, I'm ashamed of myself. The gravity got it again. It's the curse of all big cocks.
JIM: Don't bitch, feels good don't it.
CHARLIE: I guess you're right about that. Come on, honey. Suck a little on the tip to make it silent. *[?]*
JIM: Hey man, don't get hung up or it won't *get up.* Just let it happen, will ya?
LULU: Hey Timmy. Stick a finger in my ass, will ya?
JIM *[sticking a finger in LULU's ass]*: Do you like that sister?
LULU: Aw . . . ohh.
[LULU lies on her back.]
CHARLIE: Hey. She's really acrobatic.
LULU: Yeah. I used to work in a circus.
JIM: Mm . . . That so? What d'you do there?
LULU: I helped the sideshow freaks . . . getting rid of guys like you.
JIM: Hey, that wasn't nice.

What goes on on that screen does so to makes us feel good. Life is beautiful. The sex is up close. Dialogue stilted. And the shunting never ends. It's so damned odd, it's a wonder porn isn't deemed elitist cinema and appreciated by a mere handful of enthusiasts. "Flowers? Flowers? You brought flowers to the country? Susan, I hate to disillusion you, but flowers do grow wild." It's out there on the same subjective limb as *Death Bed The Bed That Eats*.

One director, acutely aware of the absurdities of pornography on screen, is Joanna Williams. Her *Little Girls Blue* is a masterwork of sexadelia (and looks a lot like *Death Bed*, a movie with no credits).

Little Girls Blue opens to the sight of an erect, straining penis. It takes up the entire screen. Behind the twitching member, a naked woman walks into shot but remains out of focus, the camera content to fix itself on the bulbous shaft. Williams has the sex psychedelic sussed. She knows that the viewer wants, *needs*, to see the core of the sexual act. Close, and closer still. This penis is scary though, it isn't doing anything. An ethereal score creeps in. The giant cock remains in shot for some time before a second woman is suddenly seen to be giving it head.

Set within a girls' school — the kind where the pupils look to be aged eighteen-plus, Officer — *Little Girls Blue* follows the exploits of several of its students. During her American history class, Debbie begins to daydream about Mr Barrett, the history teacher. She imagines she's going down on him, while he discusses Alexander Hamilton and the Federal Government. But it's actually classmate Buffy who gets to make the teacher in real life, going to see him after class so that she might better her grades. With this encounter, *Little Girls Blue* looks almost set to lapse into a typical porno scenario, Buffy and Mr Barrett licking, poking, prodding and pulling to a most typical banal synth score. But then the choice of dialogue ("Would you lick my baby pussy? My period's almost over") quickly steers the sequence into some contention. So too, Mr Barrett's delirious facial expression when he hits the vinegar stroke. It is at this point that the viewer might realise director Williams is accentuating the inherent weirdness of porn; even stripping the characters and situations of what the audience might have come to expect by way of stereotypical dialogue and mannerisms. It may be that a few people in real life actually do look to be suffering major surgery while engaging in sex, but fewer still say "lick my baby pussy, my period's almost over" in porn movies, and that's what counts.

Little Girls Blue goes all out for sex psychedelics with its next piece. Coach Fowler, the gym teacher, sits watching his girls playing netball. One girl in particular, Marium, catches his eye. Before you know it, the playing fields have become an expanse of blueness and there, all alone, is Marium, blue-haired and blue eye make-up; naked but for blue ankle socks and a blue hair ribbon. The blue beach ball she is twirling spins round in slow motion. Then Marium is sitting on the ball and telling you, the viewer, to suck her nipples and pussy, "so hot and wet." When suddenly — POP! — the ball bursts and she is left sitting on an erect penis. Like the opening sequence, the man's face remains unseen. This time, however, his guttural ebullitions punctuate the soundtrack, unnaturally loud as they are. . . Not prominent, as in badly overdubbed, but *loud*. When Marium sees another blue ball rolling past, she loses interest in the dick and goes after that instead.

Back at netball practice, Coach Fowler tells Marium to see him after class. It seems she too may be experiencing some difficulty with her schoolwork. Later, seated at a desk, Marium puzzles over the exercise book before her. Fowler suggests, "Let's try it like this," and commences to draw mathematical symbols on the blank page. But reality dissipates again, and a topless Marium is seen to wander over the symbols in her book, exclaiming, "I don't think I'll ever get it. I *try* and *try* but I just can't get it." Then Coach Fowler appears on the page. Marium turns to him. "I don't know what to do," she says. "My pussy is all wet and it keeps tingling."

It is only really at the end of the picture that Williams brings into operation the actual fleshy throbs of in/out focus. This is when Kathy and Debbie sneak out of school to go on a date with some boys they know. Debbie is in the back of her date's car; Kathy is accommodating two boys in a barn around the corner. Again,

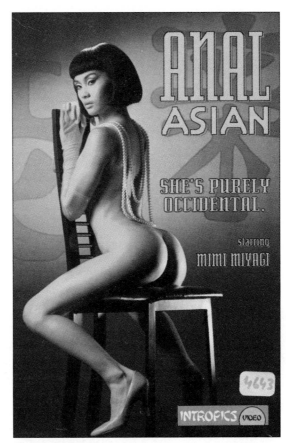

Little Girls Blue looks set to tread that tireless, well-worn path to climax when, quite suddenly, it changes tack. The camera uproots itself from its vantage point at the rear of Kathy's double penetration (where it has lain dormant for some minutes) and sweeps in real close, back out again, up and around the heaving bodies in an all-too obvious pastiche of porn film-making technique. The images become a flesh blur. But it is when the soundtrack comes into play that the sequence reaches a ruminative state proper. With the car playing doo-wop and crickets chirping in the night — to a particularly assertive accompaniment of sighs, groans and slurping — sight and sound become one together. Images flicker to a timbre, bass heavy. It doesn't mean anything anymore, least of all sex.

The final sexadelic scenario in *Little Girls Blue* again concerns Coach Fowler, who is still after Marium (his fantasy encounter with her previously was just that: fantasy). In a scam set up by Debbie — who wants a "real dick between my legs" — Fowler receives a note he believes is from Marium, requesting they meet that night in her room. Of course, when he gets there, it's so dark he can't tell Debbie from Marium anyway. And, because it's so dark, neither can the viewer. Indeed, the viewer is left to contemplate the barely discernible, shifting shapes as the fucking starts. The blow-by-blow dialogue between the couple contracts a cheap reverb effect... the suggestion being this is what the dark does to lovemaking couples. A purple hue illuminates certain shapes as Fowler and Debbie — whom Fowler thinks is Marium — go at it. The scenario wouldn't be entertained in most porn product because it is, in effect, self-defeating: you can barely see the penetration, what's the point in that?

Like the penis that opened the picture, not moving, this last episode would appear to challenge the very *incentive* of hardcore. You don't get to see it.

You might get to see it in *The Devil in Miss Jones*, but you get to see it wrong. If Miss Jones is now in Hell, no longer a virgin and suffering an eternity of frustration, it is a Hell and frustration of her own making. Having tasted the pleasures that were previously denied her, Miss Jones can now only lament on this new-found experience, forever locked in a state of anti-climax. There has been no real transitional stage upon dying and going to Hell; there has been no Abaca. Miss Jones has been in Hell from the moment she slit her wrists in the bath tub. In order to suffer an eternity of sexual frustration, she has had to experience ecstatic pleasure of the sort that exists only in the sex movie. If Heaven is everything one could want it to be, with *The Devil in Miss Jones* Damiano has hit upon the terrifying supposition that Hell is simply 'forever frustration'.

Normally, when porn movies end, nothing is resolved but the libidos of a handful of over-sexed characters.

There's an artistically valid reason for running these shots of Traci. Can someone remind me what it was...?

Damiano goes to Hell. Joanna Williams exploits exploitation.

In *Little Girls Blue* there is no pretence that those in it are anything but a vehicle upon which the sex can be made. What Williams does that is different, is spell the fact out in a big bold bulbous dick, throbbing ten feet tall. This big dick is a psychedelic signal. *You, watching, can't you see it? What's wrong with this picture?*

In the sex psychedelic, it isn't the sex act that is the impetus — the movie itself is the act.

CHARLIE: You see, if I let it hang in there, gravity keeps it going.
JIM: You must have had an 'A' in physics.
CHARLIE: No, I made 'A's in biology.
[Guitar breakout.]
CHARLIE/JIM/LULU: Oh . . . ahh . . .
JIM: Too bad it has to end.
CHARLIE: Now. One for the final drive.
LULU: Just *fuck* and take it easy.
CHARLIE/JIM/LULU: Oh . . . *ahh.* ∎

THE GOOD, THE BAD AND THE WORTHLESS

A COMPENDIUM OF COMPILATIONS

BY STEPHEN JONES

You can blame MGM. In 1974, the struggling studio released *That's Entertainment!*, director Jack Haley Jr's compilation of memorable musical clips rescued from the vaults and introduced by a veritable Who's Who of ageing celebrities. It proved to be one of the surprise box-office hits of the year, and two years later the inevitable sequel, cleverly titled *That's Entertainment Part 2*, reunited veteran hoofers Gene Kelly and Fred Astaire as hosts of another selection of classic clips.

Because they already owned the footage, Hollywood quickly discovered that nostalgia equalled easy profits, and before long other studios were grubbing around in the

Starring CONNIE MASON PLAYBOY'S FAVORITE PLAYMATE / THOMAS WOOD / JEFFREY ALLEN — Box Office Spectaculars, Inc. presents a Friedman-Lewis Production "TWO THOUSAND MANIACS!" A TOWN OF MADMEN CRAZED WITH BLOOD LUST! Produced by DAVID F. FRIEDMAN / Directed by HERSCHELL G. LEWIS — GRUESOME SLAUGHTER STAINED IN BRUTAL BLOOD COLOR! with SHELBY LIVINGSTON / BEN MOORE / YVONNE GILBERT / JEROME EDEN / LINDA COCHRAN

archives to come up with their own compilations of recycled sequences. It was inevitable that the perennially popular horror and science fiction genres would offer them a wealth of material to draw upon.

Universal was one of the first to dust off the celluloid cobwebs with *The Horror Show* (USA, 1979. Dir: Richard Schickel), which stitched together 'sixty magical years of movie monsters' with the help of on-screen host Anthony Perkins and clips from many of the studio's classic horror movies of the 1930s and '40s.

The ever-reliable British censors ensured this scene met a fate commensurate with that of the actress...

Unfortunately, the success of Harry and Michael Medved's facile and jokey movie books during the early 1980s resulted in Paramount's *It Came from Hollywood* (USA, 1982), a routine compilation of clips and trailers broken down into various sub-genres ('Gorillas', 'Aliens', 'Giants & Tiny People', 'Troubled Teenagers', etc) with inane comedy links by *Saturday Night Live* regulars such as Dan Aykroyd, John Candy, Gilda Radner and Cheech and Chong. Despite clips from various '50s favourites, it included no rarities and few surprises (no doubt due to the aforementioned Medved brothers, who were credited as 'special consultants'), while directors Andrew Solt and Malcolm Leo appeared to know nothing (and care even less) about the subject.

At least director John Landis knows his stuff, and he promised that *Coming Soon* (USA, 1983), a showcase of vintage Universal trailers hosted by '80s scream queen Jamie Lee Curtis on the studio backlot, would be "orgasmic for horror fans!" It may not have quite reached that level of excitement, but due to the input of creator/writer Mick Garris and the inclusion of Alfred Hitchcock's eight minute trailer for *Psycho* (in which the deadpan director takes the audience on a tour of the Bates house and motel), the result was an entertaining hour, marred only by an over-emphasis on ET, Steven Spielberg and upcoming Universal product.

Obviously happy to exploit any idea for all the profit it's worth, the same studio released *Terror in the Aisles* (USA, 1984. Dir: Andrew J. Kuehn. Universal/Kaleidoscope), which teamed Curtis' *Halloween* co-star Donald Pleasence with the decade's other favourite screamer, the somewhat bland Nancy Allen. Unfortunately, the two hosts (seated amidst a 'typical' sleazoid film audience) talked pretentious nonsense while the clips (often brief, muddled and all uncredited) ranged from the classic Universal horrors of the 1940s through to the slashers of the '80s (with a few odd non-genre inclusions such as *To Catch a Thief* and *Marathon Man*). Although Gregory McClatchy's editing and John Beal's music score were often inspired, the linking scenes with the two stars came across as simply pathetic.

In the meantime, the entrepreneurial Charles Band had already produced *The Best of Sex and Violence* (USA, 1981. Dir: Ken Dixon. Wizard), his own low budget cornucopia aimed at the burgeoning video market, which became the eventual audience for most compilation material. After a pre-credit sequence in which Laura Jane Leary's clothes were ripped off, seventy-five year-old host John Carradine sat in a minuscule movie studio and leered his way through forty clips from 1970s exploitation movies, many apparently used without permission. Along with glimpses of *Bury Me an Angel*, *Terminal Island*, *I Spit on Your Grave*, *Tourist Trap*, *Zombie*, *Tanya's Island* and others, Carradine's sons (David and Keith) turned up in an embarrassing scene asking to borrow the car keys and Angelo Rossitto made a brief uncredited appearance.

An ill-looking John Carradine was back five years later as the host of *Hollywood Ghost Stories* (USA, 1986. Dir: James Forsher. Castle Hill/Caidin), a mixture of clips and interviews which were meant to convince viewers that ghosts really exist. The most interesting bits were a 1927 interview with Sir Arthur Conan Doyle and excerpts from the 1939 movie *Mystic Circle Murder* featuring the real Mrs Houdini. There were also appearances by Elke Sommer, William Peter Blatty, Susan Strasberg, Frank De Fellita, Robert Bloch, Boris Karloff, Bela Lugosi and Peter Lorre, plus clips from *You'll Find*

Out, *The Exorcist*, *The Amityville Horror*, *Dark Forces*, *The Entity*, *Poltergeist* and many others. Despite his obvious frailty, Carradine joined in the climactic music video!

Cameron Mitchell is another actor whose career was on the skids by the mid-1980s (*that late? Ed.*), although even he was slumming as the weird-looking proprietor of the 'Shoppe of Horrors Video Store' in *Terror on Tape* (USA, 1985. Dir: Robert A. Worms III [?]. Comet/Continental Video). In cheap shot-on-video linking sequences, he gave three customers (Mark Fenske, Tim Noyes and Michelle Bauer) previews of such horror tapes as *Eerie Midnight Horror Show*, *To the Devil a Daughter*, *Alien Prey*, *The Vampire Hookers*, *The Slayer*, *Scalps* and The Bloodiest of H.G. Lewis series.

With a running time of almost two hours, a much better value-for-money collection of trailers and genre clips was *Horrible Horror* (USA, 1986. Dir: David Bergman. Movietime Inc/Bergman-Harris), presented by manic 1950s TV horror host Zacherley (aka John Zacherle) from his movie dungeon. Along with numerous excerpts from '50s trash classics, this also included rare footage of Lugosi and Karloff, a look at serial heroes, scenes from the 1958 Hammer/Screen Gems TV pilot *Tales of Frankenstein*, plus several out-takes from *Killers from Space* and, most interesting of all, (Abbott and Costello) *Meet Frankenstein*.

For those who liked their clips more gory, *Prevues from Hell* (USA, 1987. Dir: Jim Monaco. Off the Wall Video) featured a movie theatre full of zombies eating blood-covered popcorn and watching nearly fifty often-explicit trailers for '60s and early '70s shockers, compiled from the 'Mad Ron' archives. These included *Two Thousand Maniacs*, *Bloody Pit of Horror*, the TV campaign for *Night of Bloody Horror*, *The Wizard of Gore* ("This film will take its place in motion picture history..."), the pretensions of *Three on a Meathook*, *Ilsa She Wolf of the SS*, *Deranged*, the 3-D *Wildcat Women*, and such memorable double bills as *I Drink Your Blood/I Eat Your Skin*, *I Dismember Mama/The Blood Spattered Bride*, and the 'Orgy of the Living Dead' triple presentation, *Revenge of the Living Dead/Curse of the Living Dead/Fangs of the Living Dead*. The whole thing was some-

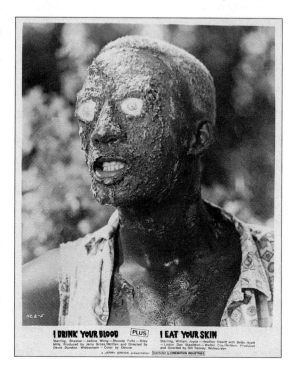

(Right) The terrifying fried egg-eyed zombie from **I Eat Your Skin**. *The budget wouldn't stretch to ping-pong balls...*

what bizarrely hosted by ventriloquist Nick Pawlow and his zombie dummy, 'Happy' Goldsplatt.

Al Lewis recreated his vampiric role from TV's *The Munsters* to host *Grampa's Monster Movies* (USA, 1988. Dir: Peter Zasuly. Amvest Video), a disappointing compilation of Universal trailers, containing most of the studio's Dracula, Frankenstein, Invisible Man and Mummy series, along with a few rarities, such as *The Cat Creeps*, *Flesh and Fantasy* and *The Climax*.

In 1971, Christopher Lee appeared as himself, Vlad the Impaler and Bram Stoker's Count in the travelogue-style documentary *In Search of Dracula* (Transylvania/Sweden. Dir: Calvin Floyd. Aspeckt Films). Originally made for Swedish TV and based on the book of the same title by Raymond McNally and Radu Florescu, Lee explored the character through history, folklore, literature and film, with clips from Murnau's *Nosferatu* and Hammer's *Scars of Dracula*. Making the most of a tedious script, the titular host of *Vincent Price's Dracula* (UK, 1982. Dir: John Muller. M&M Film Productions/Atlantis) covered much the same ground with the help of extracts from a Transylvanian epic about Vlad Tepes' exploits, and clips from Murnau's *Nosferatu*, *Vampyr*, *Mark of the Vampire*, *The Return of the Vampire* and *The Return of Dracula*.

The seventy-six year-old actor returned to host the even more obscure *Creepy Classics* (USA, 1987. Dir: Pamela Page. The Carter Companies Inc/Fox Lorber Associates Inc/Archive Films), which was produced exclusively as a promotional item for Hallmark. The half-hour tape featured Price sitting in a movie theatre and introducing quite lengthy extracts and trailers from, amongst others, the original *Invasion of the Body Snatchers*, *Dr Terror's House of Horrors*, Romero's *Night of the Living Dead* and various American International Pictures of the 1950s and '60s. This also included a special trivia game card in each box.

As far back as 1952, Georges Franju's half-hour drama/documentary *Le Grand Méliès* (France. Armor-Films) used clips and recreations to explain how pioneering film-maker Georges Méliès created his remarkable effects. More than thirty years later, Arnold Leibovit's *The Fantasy Film Worlds of George Pal* (USA, 1985. Leibovit Productions/New World Pictures) did much the same thing in a feature length look at the career of the Hungarian puppeteer/producer/director. Narrated by Paul Frees, it was full of fascinating material, with numerous clips and interviews (including Ray Harryhausen, Joe Dante, Walter Lanz, Robert Bloch, Gene Roddenberry, Ray Bradbury, Jim Danforth, Ann Robinson and Rod Taylor). Disappointingly, however, it was not quite definitive, quickly glossing over *Atlantis the Lost Continent* and completely ignoring such later Pal productions as *The Power* and *Doc Savage the Man of Bronze*.

Italian producer/director Dario Argento has been the subject of not just one, but two compilations about his work. *Dario Argento's World of Horror* (Italy, 1985. Vidmark/Image Entertainment) was directed by Michele Soavi, who went on to work with Argento on such movies as *The Church* and *The Sect*. Besides clips from some of Argento's best-known films, including *The Bird with the Crystal Plumage*, *The Cat O'Nine Tales*, *Four Flies on Gray Velvet*, *Tenebrae* and, of course, the classic *Suspiria*, this fascinating documentary also included rare behind-the-scenes footage and a subtitled interview with the man himself.

Luigi Cozzi, another Argento acolyte, directed a follow-up documentary, *Dario Argento: Master of Horror*

"THE RETURN OF THE VAMPIRE" with BELA LUGOSI Frieda Inescort, Nina Foch, Miles Mander. A Columbia Picture

(Italy, 1991. Video Search), under his 'Lewis Coates' pseudonym. Cozzi brought things up-to-date with clips from *Terror at the Opera*, *The Church*, *Two Evil Eyes* and *The Sect*, and interviews with Argento, Michele Soavi, Tom Savini, composer Pino Donaggio and Cozzi himself.

George Romero, Argento's collaborator on *Two Evil Eyes*, became the subject of his own documentary with the disappointing *Document of the Dead* (USA, 1989. Roy Frumkes Productions/Studio Entertainment). It began life as a student film shot around the making of Romero's *Dawn of the Dead*, while director Roy Frumkes was still studying at the School of Visual Arts. To supplement his original film interviews with Romero, Tom Savini, actor John Amplas and producer Richard

(Above) Not a vampire.

(Below) Neither is he.

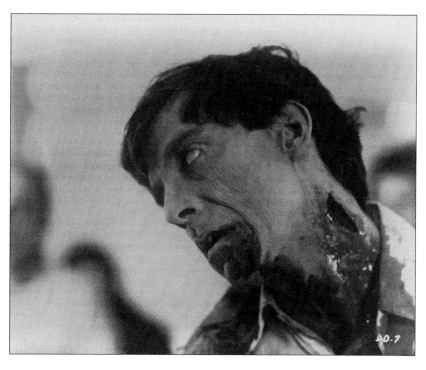

The Good, the Bad 89

MIRACLE FILMS presents

"ZOMBIE FLESH EATERS" x
Colour

(Top) People with dodgy throat prosthetics #2...

Rubinstein, Frumkes added new video footage of Romero and artists Gahan Wilson and Steve Bissette, narration by Susan Tyrrell, and clips from *Night of the Living Dead*, *Martin* and *Monkey Shines*. However, despite the rare glimpse of a spoof *Fantastic Voyage* commercial made by Romero during the 1960s, this pseudo-intellectual study was overlong and unfocussed.

One producer/director whose life would make a fascinating documentary is the near-legendary Edward D. Wood Jr. Unfortunately, *On the Trail of Ed Wood* (USA, c1991. Dir: Michael Copner. Videosonic Arts) is not it. Instead, this hour-long video featured no-talent actor Conrad Brooks (who had small roles in a number of Wood's low budget movies) talking at length about his own 'career' and taking the viewer on a guided tour of some of the seedy Hollywood locations frequented by the cross-dressing Wood and such cronies as Bela Lugosi and Tor Johnson. The result was an interminable home movie, with all too few clips to relieve the tedium.

However, it's not only directors who get the compilation treatment, and with the growth of interest in special effects it was perhaps inevitable that Ray Harryhausen's long career would be put under the spotlight. The hour-long result, *Aliens, Dragons, Monsters & Me* (USA, 1990. Dir: Richard Jones. Midwich Entertainment/Lumivision), included Eric Boardman interviewing Harryhausen at length about his films in London's Museum of the Moving Image, commentary by Ray Bradbury, Kerwin Matthews and producer Charles H. Schneer, and extracts and stills of the stop-motion animator's work ranging from rarely seen early test footage through to his last film, *Clash of the Titans*. Only Gary Owens' glib narration let the side down.

Slightly more esoteric were hour-long profiles of the work of two other special effects pioneers: *A Tribute to Winsor McCay* (USA, c1990s. Video Dimensions) and *Willis O'Brien Primitives* (USA, c1992. A-1 Video). The former included cartoonist McCay's films *Gertie the Dinosaur*, *The Sinking of the Lusitania* and *Little Nemo*, incorporating a rare hand-coloured sequence. The latter compilation consisted of a number of stop-motion pioneer O'Brien's early animated shorts for the Edison Film Company and a sound short which used O'Brien's

dinosaur footage from the 1925 *The Lost World*.

Footage by both McCay and O'Brien also turned up in two tape collections released to tie in with the dinosaurs' recent resurgence in popularity. The better of the pair was *Dinosaur Movies* (USA, 1993. Dir: Donald F. Glut. Popcorn Pictures/Simitar), a two tape set co-executive produced by Jim Steranko and hosted by 'Dinosaur' Don Glut and Christy Block. Glut really knows his subject and, along with special guests Forrest J Ackerman, Jim Danforth and Ray Harryhausen, he presented numerous rare and interesting clips and trailers covering cartoons, the silent era, enlarged lizards, stop-motion (by far the longest section), Harryhausen, recent productions, puppets and men-in-suits. As an added bonus, this also included McCay's full 1914 version of *Gertie*, plus O'Brien's 1915 short *The Dinosaur and the Missing Link* and all his surviving test footage for the never-completed *Creation*.

Although not up to the same standard, *Fantastic Dinosaurs of the Movies* (USA, 1990. Film Shows Inc/Goodtimes Home Video) still had much to recommend it. Compiled and edited by Sandy Oliviri, it featured a short documentary about dinosaurs, a behind-the-scenes look at the making of *The Golden Voyage of Sinbad*, and more than thirty trailers for such titles as *Rodan*, *The Land Unknown*, *Journey to the Beginning of Time*, *Reptilicus* and Larry Buchanan's *The Loch Ness Horror*.

Despite their growing popularity, dinosaurs still have a long way to go before they pass the immortal vampire for fans. Oliviri was also responsible for another compilation of trailers, *Dracula in the Movies* (USA, 1992. Film Shows Inc/Goodtimes Home Video), which was only spoiled by some intrusive captions. Billed as 'highlights of over fifty years of vampire films', this hour-long collection of trailers included material from Universal's Dracula series and all the Hammer vampire movies, plus Bela Lugosi talking to the audience in a specially shot promotion for *Mark of the Vampire*.

Ex-Hammer '60s scream queen Veronica Carlson hosted *Fangs!* (USA, 1992. Dir: Bruce G. Hallenbeck. Pagan Video), a one-hour look at vampire movies from Murnau's *Nosferatu* to the present. *Dracula Fact or Fiction* (USA, 1993. Screen Entertainment) purported to cover much the same material, while Rhino Video issued three *Cinematic Scrapbook* trailer tapes in 1991 covering *Dracula*, *Frankenstein* and *The Wolf Man*. The same year, the most popular vampire TV show of all time was celebrated in *Dark Shadows: Behind the Scenes* (USA, 1991. MPI Home Video), which covered both the original series (1966-71) and the short-lived revival (1990-91). It included rare footage, an interview with original star Jonathan Frid and commentary by creator Dan Curtis.

However, when talking about vampires, one name stands above all others: *Lugosi The Forgotten King* (USA, 1985. Dir: Mark S. Gilman and Dave Stuckey. Operator 13 Productions) featured rare newsclips and interviews with Bela, commentary by Forrest J Ackerman, Carroll (Carol) Borland, Ralph Bellamy, Alex Gordon and John Carradine, and trailers for *Dracula*, *Mark of the Vampire* and *Plan 9 from Outer Space*, among many others. It was a fitting tribute to an uneven talent.

Of course, there are numerous other trailer tapes and compilations available, many covering the horror/science fiction/gore/sleaze/trash/exploitation markets. The above has only been a sampling of some of those that contain material which is unusual or perhaps not easy to find elsewhere. For that reason alone, they are all probably worth tracking down. ■

FOR ADULTS ONLY!

HOME GROWN BRITISH CRUD, 1954-1972

BY MIKE WATHEN

Robert Flemyng sees the special effects for **The Blood Beast Terror**.

The success of Hammer Films in the mid-1950s must have made many a British-based entrepreneur look on with envy. Hammer proved time and again that horror and science fiction films could be inexpensively produced and yield a fast and healthy profit.

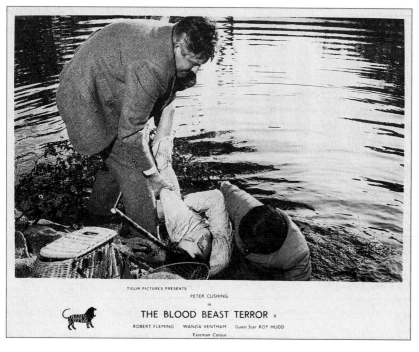

TIGON·PICTURES·PRESENTS
PETER CUSHING
in
THE BLOOD BEAST TERROR x
ROBERT FLEMING   WANDA VENTHAM   Guest Star ROY HUDD
Eastman Colour

The introduction of the X-certificate in 1951 (no admission to persons under the age of sixteen) was still controversial and a guaranteed selling point, since it was regarded in some sectors as a harbinger of moral laxity. This mild loosening of the bonds of censorship resulted in many European films reaching a wider audience in Britain than hitherto, albeit often with most of the interesting bits removed. But for the first time, adult and sensational subjects were being allowed through and, what was more, were making money. Even more importantly, the early Hammer horrors were financially successful in the United States.

Small wonder, then, that many producers thought they too could make Hammer-style films and turn a healthy profit. Some were doubtless fantasy film enthusiasts who'd been waiting for just such an opportunity, for others it was simply another commercial venture. And in much the same way that British beat groups subsequently attempted to copy American black music (and got it wrong, inventing rock music by default), so British film-makers tried (and usually failed) to copy American and European originals. But they nevertheless produced a flood of accidental art that lasted into the early 1970s.

Amicus was to become the most famous of Hammer's rivals, and has already been examined in some detail (*not by us! Ed.*). However, many other producers and production companies have been neglected. In some cases they built up a 'house style', making their films instantly recognisable. In others, the very absence of recognisability film-to-film continuity brought about an unpredictability impossible in a Hammer or Amicus production.

Edward and Harry Danziger were expatriot Americans who were making films in Britain by the late '40s. For fifteen years they turned out scores of second features and TV series as cheaply as possible. Conditions at their New Elstree Studios were too primitive to allow for adequate sound-proofing, so shooting would halt when 'noisy' traffic passed by in the road outside. Since the studios were near a dairy, this must have been fairly frequently. Not overly prolific in the horror/SF field (their usual stock-in-trade consisted of

standard thrillers like *Escort for Hire*, starring DJ Pete Murray), they are worth noting for two films: *Devil Girl from Mars* and *The Tell-Tale Heart*.

Devil Girl from Mars (David MacDonald, 1954) is of interest for several reasons. Primarily, it's the first cinematic example of a peculiarly British SF sub-genre: the cosy apocalypse, where a group of cliché ridden characters gather together by chance (frequently in a pub) and talk a lot about The Menace Outside and the imminent End Of The World. We'll encounter many more examples before we're finished. It also predates Hammer's 'enemy from space' style science fiction films (their only previous SF movies were *Spaceways* and *Four-Sided Triangle*). Lastly, it's awful. An escaped killer named Albert (aren't they always?) manages to reach a remote inn in the Scottish Highlands, where he is hidden by his girlfriend, a barmaid with a heart of gold. Also at the inn are a metallurgist, an unhappy model, a newspaper reporter and a few locals. Almost before they've been properly introduced, the plot is thickened by the arrival of a flying saucer. Nyah, representative of Mars' Intransigent Monarchy, seems friendly at first, but soon has the inn surrounded by a force field and is demanding healthy young men to take back for breeding. After much talk and the appearance of a robot that resembles a fridge on legs, Nyah ends up with Albert. Despite knowing nothing about flying saucers, he manages to blow it (and Nyah) up, sacrificing himself in the process. Many a film as cheaply made has been floated with similar elements, but the plodding direction and daft plot conspire to sink this one. Surely this dire warning of female equality can never have had more than camp value? The cast play it for all it's worth though...

TIGON·PICTURES·PRESENTS
PETER CUSHING
in
THE BLOOD BEAST TERROR x
ROBERT FLEMING   WANDA VENTHAM   Guest Star ROY HUDD
Eastman Colour

The Tell-Tale Heart (Ernest Morris, 1960) was made just before Roger Corman commenced his Poe series. This rather effective little film has every appearance of being a Hammer imitation made by people who have never actually seen one. Expensive by Danziger standards, it boasts period setting, a semi-name cast, a reputable literary source and, for its time, lots of blood and guts — including the rather silly-looking titular organ.

Eddie Marsh (Laurence Payne) is your average club-footed, drug-addled part-time writer. A lonely man (not surprising, given the circumstances), he spends much of his time spying on the attractive woman in the house opposite. Although she goes out with him once or twice, she prefers his best friend. Spying as usual, Marsh becomes insanely jealous when he observes them making love. He murders his friend, hiding the body under the floorboards. Soon every sound becomes the beating of the dead man's heart, reducing Marsh to a nervous wreck. He cuts out the heart and buries it in the garden, but still hears its beat. When he rips up the floorboards again it is to find that the heart has returned to its body. In a climax that has little to do with Poe and everything to do with earlier films like *Dead of Night*, it all turns out to be a dream, then commences again... Infrequently revived since its original release (with *Live Now, Pay*

Later), *The Tell-Tale Heart* builds up a fine, brooding atmosphere that eventually explodes into rather sweaty, over-ripe hysterics, with the murder and heart removal being quite graphic for the time. While no lost classic, it's still worth a look.

Robert S. Baker and Monty Berman were among the many to try to specifically duplicate the Hammer methods. Long before they came to reinvent the adventure series for British TV with *The Saint, Department S, The Baron, The Champions et al*, they were casting envious eyes towards Bray Studios. Hammer began their horror cycle with a black and white adaptation of the BBC's science fiction serial *The Quatermass Experiment*, so Baker and Berman used something the rival ITV network had produced: *The Trollenberg Terror* (Quentin Lawrence, 1958). Screenplay writer Jimmy Sangster was already Hammer 'star' property, and he was borrowed by Berman and Baker on more than one occasion, providing for some odd and unexpected thematic continuities. He obviously experienced problems reducing the six-part original to feature length, since the film is cluttered with incident (to say the least). A radioactive cloud (actually some cotton wool attached to a photo of the Matterhorn) is discovered at the top of Trollenberg Mountain. Climbers are decapitated. A

The Trollenberg Terror. *(Bottom) Possibly the best rubber severed head in a 1958 British SF/horror movie...*

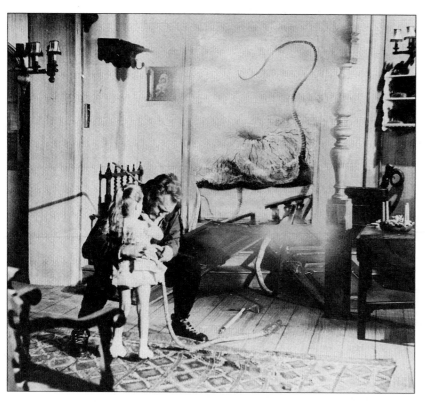

The shattering climax of **The Trollenberg Terror**.

dead man (played by Andrew Faulds, BBC radio's space hero Jet Morgan, who gave up acting to become a Labour MP) comes back to life, intent on killing everyone he comes into contact with. A young woman gifted with ESP is in mental communication with whatever it is in the cloud. An American scientist acts mysteriously. People sit around the hotel and the observatory and worry about what might be happening. None of these elements particularly relate to one another, but they drive the movie along until the aliens (one-eyed squid-like things) and their cloud come down the mountain to (presumably) kill everyone. They don't prove particularly good at this and are wiped out by incendiaries. No attempt is made to explain what the aliens are, where they come from or what they're after, although Warren Mitchell makes a couple of educated guesses. "Perhaps the world these creatures inhabit is coming to an end," he says. "Perhaps they need somewhere else to live." Perhaps. Of course, they're dead before we can ask them.

With its obviously low budget and interesting (if not exactly convincing) special effects, *The Trollenberg Terror* still manages to produce a reasonably creepy atmosphere, and can be quite effective if seen at the right age, or in the right state of consciousness.

To complete the imitation, the film (like *The Quatermass Experiment*) suffered a silly title change in the USA, becoming *The Crawling Eye*. This was nothing, however, compared to the indignities heaped on one of their later productions. In the meantime, still following their role models, Berman and Baker turned from black and white to colour and from science fiction to full-blown Gothic horror.

Blood of the Vampire (Henry Cass, 1958) is in many ways the half-way point between the 'new' approach and the barn-storming melodramatics of Tod Slaughter. Sir Donald Wolfit (always a ham, although generally considered a 'proper' actor) was the last of the actor-managers and may have considered himself

to have something in common with Slaughter. Made up to resemble a child's caricature of Bela Lugosi, with fake nose, widow's peak and blood-splattered leather apron, he comes over very much like a cross between Dracula and Sweeney Todd. The vampire angle is a red herring. Executed at the outset with the usual stake through the heart, Dr Callistratus is rather mysteriously brought back to life by another doctor, and is soon set up in business in the local lunatic asylum, experimenting on patients to find a cure for his strange blood disease. Under countless layers of greasepaint, a false eye and with his tongue literally in his cheek, Victor Maddern plays his mute, hunchback assistant. Victor Ball is another scientist thrown into the asylum for his own ungodly experimentation, and needs little persuasion to join Callistratus in his work. Barbara Shelley, his fiancée, manages to gain entrance to the hospital in an attempt to find out what's going on.

Jimmy Sangster's script contains all the distrust of the medical profession, and authority figures in general, evinced in his Frankenstein films. There are enough similarities to *Revenge of Frankenstein*, made the same year and originally announced as *Blood of Frankenstein*, to make one wonder if *Blood of the Vampire* was a script ultimately passed over by Hammer: the opening execution of the scientist, the hunchbacked assistant, the young doctor eager to learn, and the use of poor and needy patients as experimental subjects. And, to all intents and purposes, it was partially re-made by Hammer as *Frankenstein and the Monster from Hell*, substituting blood transfusion experiments for the usual brain swapping and body building.

With *Jack the Ripper* (produced, directed and photographed by Baker and Berman, 1958), the team began to find their own, more original niche — the sensationalising of true crime. This was a direct result of the slackening of censorship — real criminals could not previously be named in films. Not that censorship was that slack, for as well as inventing the 'deification of scum' sub-genre, Baker and Berman were responsible for creating alternative versions of their films: cool for the Brits and Americans, hot for the Continentals. What this mainly consisted of was mild topless 'orgy' footage in *Jack the Ripper*, *The Flesh and the Fiends* and *The Hellfire Club*, but when stills of these scenes appeared in French magazines imported into Britain, legends were born, giving rise to apocryphal tales about 'stronger' versions of virtually any film you could mention.

Jack the Ripper isn't overly concerned with the facts — though, in fairness, there was hardly the vast library of information on the murders that exists now — but at least it gets the location right and is brave enough to call the victims prostitutes: they had been 'actresses' in every other English language version. Of course, because Sangster wrote the script, the medical profession is to blame and a hunchbacked assistant is a suspect. The film also contains a remarkable cheat; when the unidentified Ripper asks his victims, "Are you Mary Clarke?", the voice is that of prime suspect John Le Mesurier — who is later revealed not to be the Ripper. The Ripper's ultimate victim was actually Mary Kelly — they obviously didn't want to push the envelope that much.

Picked up for distribution in the US by Joseph E. Levine, the film was given a lavish publicity campaign and, for the time, an unusually high level of merchandising, including two records (one a soundtrack, the other a story with dialogue) and a novelisation, appearing in both soft and hard cover. Much of the publicity centred on the use of colour at the end (the film was black and white), when the Ripper, trapped in a lift shaft, is crushed to death by the lift and his blood forced up through the floor. Despite all this, plus written testimonials from Basil Rathbone, Peter Lorre and Gypsy Rose Lee, the film was not the financial success everyone expected, partly due to its cheap, sleazy look, which would have proved a little strong

ahead of its time, and the cheap studio-bound recreation of early nineteenth century Edinburgh adds rather than detracts from the film's general ambiance of sordid viciousness. Even a bland romance between Dermot Walsh and June Laverick fails to ruin the proceedings, while the other romantic couple, young doctor John Cairney and prostitute Billie Whitelaw, are ruthlessly killed off. Burke is hanged, Hare turns King's evidence

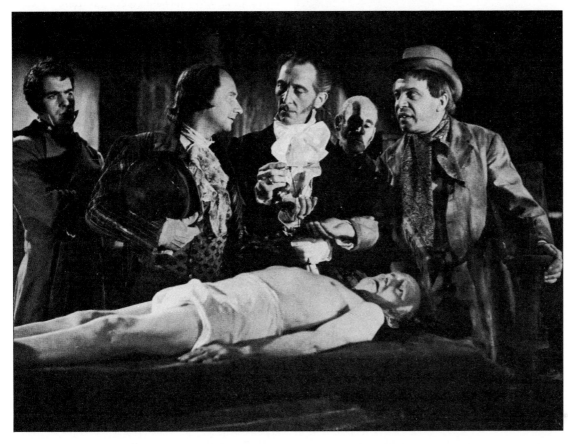

(*Left*) *Thespians hard at it in* **The Flesh and the Fiends.**

for contemporary American audiences. Its main problem is the lack of strong leads: John Le Mesurier, Ewen Solon and the rest of the supporting cast are fine, but Lee Patterson and Eddie Byrne are just not good enough to carry the film. The black and white probably didn't help much either.

However, it did well enough for Baker and Berman to begin work on *The Flesh and the Fiends* (John Gilling, 1960), a retelling of the crimes of Burke and Hare. The production immediately ran into potential trouble when it was discovered that it bore a substantial resemblance to the then unfilmed Dylan Thomas screenplay for *The Doctor and the Devils*. But since both scripts claimed to be based on real incidents, the problem was soon overcome. Shot in black and white, it boasts the best cast of the Baker/Berman horror films, and sticks reasonably close to the facts. Peter Cushing plays Dr Knox as a more noble Frankenstein — the real Knox appears to have been something of a prototype white supremacist, not at all dismayed if a few low-life scum got knocked off so that 'better' people could be cured of their ailments. George Rose and Donald Pleasence ham it up outrageously as Burke and Hare, who find that murder is a more cost-effective and labour-saving method of producing corpses for college surgeons than the usual body snatching. Despite the overplaying, Pleasence displays a cold ruthlessness that was quite

but later has his eyes burned out (quite graphically) by a lynch mob, and Knox has to face the medical council. All this was spiced up with even more topless orgy footage — although not for British or American audiences... In England, the film was released as the top half of a double bill with the French gangster movie *Rififi and the Women*. In the USA it first appeared as *Mania*, then as *The Fiendish Ghouls* — with over thirteen minutes missing, including the ending. Unsurprisingly, it did little business. It still hasn't garnered the reputation it deserves.

Perhaps in response, Baker and Berman moved away from horror films, although three of their later productions are worth mentioning. *The Siege of Sydney Street* (produced and directed by Baker and Berman, 1960) continues their interest in true crime. Reasonably factual, it boasts a rare non-horror screenplay by Jimmy Sangster, who also appears as Winston Churchill. No film that features plum-voiced Donald Sinden as a street-wise, turn-of-the-century London detective trying to infiltrate a gang of Russo-Jewish anarchists can be all bad. (*Really? Ed.*)

The Hellfire Club (Baker/Berman, 1961) had a screenplay by Sangster (with Leon Griffiths), a guest appearance by Peter Cushing and the by-now obligatory orgy sequence for foreign markets, but in spite of some minor horror overtones it is primarily an historical

Obsessed by a burning desire to create beauty from ugliness he probed deeper and deeper into the mysteries of surgery using the living as guinea-pigs for his sinister experiments

CIRCUS OF HORRORS

TOM OWEN

(Right) What's wrong with this picture?

sidered a cheap penny dreadful.

Cohen's presence probably explains the film's cheerfully ruthless sensationalism. Anton Diffring plays a plastic surgeon obsessed with female disfigurement, who is forced to flee with his two faithful assistants when a cosmetic operation goes wrong. Somewhere in France (according to the on-screen caption) he is able to repair a young girl's scarred face and take over her father's run-down travelling circus, turning it into a major success and using his refurbished beauties as star performers. If any try to leave or give the game away, they are disposed of in front of a rapturous audience. By the time the big top reaches Clapham Common, half the cast have been disposed of and the police are getting suspicious. Possibly influenced by *Les Yeux sans Visage*, *Circus* doesn't really attempt to copy Franju's masterpiece. Instead, it uses radical surgery as a peg to attach a wild and bizarre plot, thereby helping to inspire many other face transplant movies. There are some signs of financial or perhaps censor-inspired corner cutting: a sub-plot involving a clown is abruptly dropped, and a freak show (which figures heavily in the novelisation) is represented in the film only by a hairy something, possibly meant to be a gorilla. Even so, no attempt is made to soften the film via comic relief or period setting. It revels in its tasteless sensationalism and is all the better for it.

Night of the Eagle (Sidney Hayers, 1961) could hardly have been more different. Filmed in black and white, it's closer to Tourneur's *Night of the Demon* than the then prevalent garish colour look. Based on Fritz Leiber's novel *Conjure Wife*, it concerns a no-nonsense university lecturer who discovers that his wife and many of his colleagues are practising witchcraft in furtherance of their careers. While never achieving the heights of *Night of the Demon* or the Lewton chillers it imitates, *Night of the Eagle* still works well on its own level, as the sane and rational outlook of the hero (Peter Wyngarde!) is broken down by the intrusion of the supernatural. The film's second half, where Wyngarde is driven to the very techniques of witchcraft that he despises, takes on a dreamlike intensity which more than compensates for the rather slow, overly subtle first half.

Exactly who wrote what is a matter of debate. George Baxt, whose name is missing from the American prints, claims (in *Scarlet Street* #4) he was called in at the last minute to rewrite what was basically an unfilmable script. Richard Matheson believes that what was filmed was his and Charles Beaumont's script with no changes or additions. Beaumont, of course, is dead and not in a position to offer an opinion. It's unlikely that we'll uncover the truth, but a possible explanation is Baxt's rewrite was necessary to make use of British locations and actors. Matheson and Beaumont, after all, must have written their version on the assumption that the picture would have the novel's American setting. Certainly the university has a rather mid-Atlantic ambiance, reflecting the two weeks Baxt had to complete his work, additions still being handed in while the film was in production.

Unearthly Stranger (John Krish, 1963) is different again: a science fiction film, and documentary director Krish's first feature. The plot — scientist's wife is actually part of the vanguard for an invasion from outer space — is rather like *I Married a Monster from Outer Space* with the sexes reversed. Like *Night of the Eagle*, it is conveyed primarily through the emotive playing of the actors, without resorting to extravagant special

swashbuckler. *What a Carve-Up!* (Pat Jackson 1961) was a Carry On-style comedy starring Kenneth Connor, Sidney James, Shirley Eaton and Donald Pleasence. It's one of the few British horror spoofs (others include *The Headless Ghost*, *What a Whopper!* and Hammer's *The Ugly Duckling*) since *Old Mother Riley Meets the Vampire*. It's also one of the best (though that's not necessarily saying much) and is based on Frank King's novel *The Ghoul*, also the source of the 1933 Boris Karloff movie.

Julian Wintle and Leslie Parkyn formed Independent Artists in 1958. Among their films were *Tiger Bay*, *This Sporting Life* and three fantasy films notable for being so vastly different in terms of subject matter, style and execution that there's little basis for comparison. This is particularly surprising when one considers that two of them share the same producer, writer and director.

Circus of Horrors (Sidney Hayers, 1960) was made in collaboration with Anglo-Amalgamated, who had already moved into the horror film market through a co-production and distribution deal with American International. (All three Wintle/Parkyn fantasies were released in the US by AIP.) As early as 1957, Anglo had made the Val Lewtonesque *Cat Girl*, but their big year was 1959, with *Peeping Tom*, *Horrors of the Black Museum* and *Circus of Horrors*. Executive producer of *Black Museum* was Herman Cohen, closely associated with AIP for *I Was a Teenage Frankenstein*, *Teenage Werewolf* and several other films with the same basic plot as *Black Museum* — that of a strong-willed, older person dominating a younger one until he or she commits murder. Although not revealed at the time, Cohen also served as executive producer on *Circus*, apparently because Wintle, used to big budget pictures, felt more than a little uncomfortable working on what he con-

effects. Unfortunately, Krish does not attempt Hayers' semi-Wellesian camera set-ups, and the film ultimately resembles an early '60s TV drama.

Robert L. Lippert was an American producer responsible for, amongst many, *Rocketship XM* and the obscure 1962 remake of *The Cabinet of Dr Caligari*. In the '50s he made a deal with (pre-horror boom) Hammer enabling them to secure US distribution, before forming an association with Jack Parsons in the early '60s to make inexpensive horror and science fiction films in Britain. None were particularly successful, but one at least is worthy of consideration as a (very) minor classic, and the individuals involved mean some others warrant a mention.

The Horror of It All (Terence Fisher, 1963) has the distinction of probably being Fisher's worst film. Scripted by Ray Russell (best known for *Mr Sardonicus*) and starring Pat Boone, this woefully unfunny comedy bears an uncomfortable resemblance to William Castle's remake of *The Old Dark House* and is even worse. After the success of *The Raven* someone presumably thought horror-comedy was going to be the next big thing...

The Earth Dies Screaming (Terence Fisher, 1964), a co-production with Planet, is Fisher's other film for the company. Scripted by Henry Cross and starring Willard Parker, Virginia Field and Dennis Price, it would have us believe that the world has been devastated by an alien attack. Rather than screaming, people collapse and die very quietly. The survivors find London inhabited only by killer robots who can revive their victims as blank-eyed zombies. After much talk, Parker manages to blow up their transmitter, leaving the few remaining characters to start life anew in a decimated world — an effect somewhat spoiled by a distant view of a crowded motorway.

Spaceflight IC-1 (Bernard Knowles, 1965) is slow, dull and predictable, but has the dubious historical interest of possibly having influenced *Dark Star* (*Next he'll be telling us Hitchcock ripped off* Fiend without a Face! *Ed.*). Couples, who are selected for their mental and physical perfection in order to colonise a new world, spend fifty years in space without finding one. There are the usual conflicts, a mutiny and the death of the captain. The status quo is re-established and the apparently endless voyage continues.

Curse of the Fly (Don Sharp, 1965) is the third of the Fly series, and the Delambre family have still to perfect their matter transmitter. No fly-monsters as such, but lots of unconvincingly made-up mutants. 'Is This The End?' asks a redundant title.

Amidst all this mediocrity, *Witchcraft* (Don Sharp, 1964) shines out as the single jewel. Shot as *The Witch and the Warlock*, the story of family feuding surviving over centuries is as cheaply made as other Lippert-Parsons movies, but Don Sharp makes more of his limited resources than one might reasonably expect. *Witchraft* is a modern day reworking of *Black Sunday*, with a long-dead witch revived when a greedy property developer digs up the cemetery she was buried in. The developer is a descendant of the family that originally stole her land and had her buried alive — and you can probably work the rest out for yourselves... Lon Chaney (as the warlock) overacts wildly and the property tycoon (Jack Hedley) is actually one of the heroes, but there are one or two surprises and a nice brooding atmosphere.

A book could probably be written about Richard Gordon and his contribution to the horror genre. But this brief overview of some of his British-based material will have to suffice for the moment...

Born in London, Richard Gordon and his brother Alex moved to New York in the late 1940s. Primarily

involved in setting up co-productions, they also arranged British starring vehicles for fading American actors, among them Bela Lugosi, for whom they set up *Old Mother Riley Meets the Vampire*. After some years, Alex went to work with American International, while Richard formed Producers Associates with John Croydon, associate producer on *Dead of Night*. They made a deal with Eros in England, secured the services of Boris Karloff and Marshall Thompson, and gained US distribution via MGM. Producers Associates then went to work on their first double bill. Eros were a small company that often dabbled in horror and exploitation titles, including *Fire Maidens from Outer Space*, *The Strange World of Planet X*, *Man without a Body*, *Woman Eater* and *Behemoth, the Sea Monster*, the last two often incorrectly attributed to Gordon.

Fiend without a Face (Arthur Crabtree, 1957) is firmly

in the tradition of *The Quatermass Experiment*, with its sights clearly on the American market. Set on the US/Canadian border, the dialogue boasts a bewildering variety of odd accents, as the primarily British cast tries to come to terms with their newfound Americanisation.

Nothing can halt the death-grip of "the fiend without a face".

M-G-M presents "FIEND WITHOUT A FACE"

MARSHALL THOMPSON in FIEND WITHOUT A FACE with KYNASTON REEVES · KIM PARKER

X cert.

Boris Karloff opens the grave of the "Haymarket Strangler" searching for a clue to the truth.

M-G-M Presents "THE HAUNTED STRANGLER"

(Right) Karloff and his Haunted Strangler Grip. Now look at page 96 again...

Locations aside, the film's main problem is pacing. The first half drags as various corpses are discovered with their brains sucked out, but once the monsters have been identified and become visible the fun really starts. Kynaston Reeves' experiments to turn thought into energy produce stop-motion killer brains that move about like Brian the snail in *The Magic Roundabout* and — you guessed it — suck your brain out. The climactic 'siege by brain' has influenced everything from *The Birds* to *Night of the Living Dead* (*And to think I never realised Hitchcock was such a big Marshall Thompson fan... Ed.*). When it opened in America, Herman Cohen was so impressed that he signed up Arthur Crabtree for *Horrors of the Black Museum*.

Grip of the Strangler (Robert Day, 1958) was to be *Fiend*'s co-feature. Filmed as *Stranglehold*, the title of Jan Read's original story, this bleak variation on *Dr Jekyll and Mr Hyde* tries to show some of the savagery of Victorian society. The public execution of an innocent man, a prison flogging and the slashing of a gin palace floozie were all trimmed by the censor, but still create a miasma of misery amongst the melodrama as a writer (Karloff) tries to discover the identity of the Haymarket Strangler, only to realise that it is himself.

Financial returns on the double bill were good enough to persuade MGM that they wanted more of the same, only this time with some of their own money involved to improve any future profits.

First Man into Space (Robert Day, 1958) was not just in the tradition of — it *is* — *The Quatermass Experiment!* Astronaut Bill Edwards disobeys orders and flies his Y-12 rocket plane through a cloud of meteor dust. On his return to Earth, his skin becomes encrusted as his blood bubbles away, and he turns into a vampire-like monster. Once again set in America but filmed in England, the attempt to make the English landscape resemble New Mexico was not successful. But what can you expect from a film based on a story by Wyatt Ordung, the man who wrote *Robot Monster*!?

Corridors of Blood (Robert Day, 1958), filmed as *The Doctor from Seven Dials*, was meant to be the co-feature with *First Man into Space*, but MGM rushed the latter into release before the space travel fad fizzled out. Even more bleak and depressing than *Grip of the Strangler*, its mixture of surgery without anaesthetic, murder and drug addiction was probably a bit too much for the American producers. Boris Karloff plays the single-minded obsessive researcher, a part he could tackle in his sleep. Christopher Lee, in an early genre role, is a revelation, even attempting a Cockney accent. Covering much the same ground as *The Flesh and the*

Fiends, the movie strives for a high moral tone as it charts the 'trial and error' development of anaesthesia, but is actually far happier dwelling on the blood and agony of the operating table in the days when you got 'em drunk and held 'em down. For whatever reason, it languished on the shelf in Britain until 1962, when it was released with *Nights of Rasputin,* and 1963 in the USA with *Werewolf in a Girls' Dormitory.*

The agreement with MGM dissolved when the bigger company decided to steer clear of exploitation films, and Gordon's next two British-based projects involved producer and exhibitor Kenneth Rive, owner of the Gala cinema chain, and director Lindsay Shonteff.

Devil Doll (Lindsay Shonteff, 1963) is quite highly regarded in some circles, though it's hard to see why. Shot almost entirely in close-up or from a bizarre angle (possibly due to budgetary considerations), this is another picture that more resembles a TV play from the period. A variation on the 'ventriloquist's dummy' story in *Dead of Night,* with Bryant Halliday playing The Great Vorelli, who has imprisoned the soul of his assistant in Hugo the dummy. Gordon credits much of

the film's look to Sidney J. Furie, who was originally signed to direct but asked to be released from his contract when offered *The Ipcress File.* Furie had already directed two small independent horrors, *The Snake Woman* and *Doctor Blood's Coffin* — not wonderful, but better than this. But if *Devil Doll* isn't great, it's a masterpiece compared to *Curse of Simba* (Lindsay Shonteff, 1964). Running a whole sixty-one minutes in its British version (and, oddly enough, seventy-seven in its American incarnation as *Curse of the Voodoo*), it's unspeakably dull, racist nonsense about a white hunter (Bryant Halliday again) pursued by an African curse. Certain attempts are made to conjure up a Lewtonesque atmosphere. None of them work.

Both films hung around without distribution for some time. When eventually released, neither exactly set the world on fire. *Simba* ended up on a double bill with *Frankenstein Meets the Space Monster,* which must have been interesting.

By the mid-'60s Gordon had formed Protelco with Gerold A. Fernbeck, who had been involved in the financing of *Devil Doll.* They in turn arranged a co-production deal with Tom Blakeley, head of Planet Films. As well as *The Earth Dies Screaming,* Planet had produced *Devils of Darkness* (Lance Comfort, 1965), a fairly lacklustre vampire thriller set in the present and scripted by Lyn Fairhurst, better known for having worked in practically every capacity on *The Flesh Eaters.*

Island of Terror (Terence Fisher, 1966) began life as

Night of the Silicates. Although by no means an expensive film, it's certainly a step up from the impoverished *Devil Doll,* and was the best-looking film that Gordon had been involved with to date. Another variation on the 'small apocalypse' theme, it can almost

be seen as a remake of *Fiend without a Face.* An experiment has gone wrong, sundry minor characters meet mysterious deaths (bones sucked out, this time), an investigation is started and the monsters appear — a mutated version of a micro-organism designed to attack and destroy cancer cells. Unfortunately, the monsters lack the charisma of *Fiend*'s brains, looking rather like legless turtles. The special effects leave something to be desired, too. When the monsters reproduce, splitting into two amoebas, it looks as if someone has simply placed two of the creatures side-by-side and poured canned spaghetti over them. Still, there are a few effective (nasty) moments, such as Peter Cushing's hand being chopped off, and some suspense in the action sequences. Fisher apparently disliked science fiction and 'modern day' horror, and it shows. Even so, this is probably his best non-Hammer fantasy.

The Projected Man (Ian Curteis, 1966) came about when Universal acquired *Island of Terror* for American release and wanted another movie to pair it with. Since Planet didn't have another film in development, Protelco made a one-off deal with Gordon's old colleague John Croydon, and bought an unfilmed screenplay from brother Alex. The original script, by Frank Quattorochi, had been prepared at about the same time as *The Fly,* and no amount of rewriting could disguise what was by then an over-familiar idea. Bryant Halliday's matter transmitter (in fact, some sort of laser) malfunctions, turning one side of his face inside out and giving him an electrified killing touch. Curteis was a TV director given a chance at his first feature. The production went badly over-budget and behind schedule, and he was eventually dismissed, with John Croydon stepping in to supervise the last few days' shooting. The double bill did well in the US, but when released separately in Britain the success of the movies was not duplicated.

Determined to carry on making the same film until they got it right, Planet began to prepare *Night of the Big Heat* (Terence Fisher, 1967). John Lymington's 1959 novel, in which protoplasmic aliens heat up the atmosphere as a forerunner to an invasion, is the typical British 'small apocalypse' story. And yes, characters do spend much of the book sitting in a pub, sweating and wondering about the menace outside. Already adapted into a TV play, the basic plot was — like *The Projected Man* — by now overly familiar from countless other books, plays and films. Plans were well advanced for this second Planet/Protelco venture (with Fisher, Peter Cushing and Christopher Lee all signed up), but Gordon thought the screenplay needed more work and the effects budget was inadequate. Tom Blakeley disagreed and they parted company, Blakeley remaining as sole producer. Despite a good cast, the film was not a success. When the aliens finally appear, the effects are dreadful.

The third Protelco film was *Naked Evil* (Stanley Goulder, 1966), a return to black and white, with a generally impoverished look. Even worse, this tale of possession, evil spirits and voodoo also marked a return to the racism of *Curse of Simba*. Barely released in Britain, it eventually appeared in America with a new framing story and colour tinting. It didn't help. Gordon still hoped *Naked Evil* and *Big Heat* could be released on the same programme and repeat the success of their earlier double bill, but no one was interested. When *Big Heat* eventually surfaced in the USA (retitled *Island of the Burning Damned*) it suffered the indignity of being second feature to *Godzilla's Revenge*.

Despite an impressive roster of forthcoming projects, including *The Possessors* — screenplay by George Baxt, based on the novel by John Christopher — and *Who?* — to be written and directed by Val Guest from Algis Budrys' novel — Fernback was dissatisfied by the failure of the last couple of films and ended the partnership.

Gordon was still active in the '70s and '80s with *Tower of Evil*, *Horror Hospital*, *The Cat and the Canary* and *Inseminoid*, but they are outside the scope of this article and will have to wait for another time...

After Hammer and Amicus, the most notable house style belonged to the two Tony Tenser companies, Compton and Tigon. Tenser was head of publicity at Miracle Films when he met Michael Klinger, then manager of the Nell Gwynn strip club in Soho. They became partners, opening the Compton, London's first cinema club, and forming Compton-Cameo Films, initially producing and distributing nudist

films. By the early '60s they had moved up to slightly more expensive sexploitation, with two films directed by Robert Hartford-Davies, *The Yellow Teddybears* and *Saturday Night Out*. They acquired the rights to Riccardo Freda's *L'Orribile Segreto del Dr Hichcock* and *Lo Spettro* to go out with them as second features. Released as *The Terror of Dr Hichcock* and *The Spectre* respectively, they created a reputation far beyond that of the supposed major features. So nothing seemed more natural than Compton-Cameo making a Gothic horror of their own.

The Black Torment (produced and directed by Robert Hartford-Davies, 1964) offers the interesting spectacle of a British director trying to imitate Freda imitating Terence Fisher. Unsurprisingly, while many of the stylistic tricks work quite well, the film lacks the crazed imagination of Freda and his scriptwriters. There are endless coach rides, forbidding peasantry, the mysterious death of the first wife and all the usual ghostly clichés. By the end, Donald and Derek Ford's script has blamed all the weird occurrences on diabolical plots and brain fever, and the second murder victim is still undiscovered in the stable.

The Black Torment's cinematographer was Peter Newbrook, who was active in British horror for several years. As producer and cameraman he worked with Hartford-Davies and the Fords again on the extraordinary *Corruption* (1967), a mad mélange of *Les Yeux sans Visage*, *Seddok*, *The Awful Dr Orloff et al*, with the dream-coming-true-after-all climax of *Dead of Night* thrown in for good measure. Newbrook was cinematographer on *Crucible of Horror* (1971) and directed *Disciple of Death* (1972)— both starring the unfortunate Mike Raven, a Christopher Lee impersonator and blues DJ whose acting career never quite took off — and *The Asphyx* (1973), a Hammer-like thriller with intellectual pretensions.

Hartford-Davies went on to *Incense for the Damned* (1970), a troubled production based on Simon Raven's novel *Doctors Wear Scarlet*. The film was not released for some time, and studio tampering caused Hartford-Davies to remove his name from the credits. His final horror movie was *The Fiend* (1971), an enjoyably sick piece about a religious cult headed by a suitably over-the-top Patrick Magee.

Compton was encouraged by the success of *The Black Torment* to put up money for *Repulsion* (Roman Polanski, 1965), something of a risk at the time. What emerged was one of '60's cinema's most precise blending of art and commerce, as well as one of its most influential horror films. But that and *Cul-de-Sac* (Polanski, 1966) were two rare nods by Compton in the direction of critical approval. They seemed happiest playing to the crowds with movies like *A Study in Terror* (James Hill, 1965), the first of the 'Sherlock Holmes meets Jack the Ripper' films. A semi-name cast (John Neville, Donald Houston, John Fraser, Anthony Quayle) and reasonable production values seem to aim the film at the mainstream audience, but the presence of Herman Cohen as executive producer (midway, as far as his British productions are concerned, between the dreadful *Konga* and the even worse *Berserk!*) ensures that it is mainly murder and disfigurement, with only a few breaks in the plot. Fun in a simple-minded way, it led to the later — and much better — *Murder by Decree*, as well as several novels on the same theme. Oddly, the novelisation of *Study* is an Ellery Queen thriller in which Queen fills in the gaps Holmes and Watson left out.

BRITISH WINNER
of the 1966
GOLDEN BEAR AWARD
(THE BEST FILM FROM ANY SOURCE)

DONALD PLEASENCE in ROMAN POLANSKI'S
FRANCOISE DORLEAC
LIONEL STANDER **Cul-de-Sac**
with JACK MACGOWRAN

SCREENPLAY BY ROMAN POLANSKI AND GERARD BRACH
EXECUTIVE PRODUCER SAM WAYNBERG
PRODUCED BY GENE GUTOWSKI   DIRECTED BY ROMAN POLANSKI
A COMPTON FILM DISTRIBUTORS RELEASE

The Compton partnership broke up soon after, Klinger going on to *The Penthouse*, *Get Carter* and *Shout at the Devil* as well as the Confessions series (1974-77), before almost bankrupting himself with *Riding High*.

Tenser, meanwhile, formed Tony Tenser Films in 1967, soon changing the name to Tigon. He quickly acquired such titles as *Cauldron of Blood*, *Carnival of Souls* and *Terror Creatures from the Grave* for UK release, and began his own productions with *The Sorcerers* (Michael Reeves, 1967). Reeves' second film updates a basic Boris Karloff mad doctor plot from the '40s to swinging London, and equips it with the concerns and conceits of *Peeping Tom*. The setting and resulting obligatory attempt at a *Blow Up* style have dated badly, and there are some dreadful hand-held camera shots, but it improves much upon Reeves' earlier *Revenge of*

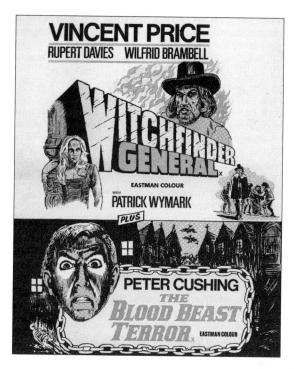

the *Blood Beast* and points the way to his far superior *Matthew Hopkins — Witchfinder General* .

The Blood Beast Terror (Vernon Sewell, 1967) was produced immediately after *The Sorcerers* with the usual eye to making up a double bill, although both films opened after *Witchfinder General* in the USA. Nice as it is to see Robert Flemyng repeat his Vincent Price act, this tale of an unfortunate young woman who periodically turns into a giant death's head moth is a

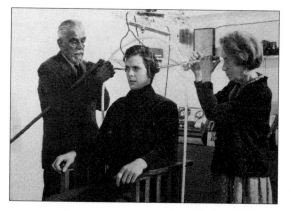

misfire on almost every level, and can't even be described as unintentionally funny.

Tigon then formed a brief alliance with AIP, which lasted for their next three films. The first was the best they were associated with. *Matthew Hopkins — Witchfinder General* (Michael Reeves, 1968) continues the theme developed in *The Sorcerers* — the ease with which people are drawn to violence. The superbly evoked English Civil War setting points out the casual viciousness of the period. And the message that revenge automatically makes the avenger as bad as the perpetrator of the original crime — more than a little heavy-handed today — was evidently misunderstood at the time. Despite extensive cutting, the film was still criticised for its violence. Of course, in America they didn't even realise there had been an English Civil War and cared less, so the title was changed to *The Conqueror Worm* and Price got to read part of the poem behind the credits. Actually, Reeves did not want Price on the film at all. Equally, Price had heard of the new 'boy genius' and was not impressed. In this atmosphere of mutual dislike they produced Reeves' best film and Price's best horror performance.

Although involved in preparing *The Oblong Box* for production by AIP, Reeves died before shooting commenced. He was twenty-five.

Curse of the Crimson Altar (Vernon Sewell, 1968) has a good cast (Karloff, Christopher Lee, Barbara Steele), a fine location (a supposedly haunted house once belonging to W.S. Gilbert) and excellent — if uncredited — source material (H.P. Lovecraft's 'Dreams in the Witch House') all thrown away in a stodgy and almost incomprehensible occult thriller. Sewell went on to the dreadful *Burke and Hare*. When Karloff died soon after finishing *Crimson Altar* (released in the US as *The Crimson Cult*), Tenser announced a special memorial. He would open a cinema in London called The Karloff that would only play horror films. This splendidly daft idea unfortunately came to nothing.

With *The Haunted House of Horror* (Michael Armstrong, 1969) the locations (the old Birkdale Palace Hotel at Southport and Bank Hall at Bretherton) are, again, the best thing about the gory 'teenagers in a haunted house' yarn. Karloff was supposed to play the police inspector. Recommended to anyone who likes to see faded pop stars (Frankie Avalon and Mark Wynter) sliced into pieces. It was shot under the much better title of *The Dark* and double-billed with *The Crimson Cult* in the USA to a resounding lack of interest. Director Armstrong had made his début with *The Image*, a strange short starring a very young David Bowie, and later went to Germany for *Mark of the Devil*.

Tigon attempted to diversify with *The Body Stealers* (Gerry Levy, 1969), an undistinguished *Invasion of the Body Snatchers* ripoff. Parachutists trying out a revolutionary new design vanish when they pass through a red mist and are kept in suspended animation when alien replicas take their place.

Even more misguided was *Zeta One* (Michael Cort, 1969). *Zeta* was a short-lived British softcore photo-story magazine, and this is based on one of the stories contained therein. A James Bond type attempts to foil extra-terrestrial amazons when they try to take over the world. Presumably someone thought that this could turn into a series. They were wrong — the world wasn't ready for softcore SF/spy movies.

Business should have been back to normal with *Blood on Satan's Claw* (Piers Haggard, 1970), an attempt to repeat the *Witchfinder General* formula with

(Top) Matthew Hopkins — Witchfinder General.

(Left) The Sorcerers.

(Above) **Curse of the Crimson Altar**.

(Right) Piers Haggard directing **Blood on Satan's Claw**.

his scenes had yet to be shot. In order to save what they already had, one story was expanded to feature length, with footage intended for other episodes combined into a single narrative, which explains the many loose ends and the first thirty minutes having little relevance to the rest of the picture.

Still, even if it makes little or no sense, *Blood on Satan's Claw* is certainly worth a look (but beware the censored print), which can't be said for its companion piece. *The Beast in the Cellar* (written and directed by James Kelly, 1970) is a strangely stylised gore film in which two dotty sisters cover up murders committed by their even more crazed brother. The double-bill was hardly released in Britain or the USA, but even so was probably seen by more people than Tigon's last three fantasy pictures.

Virgin Witch (Ray Austin, 1970, released 1972) is a desperately cheap looking co-production that is more interesting than its basic sex 'n' horror plot (model girls involved with satanic cult) would indicate. Vicky Michelle (who co-stars with sister Ann) went on to a TV career which scaled the heights of 'Allo 'Allo...

The Creeping Flesh (Freddie Francis, 1972) is practically the last gasp of what had by then become the traditional British horror movie. An oddly bleak and depressing look at Victorian — and by implication, modern — England's inability to cope with sexuality and insanity, tied up with a far-fetched plot concerning the nature of 'absolute evil'. Like *Blood on Satan's Claw*, there is evidence to suggest that more than one plot has been melded together, though whether at script or editing stage is not clear. Of course, Francis had made so many anthology movies by this stage he probably couldn't help it. It's still his best film as director.

Doomwatch (Peter Sasdy, 1972) brought the wheel full-circle with a movie adaptation of a then-popular TV series. Slowly paced and over-worthy, the horror trappings (Cornish island where the natives don't like outsiders, mysterious noises in the night, lumpy-faced mutants) work against the story's serious intent; the illegal dumping of chemical and radioactive waste. Once again, it received only a very limited release in Britain and next to none in the USA.

By this time, Tenser was reportedly tiring of the explicit violence he was having to inject into his films. He may also have been disturbed by the lack of financial return on some of them. For whatever reason, he sold the company in 1972. It survived until the early '80s before finally folding.

Although the British horror movie was far from dead, the original impetus provided by the success of Hammer certainly was, and so was the concept of 'family' businesses making films with a uniform look — apart from occasional misfires like Tyburn. Further relaxations in censorship also allowed films greater freedom. British horror of the '70s, now no longer part of cosy post-Victorian repressive 'moral' society, could comment on the darker side of 'Britishness'. Films like *Death Line*, *Horror Hospital*, and the work of Peter Walker and Norman J. Warren are worthy of study from precisely this 'outsider' viewpoint. Perhaps next time (*!?! Ed.*).

The likes of *The Flesh and the Fiends* and *Blood on Satan's Claw* are essentially insider films, a comfortable excursion into morbidity, violence and death, which titillates and entertains at the same time as they (usually) reinforce the belief that everything is basically okay, like a celluloid *News of the World* — an attitude as peculiarly disturbing as it is peculiarly British. ■

even more violence and sensationalism. It was originally intended as an anthology film, with the Patrick Wymark character continuing through several stories. Wymark's death part-way through filming severely compromised this idea — surprise! — since many of

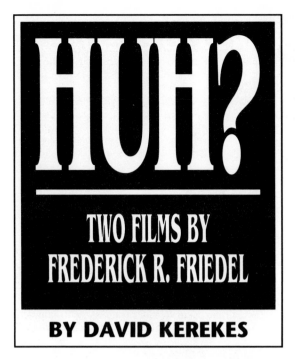

HUH?

TWO FILMS BY FREDERICK R. FRIEDEL

BY DAVID KEREKES

The first line of dialogue in *Date with a Kidnapper* is "Shut up and drive the car." Nobody has said anything. Sandra doesn't even know he's there,

Starring **JACK CANNON** – **LESLIE ANN RIVERS** and **GLADYS LAVITAN**
Produced and Directed by **FREDERICK R. FRIEDEL**

but Eddie leans over from the back seat, pushes a gun to her ear and tells her to "Shut up and drive the car." That's kind of endearing, if you ask me. Then the credits roll. One could hazard a guess that this movie is prey to a title change. With the credits comes the declaration 'Jack Canon as [*sudden freeze frame*] *Date with a Kidnapper*'. Another endearing quality.

Jack Canon — gaunt, mean — is in both *Axe* and *Date with a Kidnapper*. Wearing the same suit. Two movies from director Frederick R. Friedel. In the former, Canon plays Steele, leader of a gang who beat up a cross-dresser, inadvertently kill him (and his friend), then go on the run. In the latter he holds the daughter of a millionaire to ransom, but bungles the attempt. Indeed, the similarities don't end there. Each picture has a whacked-out teenage girl as its fulcrum (in turn subjected to abuse and rape); neither picture resolves or determines anything.

In *Date with a Kidnapper* the sidewalks are paved with dead men, creeps and "little bastards." Eddie (Canon) tells his hostage, "Don't try anything stupid that'll make me kill you — because I will." They book into a two-bit hotel; middle-aged man with teenage 'daughter'. Only when Eddie requests single beds does the guy behind the desk raise an eyebrow.

Sandra (Leslie Ann Rivers) manages to scribble a message on a roll of toilet paper and throw it out of the window. Later, two men brandishing pistols turn up at the door. "Thank God you found my note," cries Sandra. Bemused, the men turn to one another. "Yeah, it was very well written." They knock Eddie around and tie the girl to the bed and rape her. Eddie is forced to watch. "You *fucking bastards*," he snorts.

This sequence is uncomfortably protracted. It makes its point and continues to roll, cutting from Sandra's teary face to the fat man's pummelling butt to his accomplice holding a gun to Eddie's head. To Eddie himself and his wrists, red raw from trying to pull free of his binds. Sandra. Fat man. Other man. Eddie. When Eddie does slip free, he turns the gun on his captor and shoots him in the balls. Then he shoots the fat man up his big fat ass.

Eddie doesn't appear to know these people. Not who they are or what they want. It's a town full of dead men and creeps, turning tricks and trying their luck. When Sandra attempts to plead with the hoods, she gets the butt of a gun to her crotch. It's as if director Friedel is trying to tell us that of all the bad guys in the world, there are many worse than Eddie.

Driving from the scene, though sorry for what has happened, Eddie refuses to let the girl go. He calls her old man (played by Friedel) and demands that the money be ready in two days or the girl is dead. But his voice is shaky. And he has a sick mother, too. That's why he needs the cash.

Date with a Kidnapper opens with a pair of feet bounding down a stairway and out of a front door, the camera then pulling back to show Sandra getting into her car and Eddie pulling his gun on her. Shut up and drive. *Axe*, Friedel's début picture, opens to three pairs of feet striding along a dimly lit corridor. Camera pulls back to reveal Steele (Canon), Billy (Friedel) and Lomax (Ray Green), dressed like *Reservoir Dogs* and busting their way into an apartment. Here they wait for Aubrey — Steele picks his fingernails, tells the others to shut up and sit down. Lomax proceeds to burn holes in a baby doll negligée he finds in the wardrobe. When Aubrey does show, trailing a companion, he gets a cigar stubbed into his mouth and beaten up.

TOTAL TERROR-YOU'LL BE SCARED TO BREATHE..!

"More horrific than
Texas Chain Saw
Massacre"...

Childs Associates (Films) Ltd present
A HARRY NOVAK FILM

CALIFORNIA AXE MASSACRE

Produced by J.G.Patterson
Written and directed by Frederick R.Friedel

Starring Jack Canon · Ray Green
Introducing Leslie Lee as Lisa

The slaps and punches flop with the resonance of a cheap kung fu flick, twisted facial expressions mugging for the camera. Aubrey's effeminate friend cowers in the corner, a pitiful "ooh" repeated on the soundtrack whenever the camera turns to his quaking form. Aubrey dead, the friend jumps out of the window. "Now why'd he do that? It's twelve floors."

Driving from the scene, Billy peers distractedly through the window in the back. "What's the matter, kid?" Steele asks. They decide to lie low for a while in the country, hit up a secluded farmhouse somewhere.

Teenaged Lisa (Leslie Lee) tends to a farm and her infirm Grandfather. A single ear-piercing note leaps up several octaves whenever she walks into shot. That kid's not right.

Lisa looks to the floor, off to one side. Holds her head down and looks sad. She chops off a chicken's head in the yard, then sits down to milk and cookies. Upstairs plays the broken TV set. The screen sends its picture round and round, but Grandfather stares. Through it, beyond it. Finishing her snack, Lisa feeds Gramps raw eggs and bathes him with a sponge. The outlaws are closing in.

Date with a Kidnapper and *Axe*. Curios. Quite possibly the only pictures Frederick R. Friedel has made to date. *Axe* is cumbersome, plodding, a picture that doesn't make much sense (many sequences don't make *any*

sense). The violence is unconvincing and often funny to watch. Yet the movie has reached mythic status due to its Director of Public Prosecution's ban. Ironic. Chisel away the bloody grist from those so-called 'video nasties' — the cannibals and D'Amatos — and what are you left with? Humiliation. Effrontery is a major contention for the DPP. *I Spit on Your Grave, Fight for Your Life, Island of Death, Last House on the Left* and their like, they all do it: subjugate, humiliate and degrade real people, not with monsters, but with other people. For lengthy periods and to excess. (So does *Date with a Kidnapper*, but poor distribution saved many a video from the dreaded blacklist.)

In *Date with a Kidnapper*, degradation comes with two hoods in a roach hotel, pussy-whipping and raping the blonde haired girl who thinks herself saved. In *Axe*, it is only minutes away from Lisa's farmhouse.

Steele pulls off the road at a grocery store. He and Lomax go inside, while Billy waits in the back, peering. A lone cashier stands behind the counter. Across the store Steele chomps on an apple and spits it out. Reckons the fruit is old. "We're very sorry," says the woman. "Please take another if you like." Her hands are flat against her sides and the camera up close against her face. She looks real North Carolina. Steele starts to hurl the fruit at her. Then he and Lomax drag her from behind the counter, tear open her blouse and pour cola over her brassiered breasts. The woman cries, a very genuine kind of cry. The men position an apple on her head and aim their pistols. Steele manages a shot and busts the ketchup bottle above her head. They leave.

Axe is a wilderness. When the crooks find Lisa's secluded farmhouse — following on from Aubrey's murder and the subjugation of the shop assistant — the picture shifts into neutral and everyone takes to wandering around in a cerebral twilight. Miserable. Like their fee just bottomed out. Lomax touches the girl's clothes. That night he sneaks over to Lisa's room and rapes her. She kills him with a cut-throat razor, drags the body through to the bathroom, hacks at it with her axe and cleans up the mess. None of which stirs the others from their beds. The following morning, Billy discovers the corpse in a trunk. Lisa tells him that "the other one" did it, but she wasn't to tell anybody.

Many ideas from *Axe* crop up again in *Date with a Kidnapper*. Scenes that have no discernible bearing on the rest of the movie (such as that in which an unidentified man is chased from the farmhouse) are accentuated upon in *Date with a Kidnapper*.

Eddie takes Sandra and shacks up in a barn, lying low for the couple of days before her old man can come up with the ransom money. "I wonder what it's like to kill somebody?" Sandra chides her captor. He paces up and down. The sound of an approaching vehicle sends the two scuttling into the undergrowth. A painful attempt to alleviate matters, it is in fact a sorority of old dears on a bird watching expedition who have just pulled up. The soundtrack plays a suitably goofy instrumental. From this point on, Friedel fortunately keeps the jokes to himself, with our antagonist facing off a glorious display of oddball characters, one after another.

Eddie's radiator runs dry. He takes Sandra off in search of water. "Anybody home?" he calls out upon their arrival at a farmhouse. The camera skulks through the yard, coming to a door where a big old farmer pulls a shotgun. They run. Down the road, a seemingly more amiable farmer — a jolly sort, whiskers and fat belly — agrees to put them up for the night. Even feeds them. Once the couple get to bed, however, their host grabs a knife. Outside the bedroom he hesitates. "Make love to me, please," he hears Sandra say to Eddie (a curious request, coming the day she is raped). The farmer returns quietly back down the stairs and puts the knife away. (Equally odd, Sandra's request is played over twice in succession, the farmer returning down the stairs a second time.) The following morning, Eddie is attacked by the pitchfork-farmer. "You crazy sonofabitch...you crazy..." Eddie attempts to 'pacify' the old man, pulling his gun and shooting him dead. Sandra runs off, hysterical. The old man falls to the floor, near to his mute daughter who sits unperturbed by the commotion. Eddie chases after Sandra. She reaches a clearing and calls to a man up ahead for help. But the man doesn't stop, just keeps hobbling along. What follows is a colossus of transcendentalism. "Help! Please, please wait!" Sandra grabs hold of the man, who turns around, panics. "Can't you see I'm blind!" he hollers, before shrugging the girl off and hurrying out of the frame.

In the next sequence, Eddie is phoning his mother to tell her he's getting married. "Damn you," she says. "You're just like your father." But his mother is sick anyway. Suddenly in love, Eddie and Sandra collect the ransom money and celebrate with a drink in a nowhere bar. Eddie is so happy he does an impression of Jimmy Cagney. "That's very good. I enjoyed it," Sandra says when it's over. They slip a coin into the jukebox and dance to an irksome variation on 'The Blue Danube' waltz (on a jukebox). The bar gets held up by a gang of hoods, who steal the Cadillac parked outside and all the cash that's in it. Eddie and Sandra laugh. A hearty laugh.

No such luck in *Axe*, however. With Billy out in the woods, Steele decides to make a pass at Lisa. "We'll give your Grandfather a real good TV show to watch," he tells the girl, dragging her out in front of the old man. Like the beating administered to Aubrey, Steele's advances are all over the place. Extensive mugging ensues and shots of hands pawing, reaching out. The TV provides counterpoint to the scene with a horse race commentary. Lisa struggles to reach the nearby axe, eventually bringing it down on Steele. The lifeless form flops at Grandpa's feet and the TV announcer concludes, "There are many disappointed fans in the field today."

When Billy discovers the body, he runs out into the yard and is shot down by two cops. "That's one of 'em alright," the officers deduce. Lisa feeds her Grandfather tomato soup, humming to herself as she goes.

Like his portrayal of Billy (the kid), Friedel's direction distractedly peers out of the window in the back. His command of action sequences and tension is good, but when he puts his players into an old farmhouse with a homicidal teenager, or into a barn following the rapture of a kidnapping, what ought to constitute atmosphere just comes out a sticky mess. However abhorrent their previous actions, once the hoods reach Lisa's home they become lax characters in a dull movie. Estranged maybe, but dull nonetheless. When Eddie attempts to interact with Sandra, small talk about how tough her father was, the words come on like a second-rate gag (one half expects Eddie to follow up with a mother-in-law joke). Which possibly explains why *Date with a Kidnapper* avoids dumping a bunch of characters together in a farmhouse in search of ambiance, and chooses instead to keep the set pieces rolling. Friedel's films have no atmosphere. Strange. ∎

AXE
(aka CALIFORNIA AXE MASSACRE).
USA 1977.
Dir, Scr & Co-Ed: Frederick Friedel. P: J.G. Patterson Jnr. Exec P: Irwin Friedlander. Ph: Austin McKinney. Mus: George Newman Shaw & John Willhelm.
With: Leslie Lee (Lisa), Jack Canon (Steele), Ray Green (Lomax), Frederick R. Friedel (Billy), Douglas Powers (Grandfather), Frank Jones (Aubrey), Carol Miller (Storewoman).

DATE WITH A KIDNAPPER
(aka THE KIDNAPPER??).
USA 1978?
Dir, P & Scr: Frederick R. Friedel. Exec P: Irwin Friedlander. Ph: Austin McKinney. Ed: Avrum M. Fine. Mus: George Newman Shaw & John Willhelm.
With: Jack Canon (Eddie Mattlock), Leslie Ann Rivers (Sandra Morely), Gladys Lavitan (Mrs Mattlock), Frederick R. Friedel (Mr Morely).
'FOR ADOLPH'

TRUE TO HIS OWN OBSESSIONS

THE FILMS OF WALERIAN BOROWCZYK

BY COLIN DAVIS

Sirpa Lane discovers her hovercraft is full of eels in **The Beast**...

Some images: Countess Bathory bathes in virgin's blood. On an isolated island, everyone's name begins with G and a dead girl opens her eyes. A Victorian lass shoots her father full of arrows. A maiden, ravished by a hairy monster, responds so enthusiastically he dies. Another girl loves only her pet rabbit. Lucrezia Borgia stays at home with her father and brother. Dr Jekyll's fiancée joins him in his transformation. A pious young lady masturbates with a cucumber, another girl does it with a rose (a gift from her mutant fiancé), while a nun employs a dildo bearing a picture of Christ.

Some responses: 'An impertinent genius'; 'Overrated'; 'Innocently sensual'; 'Cold tendentiousness'; 'Boring'; 'Simply the most ravishing film images in the world.'

Walerian Borowczyk is a director whose work has ranged from arthouse shorts and animation, through horror and romantic melodrama to soft pornography. At one time the recipient of the highest praise, he seems to have become a marginal name in film history. I believe he has had less than his due in discussions of fantasy film and that his eroticism deserves to be taken seriously.

Born in Poland in 1923, Borowczyk studied painting at the Academy of Fine Arts in Cracow, going on to exhibit his own pictures and to become a prize-winning designer of film posters. Through the '50s and '60s he established an international reputation with his short animated films, many of them collaborations with the celebrated Jan Lenica. Other animations were of everyday objects, like *Dom* (1958), in which a girl (the first appearance of Borowczyk's wife Ligea Branice) imagines surreal events. Machines build themselves, and a pile of hair crawls about, eating a newspaper and pursuing an orange. In *Renaissance* (1963), bric-a-brac blown to pieces by a bomb is reconstituted by back-motion. A bunch of grapes leaps onto a stem, a flattened trumpet becomes whole and plays itself. Like the great Jan Svankmajer, Borowczyk is obsessed with objects, particularly curios and antiques, though the Pole's approach is generally less sinister than the Czech's.

Not that Borowczyk was never savage: his best known short cartoon, *Les Jeux des Anges* (1964), evoked such responses as 'almost intolerable savagery', 'scathing despair' and 'an obscene masterpiece.' Developed from a series of watercolours for an exhibition, the film depicts an endless series of beheadings and mutilations. Shaven heads roll and sawn-off wings are everywhere.

Equally dark was his first live action short, *Rosalie* (1966), in which a weeping servant girl (Branice), accused of murdering her illegitimate baby, tells her story of betrayal, intercut with shots of surgical instruments and horridly suggestive parcels. But it may all be fantasy, a protest at her bleak life. Borowczyk, it was said, showed an unsuspected compassion. Later in his career, his treatment of women was to be viewed less sympathetically.

Having moved to France in 1959, Borowczyk made his first feature, the cartoon *Théâtre de Monsieur et Madame Kabal* (1967). In a surreal battle of the sexes, Madame Kabal, playing the piano, is angry to hear her husband snoring, so drags him on screen and, unable to wake him, dismembers him. Later she summons Borowczyk into the picture and tries to seduce him. French critics spoke of 'a glimpse of the cinema of tomorrow' and compared Borowczyk with Ionesco and Beckett.

The animator, Borowczyk once said, is an alchemist, putting different things together and creating something new. Disney was no alchemist, no creative artist. "Animation, like painting, is my safety valve. My ideal is to be alone with my problems. I

Ligea Branice and Michel Simon in **Blanche.**

don't like collaborators." Considering this attitude — often expressed — and his artistic success as an animator, it was perhaps surprising that he now moved into live action films. However, Borowczyk had said he was tired of making short films because nobody took them seriously, and of course he could hardly make a career out of art-house cartoon features.

Goto, Island of Love (1968), from Borowczyk's own screenplay, may have used real actors, but its world was hardly 'realistic.' Key images and themes had already been established in Borowczyk's work — casual brutality, oppressive authority and sterile ritual, voyeurism, a concentration on objects giving them the status almost of characters. Goto is an island under totalitarian government, its inhabitants, whose names all begin with G, slaves of claustrophobic routines, dedicated to resisting change. Goto is as self-contained as Mervyn Peake's Gormenghast (G again!). But change comes, through the unwitting agency of the governor's wife Glossia (Ligea Branice), who is coveted by a soldier and a convict. The fantasies of the convict Grozo are the only scenes shot in colour: whatever his faults, he is more alive than the others. Failing to escape with her soldier, Glossia kills herself to avoid Grozo, but in the final shot her eyes open briefly. Life is not easily defeated, even in life-denying Goto. To Borowczyk's wry amusement, the film was banned in Franco's Spain and in communist Poland.

In *Blanche* (1972), Borowczyk's most acclaimed picture, Ligea Branice, with her large eyes and air of unworldly vulnerability, portrays another pathetic heroine, her situation pointed to early on by shots of a caged white dove. This is not a fantasy, but again we are in an enclosed world, the castle of an elderly medieval lord (Michel Simon) whose pure young wife is the innocent object of others' passions — her stepson, a visiting king and his amorous page. At the end, all are dead except the king, victims of humanity's tortured, ritualised response to natural urges. These people are enslaved by tradition as surely as the inhabitants of Goto. The king and his page pursue Blanche almost from obligation — it is the done thing

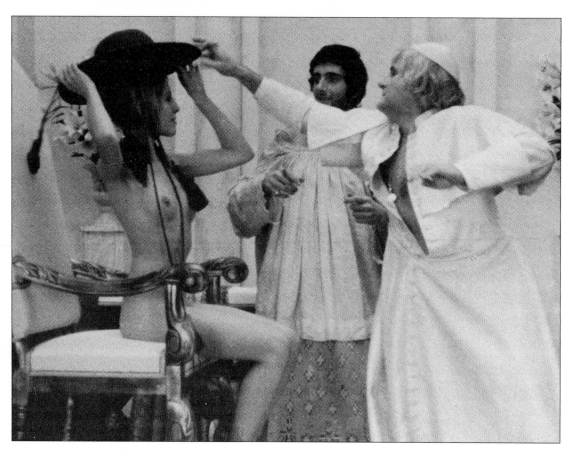

(Right) **Immoral Tales:** *the result of allowing women into the priesthood...*

to covet your neighbour's wife. The stepson's passion
is harmless as long as it is hopeless; after all, unrequit-
ed passion was an accepted aspect of courtly love.
However, he is quick to spurn her when he thinks her
purity is sullied. Her husband's reaction to the
assumed adultery is more conventional: pride and the
view of wife as property. Even the king bows to this
convention, giving the page to the old man's revenge:
he is dragged to his death by horses. Blanche's tragedy
is doubly poignant because her innocence is real, yet
in this artificial world perhaps it is irrelevant that no
adultery took place.

Most of the court are shown to be deceitful and
immoral, including the monks, a favourite target of
Borowczyk's. This time, as well as writing and directing, he was editor and set designer, and the colour
photography did justice to his pictorial sense. Even his
most critically unpopular films have always been
acknowledged as beautiful to look at.

If *Goto* had been well received, *Blanche*'s reviews were
ecstatic: 'A unique, irresistible and unforgettable film';
'The finest film one can see in London at present';
'Magnificent beauty.' But things were to change...

In 1973, the London Film Festival showed the
unfinished *Immoral Tales*, including an episode not
used in the final version but later expanded into *The
Beast*. The *New Statesman* (the Thought Police lurk at
both ends of the political spectrum) was outraged:
'What on earth does the British Film Institute think it
is up to?' The film 'seems positively designed to do Mrs
Whitehouse's work for her.' The audience was sent
'shuffling out shamefaced,' (a likely story!). Still, the
good old *Guardian* called the showing 'patently justi-
fied.' The completed film, with a new episode replacing
the bestial one, was screened at the 1974 Festival.

Intended as a prologue to *Immoral Tales*, but not

always shown with it, was a fascinating and hilarious
short, *Une Collection Particulière*, a tour around a museum of vintage erotic toys. The presenter, glimpsed
only as a pair of hands displaying the artifacts to us
like an auctioneer, is André Pieyre de Mandiargues, a
distinguished (Prix Goncourt) writer who was to provide stories for a number of Borowczyk's films. His
novel was the basis for the much reviled British picture *Girl on a Motorcycle* starring Marianne Faithfull,
one of the icons of Swinging Britain. The American
drive-in distributors, knowing what the punters want,
retitled it *Naked Under Leather*. *Une Collection Particulière* has further cultural cred: one of the erotic pictures is attributed to Rembrandt.

Immoral Tales is prefaced with a quote from La
Rochefoucauld: 'However enjoyable love may be, it is
enjoyable more for the ways through which it mani-
fests itself, than for itself alone.' Borowczyk's fascination with the ritual moulds into which mankind forces
natural impulses is more explicit than before: he had
dealt with the results of passion, now he showed it in
action. "*Immoral Tales*," he said, "was present in its
embryonic state in all my previous films."

The first tale, 'The Tide', is from a story by Pieyre de
Mandiargues, written expressly for an erotic exhibit at
an international surrealist exhibition. A Parisian student on holiday takes his sixteen year-old cousin to
the beach. Familiar with the tides, he deliberately gets
them stranded and the docile girl falls in with his idea
of passing the time. As she fellates him, we glimpse
continually not only — nor most importantly — the
expected flesh, but newspaper cuttings of tide timeta-
bles and the young man's watch as he times his
orgasm to arrive precisely with high tide, hilariously
recalling the numberless films in which crashing
waves have symbolised off-screen naughtiness.

'Thérèse Philosophe' is set in 1890, when a pious young innocent, as punishment for being late home from Mass (she was only studying church ornaments) is locked in the lumber room by her strict aunt. Aunt, obviously pretty innocent herself, gives Thérèse nothing to eat but, wait for it, some cucumbers. Resigned to her captivity, the girl examines the boxroom's Borowczykian contents — old books, dolls, vintage clothes, and finally *Thérèse Philosophe*, an antique pornographic book with illustrations.

Having eaten, 'real life' Thérèse undresses for bed and devours the pictures while we, in turn, watch her. One cucumber is uneaten. Sure enough, the vegetable cliché serves its purpose, but in the meantime Borowczyk has rendered erotic everything the girl touches — a doll, a wooden duck, even a lithograph of a king whose whiskered face is plausibly a symbol of masculinity to an 1890's girl. Thérèse escapes through the window, but is raped by a passing tramp. Later, we are told, she is beatified as a holy martyr.

Erzsebet Bathory, the subject of the third tale, needs little introduction. Countess Bathory (1550-1614) has inspired a number of films, including the impressive Belgian art movie *Daughters of Darkness* and Hammer's lacklustre *Countess Dracula*. Film is less lurid here than reality: the goriest nasty could hardly cap the career of Erzsebet, who slaughtered several hundred girls with horrible tortures. She really did bathe in their blood, seeking to retain her beauty, though whether she was merely rationalising her urges is a moot point. In *Immoral Tales* she is played by Picasso's daughter Paloma, who looks appropriately sombre, but cannot bring the right intensity to the part. Barbara Steele might have been perfect.

We see first a peasant community bustling with coarse but healthy life. The Countess arrives with her soldiers, lining up overawed village girls for inspection. The prettiest are taken to the castle and made to bathe: milling naked bodies fill the screen. The Countess moves among the girls, distributing aphrodisiac wine, and joins them in a gentle orgy. But here comes Istvan, the page with a sword...

Attended by Istvan, Erzsebet steps into a deep bath filled with blood. Afterwards they retire to bed, where the page is revealed as a girl. When the Countess is asleep, Istvan admits a detachment of soldiers, whose captain she embraces. Countess Bathory is betrayed.

The coy dots between the previous two paragraphs conceal nothing, gorehounds will be sad to hear. The slaughter is not shown, at any rate in the version shown at the 1973 Festival. Opinions differ, but I am inclined to think no cuts were made. Borowczyk does not show much interest in gore as such, although there were nasty moments in the later Jekyll and Hyde film, so extra *Immoral Tales* footage might have been shot. As always, objects and textures are co-stars; as Philip Strick pointed out, the blood running down Erzsebet's skin and the water running down the bath are given equal pictorial interest.

The last tale, 'Lucrezia Borgia', is the weakest. In Rome of 1498, Lucrezia (Florence Bellamy) visits her father, the Pope. Disposing of her husband, Lucrezia's father and brother join her in an incestuous orgy, conceiving a child whose baptism closes the episode. Intercut with these disgraceful goings-on are shots of puritanical reformer Savonarola, preaching against ecclesiastical corruption and in due course being burned as a heretic.

This is another Borowczyk dig at the church, rather heavy-handed and schoolboyish. The Savonarola scenes are minimal enough for Monogram: close-ups of the man in a pulpit stuck in a corner of the studio. Perhaps it all seems more daring in a Catholic country. Even this crude fable has an optimistic twist. The last thing we see is the happy face of Lucrezia's healthy child — life goes on, and with renewal comes a fresh possibility of goodness.

The censors wouldn't touch *Immoral Tales* and the completed film was finally shown in London in 1977 with a local GLC certificate, to violently differing reviews: 'One film towers head and shoulders over its fellows this week' (*Financial Times*); 'Porn is porn is porn' (*Spectator*) and of the Bathory episode, 'A concentration camp nightmare with a sexual veneer.'

Story of a Sin (1975), made in his native Poland, was for Borowczyk almost mainstream. Based on a celebrated spicy Polish novel of 1906, it is a melodrama, a tale of *amour fou* enhanced by Mendelssohn's romantic violin concerto on the soundtrack. A fallen virgin pursues her lover through all the degradation the world can throw at her, including a harrowing miscarriage filmed from her viewpoint, and in the end dies for him. Eva (a terrific performance by Grazyna Dlugolecka) is somehow ennobled, her foolish sacrifices rendered almost reasonable. Although a victim, she is a heroine, and Borowczyk certainly isn't anti-feminist here. The film was generally well received. 'In the mannerist department, no director can hold a candle to Walerian Borowczyk' (*Financial Times*) and, of course, 'the piece is visually exquisite' (*Sunday Times*).

With *The Beast*, it was back to controversy. At the 1975 London Film Festival, black market tickets fetched several times their face value — not sold, one hopes, to any of those who'd shuffled shamefaced out of *Immoral Tales*, whose unused episode, the cause of the *New Statesman*'s hot flushes, was now expanded to feature length.

Stamping and snorting resound as opening credits roll on black, then we see (in startling detail) horses mating in a château courtyard, watched by a man with a bandaged hand. He is Mathurin, backward son of the Marquis de l'Espérance, who hopes to mend the family finances by marrying Mathurin to a rich American, Lucy Broadhurst. Under her father's will, she must be married by the Marquis's uncle, a cardinal. Already we have the contrast: the honest rutting of the beasts and the elaborate conventions of mankind. Mind you, the

The Beast: *do you really need me to tell you what's going on here?*

mating of domestic horses would be supervised, but let it pass.

Lucy (Lisbeth Hummel) arrives, enchanted with the French countryside, snapping everything — including the mating horses — with her Polaroid. Meanwhile, the cardinal refuses to come, regarding Mathurin as a pagan, despite the telephoned pleas of the Marquis's other uncle. The Marquis forces the old man to phone again, threatening to reveal that he poisoned his wife. A strange family, though the Marquis's other child, Clarisse, seems normal enough, usually busy in bed with a black servant, though he is always being called away at the crucial moment, leaving her to console herself with the bedknob.

Mathurin shall be baptised. The local priest arrives for the ceremony but the Marquis performs it himself behind closed doors, squaring the priest with promises of a donation from Lucy's fortune. Anyway, the priest is more interested in his favourite choirboy — Borowczyk can never resist a dig at the church. In another room old uncle snoozes, a snail crawling on his hand. A symbol of the family's corruption or his own decay? Snails will be back.

Meanwhile, in an old album belonging to the eighteenth century Marquise Romilda de l'Espérance, Lucy finds a drawing of a bearlike monster with the handwritten caption 'I fought and defeated him.' The Beast, Lucy learns, is said to appear every 200 years, and a glass case displays Romilda's corset, complete with clawmarks. Back in her room, Lucy is becoming aroused by her Polaroids of the horses when a rose arrives, ostensibly from Mathurin, but really from the Marquis acting on his backward son's behalf. Lucy dozes and dreams of Romilda.

At the beginning of *The Beast* there is a quotation from Voltaire: 'Anxious dreams are really a transient madness.' This dream sequence is the original *Immoral Tale*, first called *The True Story of the Beast of Gevaudan*, based on an actual French legend which crops up sometimes in those cheap paperbacks with titles like *Unsolved Mysteries*.

The Marquise Romilda, searching for a stray lamb in the woods, comes upon the Beast devouring it. The monster pursues her, clutching at her garments until, clad fetchingly in the famous corset, she is caught and ravished. A heavily artistic shot of a snail crawling on a satin shoe, contrasts with numerous displays of a huge ejaculating phallus. These, er, shots were cut in the later release version, upsetting the formal Scarlatti harpsichord music accompaniment. Borowczyk has always favoured classical music, and here it provides an ironic contrast with the action. Some sources say it is Borowczyk in the monster suit; make of it what you will! An academic point: I don't know what the make-up department used in those ejaculation shots. Maybe the effect went on the catering budget: hardcore photographers often use potato soup when there's a shortage of the real thing. Regarding that snail, watch for my 10,000 word essay on the significance of gastropods in the films of Borowczyk. Snails, by the way, are hermaphrodite, which must prove something pretty disgusting.

While Lucy dreams, the Marquis catches his uncle phoning the Cardinal telling him not to come. The old man has already warned that Mathurin will die if he marries. The Marquis cuts his uncle's throat. Meanwhile Lucy awakens and, aroused by her dream, employs the rose in one of those feminine autoerotica scenes Borowczyk is fond of. When I am reincarnated, I think I'll come back as a greenfly. Originally this scene ended with a long held closeup crotch shot that would not be out of place in a hardcore movie.

Lucy dreams again and wakes with the Beast's dying moan in her ears — Romilda responded so enthusiastically that the monster collapsed in ecstasy. Or was the cry in her dream? She goes to Mathurin's room and finds him dead. Laid out, he is found to have a tail, and the bandaged hand is a hairy paw: is this the promised reappearance of the Beast or is it heredity — did Romilda's encounter bear-fruit? Lucy flees, and as the film ends we see Romilda again, covering the dead Beast tenderly with leaves and walking slowly away.

The film's reception, then and on its 1978 release, was polarised. Many hated it: 'Silly rather than sexy'; 'Somewhat distasteful'; 'The acting is diabolical'; 'Regrettable that a director of this calibre should pander so blatantly to the sensation seekers.' Others were admiring: 'Is there any living director with more of a painter's eye than Borowczyk?'; 'His ability to take the elements of hardcore pornography and transmute them into a beautiful and disturbing erotic comedy

The Beast: (above right) Hermaphrodite gastropod on the rampage!

(Below) Lisbeth Hummel bathes in potato soup...

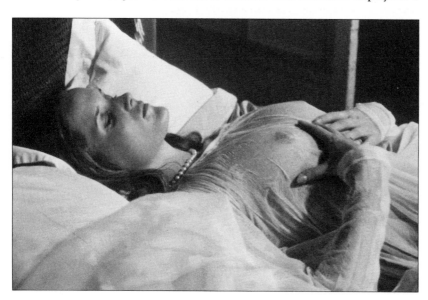

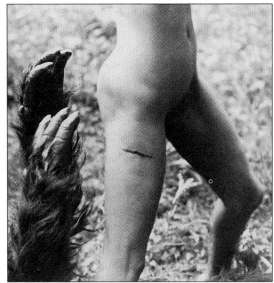

makes him unique'; 'One of the most compulsive and sophisticated films to be seen in London.' Said a *News of the World* columnist: 'Dreadful film, which sounds to be the ultimate in depravity... I am speechless.' You will note that he hadn't actually *seen* it.

The BBFC decided it couldn't certificate the picture without mutilating it, so a local GLC certificate was obtained after distributor's cuts. Remembering the *New Statesman*'s tirade, it is worth remarking that the GLC then had a Tory majority.

Feminists will have difficulties with *The Beast* — yet another depiction of a woman raped and enjoying it, and a view of female sexuality as lethally all-consuming. Makers of such movies are customarily accused of having a profound fear of the sexual woman, but Borowczyk, though he often deals with the power of aroused femininity, doesn't seem to me to be afraid of it. The ravishing is not rape, because the Beast is not a man, not self-aware. It is not even a real animal but a creature of myth, a walking symbol, and Romilda's response only a release of her natural instincts. Also, though it may not be intentional, Sirpa Lane's inept acting considerably lightens the scene. As for the apparently lethal passions of Romilda and Lucy, they may symbolise, not female sexuality as such, but rather the impact of the civilised on the natural.

The Beast is usually described as a version of *Beauty and the Beast*, but this not quite accurate. The original *Immoral Tale* had no particular connection with the fairy story, being merely another in the endless list of myths and stories of women and animals, going back to antiquity. In the expanded version, Borowczyk gives us a reversal of the familiar tale.

In *Beauty and the Beast* the girl is a victim, to be handed over to the monster to save her father. In *The Beast* the creature itself turns out to be the victim, whose fate is echoed by that of Mathurin, perhaps its descendant, who is being married off for money to save *his* father financially.

A questionable element is the admittedly funny running joke of the black servant and his *coitus* continually *interruptus*. Is it meant to parallel Romilda's encounter, the negro to represent 'natural' lust? That would be, at best, stereotyped and patronising. However, the servant, far from being brutish, is elegant and self-possessed, comparing well with most of his employers. The Beast is black, but so are real 'mon-sters' like bears and gorillas, and anyway the costume was designed for the original short film, before the servant's character was conceived. I am inclined to think Borowczyk simply intends Clarisse's behaviour to be as scandalous as possible from the viewpoint of conventional French society. With slight misgivings, I'd acquit him of racism.

The Streetwalker (1976) was another tale of *amour fou*, from a novel by — yes — Pieyre de Mandiargues, starring Sylvia Kristel and Warhol stalwart Joe Dallesandro. He plays Sigismond Pons (!), a married man who becomes insanely obsessed with a whore — guess who. Students of trash cinema will remember a little gem called *Seeds of Evil* in which Joe turned into a tree. Unkind critics of his acting might suggest this was typecasting: certainly he isn't the first actor who springs to mind in the context of sensitive drama. For that matter, Sylvia Kristel didn't become famous for her acting, but the *Daily Mail* critic (a woman, please note) wrote of *The Streetwalker*: 'For the first time I am aware of (her) as a sensitive actress... I think it is a fine and caring movie.' The *International Herald Tribune* called it 'a psychological study of rare cinematic artistry, one of the year's most distinguished films.' Further positive response came from *The Guardian* — 'Borowczyk, for me, is still one of the most fascinating directors working today, even at half stretch' — and from the *Sunday Telegraph* — 'Because of its subject it is a film that will, inevitably, be misunderstood, but it suggests Borowczyk as a singular talent, entirely true to his own obsessions.'

However... 'Soft porn... strictly and disappointingly for the raincoat brigade' (*Financial Times*); 'Laughably seamy' (*New Statesman*); 'Do shun' (*Observer*); 'Pretentious... such parts of Borowczyk's reputation as survive the wretched *Immoral Tales* are likely to be torpedoed by this glossy farrago' (*The Times*).

In 1977 came *Behind Convent Walls*, the mere title of which must have confirmed the opinions of those who thought Borowczyk was going to the dogs. As always, the screenplay is his own, but this time based on Stendhal, no less; it is a study of repressed and distorted emotions bursting into violence. Needless to say, there is an abundance of nudity and sexual activity on the part of the nuns — with any man available, with each other and, of course, with themselves. We see one sister whittling away at a homemade dildo —

I think we can safely surmise these 'shots' are from **The Beast**...

do-it-yourself in two senses — and there seem to have been some fairly startling penetration shots in the original film. There is one dildo with a picture of Jesus Christ on it, which is after all only a literal interpretation of the Bride of Christ idea. The most casual reading of the history of religion makes it clear that the language and imagery of Christian mysticism, and the behaviour of many celebrated ascetics, quiver with suppressed eroticism.

Among the Nuns are Ligea Branice, seen in strenuous congress with the butcher boy, and Marina Pierro, who was to become a Borowczyk regular. Branice even contributes to the music, singing an arrangement of a Tuscan folk song. The film was made in Italy and there are many Italians in the cast, so faces and exteriors are authentic.

Borowczyk's fascination with the antique and esoteric extends to customs as well as objects: when the butcher boy delivers meat to the convent, he is fitted at the door with black spectacles acting like blinkers — he can see where his feet are going but not look upon the nuns. This aspect of Borowczyk recalls Val Lewton, who never missed a chance to display odd customs or curious objects in his 1940s films. The two men might seem to have little else in common, considering Bor-

Behind Convent Walls: You should see the stuff we daren't print... For further 'proof' of what nuns get up to, check page seventy-two...

(Right) Ligea Branice.

(Below) Marina Pierro.

owczyk's erotic preoccupations, but remember *Cat People* with its 'suggestions of sexual anxiety and antagonism, the identification of physical passion with destruction, and overtones of lesbianism' (Joel Siegel). And Lewton — a Slav by birth — once edited a pornographic book that was burned by the New York Police Department.

Three Immoral Women (1979), another omnibus movie, continued the tradition of female protagonists. One episode, from a story by Pieyre de Mandiargues, is in his and Borowczyk's most extravagant vein. Marceline loves only her pet rabbit — a genuine bunny girl. Her unfeeling family serve the animal for dinner, so she runs away and lets the local butcher seduce her, butchering being presumably a symbol of

brutishness. But he is filled with remorse and hangs himself, whereupon Marceline selects his sharpest knife and returns home to carve up her family. In 'Margherita', a baker's daughter (Marina Pierro) becomes a model for the painter Raphael, takes money from a rich man for sex, then poisons both him and Raphael and returns with the gold to her own lover. The *Monthly Film Bulletin*'s Tom Milne, who thought the film, though beautiful to watch, a waste of Borowczyk's talent, remarked on the ineptly written English dubbing, a recurring problem. The film was cut in Britain from 111 minutes to eighty-nine.

Lulu (1980), scripted by Borowczyk from Wedekind's plays, was never released in Britain. Lulu is the embodiment of amoral female sexuality, bringing destruction to the men in her life. Eventually, having become a prostitute in London, she is murdered by Jack the Ripper. Lulu had been brought to the screen — and the opera — before, notably in *Pandora's Box*, a silent movie starring the phenomenal Louise Brooks, a hard act to follow. Borowczyk's Ann Bennent was thought inadequate; she is, incidentally, the elder sister of David Bennent (*The Tin Drum*, *Legend*). Jack the Ripper was played by Udo Kier, a familiar face in offbeat cinema; in Borowczyk's next film he was the star. The director had noticed Kier's work in *Blood for Dracula*.

If *Lulu* had been filmed several times, Dr Jekyll had, you might think, been done to death. Borowczyk's version was originally titled *Le Cas Etrange de Dr Jekyll et Miss Osbourne*, but the producers changed it to *Dr Jekyll et les Femmes* (1981), angering Borowczyk, who called them "amateurish and uncultured" in an interview and claimed they had demanded a sexier film. They retorted that, on the contrary, they'd made him tone it down. For its brief British showing it was called *Blood of Dr Jekyll*, and on video *Bloodbath of Dr Jekyll*.

The picture opens with a little girl fleeing through

dark alleys from a shadowy figure whose identity we can guess. The brutal scene — in the original print we see the beating of the prostrate girl — is photographed in Borowczyk's usual style, all velvety shadows and opalescent highlights. When the action switches to Jekyll's house there are endless shots beautiful enough to frame; indeed, they often are framed, the actors seen in medium shot through doorways or down panelled corridors. A dinner party is being held to celebrate the engagement of Jekyll (Udo Kier) to Fanny Osbourne (Marina Pierro), but he is busy in the lab dictating to a cylinder phonograph in words from Stevenson's original story: 'Men have before hired bravos to transact their crimes, while their own person and reputation sat under shelter.'

Jekyll joins his guests and an adolescent girl entertains with gawky ballet, the camera homing in on bare legs and frilly Victorian drawers. This seems anachronistic, but no more so than, say, the public showing of nudie movies in Victorian England depicted in Coppola's *Dracula*, a film as extravagant as any of Borowczyk's. At dinner there is heavy philosophical discussion, Jekyll defending his theories against his friend Dr Lanyon, played by good old Howard Vernon, a stalwart of Euro-horror. Loyal Fanny supports her fiancé, though she can't follow the argument. As the meal ends, the young dancer goes to bed and we see a dark figure sign the guest book (in Borowczyk's own jagged writing) — Edward Hyde.

The dancer is raped — by someone with 35cm of the necessary, says Dr Lanyon. The pompous General (Patrick Magee) takes charge, but after firing some shots outside he returns to deliver, as only Magee can, the priceless lines: "Misfortune follows misfortune... another innocent victim has been done away with. I have killed your coachman, madam... terribly sorry." Encountering Hyde, he cravenly allows himself to be tied up, and has to watch Hyde ravish his nubile daughter (Agnès Daems — where *does* Borowczyk find them?), who doesn't mind at all. Encouraged by Hyde, she shoots her bound father with poisoned arrows — don't even ask where they came from. Hyde, nothing if not impartial, then rapes a male guest.

Jekyll, himself again though understandably looking drained, sends a note to Fanny, telling her to stay away until he contacts her, but she hides in the lab and watches his next transformation; she is spying and so, by implication, are we. Jekyll takes no potion or injection, but wallows in a bath of red fluid, a surrogate womb. Hyde is played by another actor, with no special makeup except an odd, plastered-down haircut and — an unsettling touch — no eyebrows: his face is superbly sensual and evil.

Fanny follows Hyde, who tries to kill her, but she grabs some of those poisoned arrows (all right, they were the General's engagement present — honest!) and wounds Hyde. He fires one into her and continues his rampage, evidently immune. Becoming Jekyll again, he carries the stricken girl to the lab where, to his horror, she flings herself into the bath. Her metamorphosis extends only to red eyes. At her urging he bathes, though since the antidote has run out there is now no going back. Hyde and his new partner embark on an orgy of destruction in the corpse-strewn house, 'Jekyll' killing his mother and 'Fanny' hers, and they escape in a carriage, licking the blood from each others wounds. As Borowczyk remarked, perhaps they are among us still.

The film does not quite come off, though Pieyre de Mandiargues thought it Borowczyk's masterpiece. The usual irreverent humour makes us laugh with Borowczyk, but sometimes it is difficult not to laugh at him. Once again the dubbing is poor and unidiomatic, as when Fanny, talking informally to her fiancé, refers to "your pater." Ironically, the producers told *L'Ecran Fantastique* that the dubbing was being specially done in New York, stressing its importance in selling the picture in the States. This seems to exonerate Borowczyk, yet Magee speaks with his own voice and we've sampled his dialogue. Borowczyk specifically stated that the dinner party conversation's heaviness was satirical. Maybe it all sounds better in French.

Despite adherence to the Unities — single setting, single night's duration — the plot is confusing, though the *Monthly Film Bulletin*'s 'frantically muddled' is a little severe. Then there is Patrick Magee, whose ripely hammy performance, replete with his extraordinary mannerisms, clashes with some of the other playing. Either he could not be curbed, or that's how Borowczyk sees Victorian generals.

Marina Pierro's dark Neapolitan beauty is plausibly in period and she easily projects the sensuality, damped-down or untrammelled, of Fanny's two selves. Fanny, she has said in an interview, is a bourgeois out of her depth. A former *Harper's Bazaar* fashion model, Pierro was spotted by Visconti, who gave her a small part in *L'Innocente*. Udo Kier is his usual smooth-faced, decadent self, possibly not the most likely Victorian doctor.

Because the action takes place during one night, there is none of the usual dramatic development. We see nothing of Jekyll's normal life, and he has already embarked on his dual career. He *wants* to be the bestial Hyde: this, Borowczyk seems to say, is what these pillars of rectitude were really like, and we'll have no nonsense about Jekyll's agonies of conscience. As satire, the film is mercilessly exaggerated and best enjoyed as a delirious trip through Borowczyk's cinematic world. In the original print, the sexual violence is more explicit, with glimpses of the giant organ with which Hyde, according to Dr Lanyon, has pierced the stomach wall of his victims. Borowczyk has never seemed interested in violence for its own sake, so he clearly intends his film to be more than knockabout black comedy. Fanny Osbourne was, of course, the name of Stevenson's wife. Giving it to the character of Jekyll's fiancée is, I should say, merely Borowczyk's little joke, though since Mrs Stevenson is supposed to have persuaded the author to burn the first, stronger, draft of his story, it may be a dig at her Victorian sensibility.

1984 saw the release (somewhere...) of *L'Art d'Aimer*, a French/Italian co-production based on the work of Ovid. It again starred Marina Pierro, alongside Michele Placido, Massimo Girotti and Milena Vukotic, while the barely comprehensible production notes claim 'Ovid in person appears on the screen', which probably came as something of a shock to him. Ovid aside, no one appears ever to have seen it, so we mortals must remain in the dark...

The last Borowczyk film to have any distribution here was *Emmanuelle 5* (1986), which statement suggests ultimate humiliation — a master chef behind a fast-food counter. Borowczyk apparently took the project seriously, and at least one loyal French critic spoke of landscapes, sets and actors 'united in sumptuous and refined choreography.' Borowczyk, he said, 'remains cloistered in his impertinent genius. One can only submit to its charm.' British critics, not to say distributors, were by now reluctant to submit.

When it finally surfaced in the US in 1992 it had not only been hacked down to around 70 minutes running time, but also contained extra material filmed by one Steve Barnett, of whom *Shock Cinema* says 'has yet to prove that he can even direct his own bowel movement'. We'll take their word for it...

Whether by choice or market necessity, Borowczyk remained in his cloister of elegant erotic dramas. *Cérémonie d'Amour/Rites of Love* (1988) was described in *Variety*, usually quite sympathetic to his erotic output, as 'a sad attempt to regain some of his former prestige.' Scripted by Borowczyk from Pieyre de Mandiargues' novel, the movie depicts another case of fatal sexual obsession involving a young aesthete (Matthieu Carrière) and a prostitute (Marina Pierro). Refusing him promised delights, she humiliates him and he ends up wrongly arrested for the murder of another woman. There is much talk and little erotic action. The original title was *Tout Disparaitra* ('Everything Must Go'), which seems rather sadly appropriate.

Actors respect and enjoy working with him. He arrives on set with the scene already prepared in his head and, in his strong Polish accent, instructs his performers in every detail, calmly and without pressuring them. Behind the camera there is perhaps more tension. Borowczyk has often expressed a wish that he could create films on his own. "I look through the viewfinder and I eliminate. I also eliminate collaborators who dare to haggle over my ideas. *I know it all.* And that's often had members of my team in tears." "A cameraman is good when he does exactly what I want." He is reluctantly aware of commercial pressures: "You are obliged to work within the framework of degenerate film distribution circuits."

Borowczyk has described his films as being, generally, symbolic fables. This does not necessarily mean moral fables: "We always want to explain everything, justify everything. I don't." Of his humour he said" I don't use gags. It's more a way of seeing things... an artistic exaggeration." Buster Keaton and Charlie Chaplin are among the few film-makers he will admit to admiring. Taxed with his unpopularity with feminists, he points out that many women occupy key roles in his crews, though in view of his remarks about his treatment of crews, this hardly marks him down as a feminist. More seriously, he has said of the women in his films, "I am on the side of these women. I hope people recognise their heroism: that is, the heroic energy they devote to realising their desires, whatever they may be. Pornography? "Anything that's beautiful is definitely not pornography. The very term belongs to legislation, not to art."

Borowczyk, now in his seventies, is unlikely to strike out in a new direction or to regain the international critical acclaim he once enjoyed. A few of his pictures turn up at arthouses (themselves a threatened species) and *Blanche* has been shown on network TV. *Story of a Sin* might be televised with cuts, but earlier movies would probably now be deemed obscure; later ones would, of course, be unsuitable in the current, worsening climate of broadcasting.

It would be an oversimplification to blame Borowczyk's critical decline on British stuffiness in the face of his increasing concentration on the erotic. I have quoted enough reviews to show that some British critics stuck with him despite catchpenny titles like *The Streetwalker* and *Blood of Dr Jekyll* being slapped on his work like lurid wrappers. Nonetheless, I suspect that if his obsessions were of a different nature, his failings — repeating himself, insufficient attention to character, occasional sheer silliness — would have received more generous treatment. The fact that the Carry On films are nowadays treated almost as comedy classics must say something about British attitudes. Sex can be laughed at, because it is inherently laughable, not to say smutty. Borowczyk laughs readily at the complicated approach of human beings to their sexuality, but sex itself he treats seriously, though seldom solemnly. For many reasons, truly erotic cinema, whether hardcore or soft, is almost impossible to achieve, but at his best Borowczyk gets very close. The fantastic and horrific elements in his work are interestingly offbeat, spiced with his sardonic humour. And nobody could make it all look more beautiful.

A few years ago he noted ironically that there had been some progress in the reception of his work, at least in France. "My films were classified by *Pariscope* as ER (erotic); now they qualify as DP (psychological drama). Who could wish for more?" ∎

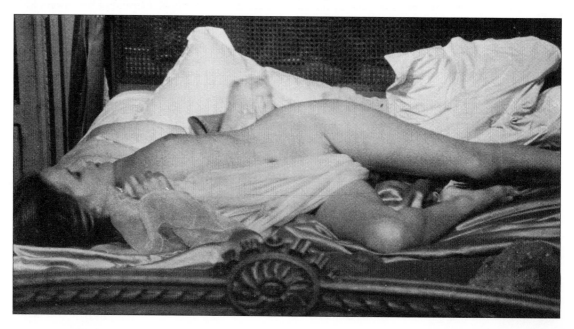

More masturbation. (**The Beast,** *again...*)

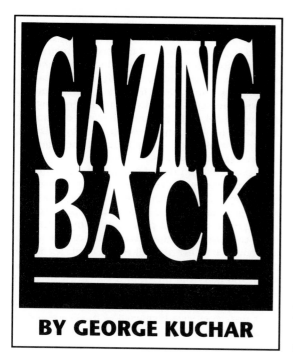

GAZING BACK

BY GEORGE KUCHAR

My dad smoked and didn't like the movie *Ben Hur* because it was lacking in simulated humping sequences. My mom liked Barbara Stanwyck and I don't think she (Stanwyck) ever simulated humping either. My mom respected her.

In the 1950s everybody was making 8mm movies. You'd develop them cheap at the local camera store and in five or ten years the emulsion would crack and chip in time for the 1960s avant-garde film explosion. No need to bake your footage in an oven like so many artists were doing: your home movies had already deteriorated into art.

My eyes were good then. I could edit 8mm film without the aid of a viewer and my splices resembled crushed cockroach legs, what with the excess glue and embedded hairs. They went through the projector gate in fine order though. In fact, many would just flip the gate wide open, throwing the lens at right angles to the projector body, which was hot and heavy and smelled like an overheated radiator. Top or bottom reels would fall off if not anchored securely and they'd radiate across the room like runaway tape measures spreading your work to the four corners of the compass.

Pets would love to chew the work when it was strung up at the editing table. I think they liked the

Barbara Stanwyck — simulated humping scenes: none.

I make moving pictures. When I was a kid (American for youth...a kind of goat in farm lingo) I'd draw on the margins of my dad's books and create flip movies. My dad enjoyed graphic sex diaries and literature on World War Two. My flip movies were violent and one was so sexual that when a friend threatened to flip the pages I ripped the book out of his hands and rushed down the street to deposit the novel novelty in a curbside slot that led to the New York City sewers. I hoped it would be devoured by alligators (or were there crocodiles down there? That was never made clear in folklore). I think my flip movie was about a stick figure masturbating. I can't remember if I put meat on the stick figure or if it just looked like he had an extra leg.

George — simulated humping scenes: innumerable...

things of clicking excellence. They had kind of a black hide bordered by gleaming metal and spun numbers around in little portholes of mystery and mathematical perfection. To kill it all you had to do was enter an arboretum on a frigid winter day and the camera would break into a terminal cold sweat and drown in its own secretions... It usually survived everything else, although it did choke on sand and would occasionally display ill-temper during cold weather by splashing electrostatic blotches onto the face of the film stock pressed against its innards.

Of course, when I started working in video the hide and metal were gone, and black plastic reigned supreme. I always had a fondness for plastic because when it burned it curled up and blistered like a potato chip. I loved potato chips and pork rinds in my youth but never cared for taco chips because they cut the roof of my mouth and then the salt would burn. My instrument for creating moving pictures was now Japanese and it was quiet and the chips it contained were tiny and as mysterious as the Orient itself.

It was hated, though. The people who clutched Swiss perfection were frightened of its silence and by its appetite for cheap ingestion. It was an object of potential electric shock and an eyeball carcinogen. I was tainted by holding it close to my heart and pressing its bright red button. It made that other red light go on and freeze living subjects in its laser-like glare of scarlet penetration. To those other motion picture-makers it was poison...like bad sushi. To me it was my friend, like my Swiss friend, but now I was older and it was harder for me to lift up my Swiss friend because it ate too much expensive stuff. It no longer was able to eat what I used to feed it because they didn't make that roughage any more. It had to eat this negative stuff and then it coughed it up and I had to turn that mess into a positive thing and make it right; and making things right costs money. I'm wrong therefore I have no money.

I must not forget to tell you that I also painted as a youth. That was my vocational leaning: to become a commercial artist...an illustrator. But mostly I painted the Loch Ness Monster rising from the depths of the loch, its long neck sticking up into the air, framed between the cleft of two massive hillsides. A more experienced artist, upon seeing this work, turned beet red as he sheepishly noted the phallic significance of this massive reptile. Now it is so obvious to me that I can see nothing else but those huge thighs rising above the water and that semi-erect thing poking toward the heavens.

When all things fail, like the electricity, I will go back to painting (by daylight); for my film and video work, like the Frankenstein monster, comes alive through electrical fluid. That reminds me: did you know sex was electrical? I think I mentioned this before. But once, when my brains were fried, I could actually see the white hot, electrical fluid moving from the outer appendages toward the protruding, central appendage and it was brought into being by friction.

Anyhow, while there is still electrical current coursing through the planet, the walls and me, I will use it to create moving pictures, and when it ceases the pictures will no longer move (unless I go back to the early days and draw them on the margins of literary endeavours). I will no longer move either when the Good Lord pulls the plug on me, but until then I must strive for independence from the main switch by storing up electrostatic charges by friction. Friction feels so good. ■

way their teeth fit into the sprocket holes. My dog once defecated on a pile of out-takes, ensuring their exclusion from the final film. (*Strangely enough, a demented, incontinent cat that came with our first house left a heap on some Al Adamson press books I'd borrowed to illustrate the interview we ran with him. Maybe some animals just have a different approach to art...Ed.*)

Of course I'm talking about 8mm and 16mm movie-making now. 16mm projectors were impressive housings composed of heavy metal and they loved to engage in audio combat with your soundtrack. They emanated the ultimate in all-consuming 'white noise' and the cacophony condemned many literate subtleties to inaudible murmurs of the heart. When they broke they broke real good, and if you had enough money your home resembled a burial ground for those mechanical behemoths. They were too heavy to lug back and forth to the fix-it shop, so they rested in peace where they had fallen or been laid to rest. Once in a while one in their midst would be resurrected to play silent rushes if it was only the speaker parts that were dysfunctional. Now I know someone, an artist, who uses old projector carcasses to construct massive sculptures in the shape of domestic pets and birds of prey. This is in keeping with the true nature of these projection devices that purred and roared at your touch and occasionally ripped to shreds the living art you dangled in front of it.

The 16mm movie cameras themselves were Swiss

REVIEWS

THE BLONDE AND THE BLACK PUSSYCAT
(aka ALLE KATZCHEN NASCHEN GERN).
West Germany 1967.
Dir: Josef Zacher. With: Edwige Fenech, Angelica Ott, Barbara Capell, Sieghardt Rupp, Ernst Stankovski, Helen Vita.

Along with Zacher's *Sex is a Pleasure* (also featuring Fenech), this is yet another clichéd entry in the 'oom-pah-pah' school of Teutonic sex comedy. The action takes place in an old French castle where a count and an army officer battle over the ownership. Also extreme sexual rivals, they both lust after the only two virgins left in the neighbouring village. Things get a shade warmer with the arrival of Fenech, who gamely strips off in her carriage to leave a trail of clothing for the young bucko pursuing her on horseback. This prompts such side-splitting classic dialogue as "I hope she leaves her stockings 'til last, they show up so clearly in the grass." The rest of the movie catalogues the bawdy goings-on in and around the castle, packing in the usual displays of fumbling striptease, frilly underwear, heaving bodices, rolls in the hay and colourfully photographed bare buttocks. The climactic duel, complete with scores of half naked young ladies clambering out of a lake, must have elicited at least a murmur of appreciation in British softcore halls at the end of the '60s, but it's difficult to imagine *anyone* finding these ham-fisted frolics erotic. As if to complement the often strident Gerhard Heinz score, most of the cast mug away frantically, although the teenage Fenech manages to escape Zacher's lack of style and emerge as engaging and seductive as ever. Born in Algeria but raised in France, Fenech is officially Maltese. Sadly, her participation in projects such as this does not appear to have endeared her to Malta's inhabitants. In the Maltese language, 'feneck' means rabbit, and the natives have a saying: "Edwige Fenech, she fucks like a rabbit!"
Mark Ashworth

CAREFUL.
Canada 1992.
Dir: Guy Maddin. With: Kyle McCulloch, Gosia Dobrowlska, Sarah Neville, Brent Neale.

The citizens of the Alpine village of Tolzbad have to live their lives carefully. The slightest sound above a whisper is likely to cause an avalanche from the snow-capped peaks above. Thus they go about their business in almost total silence, frowning on anything that threatens to disrupt the precarious status quo.

Enter Johann, a handsome and impeccably well-mannered village lad who is looking forward to a career as a butler (he's currently studying hard at Tolzbad's internationally renowned School for Butlers) and wedded bliss with his pretty childhood sweetheart Klara. The future looks rosy for strapping young Johann, if only he can resist those sweaty incestuous longings he feels for his voluptuous Mama...

Another fine example of the 'Oom-pah-pah' school of Teutonic film-making...

S.F. FILMS PRESENT
'THE BLONDE AND THE BLACK PUSSYCAT'
EASTMANCOLOR   Cert. 'X'

Welcome back to the weird and wonderful world of Guy Maddin. Whilst *Careful* has all the hallmarks of having emanated from the same demented brain that spawned *Tales from the Gimli Hospital* and *Archangel* — the same wildly over-ambitious sets (here ranging from from a Tyrollean village complete with working cable car to a secret ice cavern buried deep in the mountainside), the same wilfully over-indulgent acting, the same scratched, decaying celluloid — it marks a quantum leap in Maddin's particular *oeuvre*. For one thing, it's in colour (well, it's been hand-tinted, actually), and for another it's been screened at some of the world's most prestigious film festivals (and left most of its audiences staring blankly at the screen and making strange flatulent noises through their mouths).

But seriously, *Careful* is vintage Maddin. There is simply no one working in modern cinema who comes close to producing films as startlingly original and mind-bendingly profound as him. Whilst *Careful* touches on all manner of forbidden topics — the aforementioned incest, sexual guilt, patricide and self-mutilation, to pick the most obvious — it deals with them as unfortunate eccentricities of personality rather than manifestations of psychopathology. They're the price we pay for being human and the only alternative is oblivion.

Aside from which, it takes a very special kind of imagination to tell a story that the viewer just knows is going to end in tears — and then, quite literally, end it in tears.

One day all movies will be made like this.

David Taylor

CULT OF THE COBRA.
USA 1955.
Dir: Francis D. Lyon. With: Faith Domergue, Richard Long, Marshall Thompson, Kathleen Hughes, William Reynolds, Jack Kelly. Universal-International.

Despite the low budget and contract cast, director Lyon brings a nice film noir look to this enjoyable slice of '50s hokum. Sultry Domergue plays an Asian high priestess who can transform into a deadly cobra. She travels to America to revenge herself on five GIs (future TV stars Lang, Thompson, Reynolds, Kelly and David Janssen) who photographed her secret ritual.

B-movie favourite Thompson gets the role of his career as Domergue's insanely jealous boyfriend and Ed Platt (from TV's *Get Smart*) turns up as an unbilled high priest.

Stephen Jones

"CULT OF THE COBRA" A Universal-International Picture
"Copyright 1955 Universal Pictures Company, Inc. Permission granted for newspaper and magazine reproduction. Any other use including television Prohibited." Printed in U. S. A.

THE DEVIL'S COMMANDMENT
(aka I VAMPIRI, LUST OF THE VAMPIRE).
Italy 1956.
Dir: Richard (Riccardo) Freda. With: Gianna Maria Canale, Carlo D'Angelo, Dario Michaelis, Wandisa Guida, Paul Muller, Antoine Balpêtré. B.P. Productions/RCIP.

This is notable for marking the beginning of the Italian horror film renaissance. Although loosely based on the Elizabeth Bathory legend, it has more in common with Georges Franju's much better *Les Yeux Sans Visage*, as a mad scientist (Balpêtré) uses the blood of female victims to restore the youth of his beloved Countess (Miss Italy finalist Canale).

Because of added bath murders and rape scenes, the American version (which also includes Al Lewis from TV's *The Munsters*) was originally released as an adults-only feature, although it looks very tame by today's standards. (*The UK version was rendered almost incomprehensible by excessive distributor cuts. Ed.*)

If the finished result seems uneven, it's because Freda walked off the production and cinematographer Mario Bava completed the twelve days shooting, replacing Freda's baroque style with his own more linear approach. In the decade to come, both directors would carve their own distinctive niches within the Italian horror film, but, if nothing else, this serves as a unique collaboration by these two great stylists. Freda also plays the part of a doctor in the film.

Stephen Jones

GIMME SHELTER.
USA 1970.
Dir: David Maysles, Albert Maysles, Charlotte Zwerin. With: Rolling Stones, Jefferson Airplane, Hell's Angels and lots of stoned hippies.

This important 'rockumentary' focuses on the violence that occurred at the Rolling Stones concert at Altamont in 1969: a notorious event in which four births, four deaths and the fatal stabbing of one Meredith Hunter by Hell's Angels took place — an attack that also prompted the final dissipation of the Love Generation dream. On Saturday 6 December 1969 the dream turned into a violent nightmare as the Stones paid homage to Satan under a sickle moon, only to have the wrath of the god they were worshipping turn against them. The day was doomed from the outset, as the footage captured by Zwerin and the Maysles brothers clearly shows. Miles away from the safety of San Francisco, 30,000 hippies converged on Altamont Speedway (a car race-track in the middle of nowhere) to get high, get naked and listen to the Stones, fresh from burying the memory of their erstwhile leader Brian Jones. After cruising around fourteen American states, they ended up at Altamont to stage a free concert. To police the event they engaged the services of California's Hell's Angels (for beer), a move that proved to be one of the biggest mistakes in their career. For starters, head Angel Sonny Barger was not particularly enthralled about taking on the role of 'cop'. "I ain't no cop," he complained after Altamont. "He [Jagger] used us for dupes." When things started to unravel, the Angels took their frustration out on the 'innocent' hippy throng with bottles, chains, lead-filled pool cues and anything else that came to hand. The camera perfectly captures the

and the Rolling Stones' worst acid flashback.
Edwin Pouncey

KNICKERS AHOY
(aka FRAU WIRTINS TOLLE TOECHTERLEIN).
West Germany/Italy 1973.
Dir: Franz Antel. With: Terry Torday, Femi Benussi, Gabriele Tinti, Paul Loewinger, Marika Mindzenty, Maja Hoppe.

There's little to get your Calvin Kleins in a twist over about this jauntily dubbed but predictably lumpen costume romp, in which Antel — hiding behind his customary 'François Legrand' pseudonym — fails to recapture the charm of his *The Sweet Sins of Sexy Susan* and *Sexy Susan Sins Again*. This time the formula looks distinctly saggy about the seams and there are moments aplenty when *Knickers Ahoy* would barely warrant the title 'Knickers Afloat'. Torday recreates her Sexy Susan role, although for some obscure reason the English language version rechristens her Susanna. Hardly have the credits — or any of the cast for that matter — rolled, however, than she dies of an apoplectic fit just as she is about to disclose the identity of her illegitimate daughter and heir. Five parentless interns at the San Gregorio Convent, all eager to get their hands on the inheritance, set out to prove their lascivious lineage by treating us to copious panoramas of their boring bare bottoms and boobs. To pad the gusset even further, Antel inserts flashbacks of Sexy Susan(na)'s past glories in amongst the bursting trouser buttons and hayloft grinds with the convent organist. The ending reveals all five girls to be our infamous heroine's offspring, but by this time it's our patience not our knicker elastic that has been stretched to breaking point. For completists, the presence of pasta sleaze regulars Benussi and Tinti might add vague interest, but it's impossible to escape the fact that the movie's best feature remains its British distribution title...
Mark Ashworth

angst and decay on the faces of the audience as they are beaten back from the idols they have come to worship by a black leather-clad army of commie/peacenik-hating, heavy-duty bikers.

The Angels' violent antics commence when Jefferson Airplane takes the stage — no sooner has the band started than an incident erupts. Singer Marty Balin tries to break it up; for his pains he is knocked unconscious by an Angel and the Airplane's set never even gets off the ground. A disgusted Paul Kantner snarls into the mic, "Hey man, I'd like to mention that the Hells Angels just smashed Marty Balin in the face and knocked him out for a bit. I'd like to thank you for that," a taunt which brings Barger on stage for a further confrontation. That doesn't occur, but the scene is set for an even uglier situation to develop.

It is nightfall when the Stones eventually lope on stage. The atmosphere is crackling with a combination of energy, excitement, fear and loathing, a volatile mixture set to go up sky high the minute Jagger opens his mouth and howls. Dressed in red and black satin, he launches straight into 'Sympathy for the Devil', the only appropriate song for the night of the demon. A scuffle immediately breaks out between audience and Angels, causing Jagger to stop and explain, "Always something very funny happens when we start that number." What he couldn't see from his vantage point was a murder taking place, the blood sacrifice to bring Altamont and the free-loving '60s crashing down in flames. The stabbing of Hunter is later shown in slow motion on the Maysles' monitors, watched in horror by a shaken Jagger. "It's so horrible," he mumbles as the Angel's knife hits its target and the shadow of Hunter's gun comes into bleary focus. Whether Jagger's horror is directed at the murder or the thought that maybe Meredith Hunter had come armed to assassinate him is never fully explained. Jagger simply gets up and walks into freeze frame as a shot of the dazed and confused hippy multitude tramping back to civilisation cues the credits. Although he never admits as much, *Gimme Shelter* must have been (and probably still is) Jagger's

BORDER FILMS present **Knickers Ahoy** Cert **X**

LEGAL INNOCENT.
Hong Kong 1993.
Dir: Cha Chuen Yee. With: Celia Yip Tung, ??

The Hong Kong film industry thrives on extremes of violence. From the carefully choreographed mayhem of their martial arts epics to the comic strip gore of their horror movies, they take genre entries to delirious new levels of carnage. One can therefore forgive the Hong Kong censors for barely batting an eyelid when they viewed and passed — *sans* cuts — a low budget gore movie purporting to tell the true story of a demented restaurateur who ran amok on the nearby island of Macau, murdering an entire family and feeding their dismembered bodies to his clientele in their dim sum.

Somewhat ingeniously entitled *The Untold Story*, the film caught even the most hardened Hong Kong gorehounds by surprise with its scenes of a young child being murdered in front of his screaming parents by having a broken bottle rammed into his throat and another toddler being decapitated with a meat cleaver while his siblings look on. Despite (or perhaps because of) the subsequent press furore, it took over $HK14,000,000 at the box-office (which converts into approximately £1,500,000) and inaugurated a trend for graphic depictions of real life crimes. Another film, *The Bo Hill Murders*, which told in lingering detail of the rape and murder of two teenage expatriates in Hong Kong, was swiftly released to an audience hungry for more. It looked set to match *The Untold Story* at the box-office until complaints from both the press and the public forced its makers to withdraw it from circulation.

When *Legal Innocent*, another somewhat spurious 'true story', was released in June 1993, it became something of a *cause célèbre*. Here, a ne'er-do-well playboy called Patrick Wang conspires with his sluttish mistress, Kitty Yeun, to humiliate and murder his live-in girlfriend, dissolving her battered body in an acid bath. When Wang is caught and convicted of the murder, he uses his natural guile to seduce a naive social worker who visits him in jail. Having convinced her of his innocence, he gets her to successfully petition for his release. The trouble was that Patrick Wong, the person on whom the character of Wang was based, had been exonerated of the crime in court and it was his mistress, Kitty Yu Mo-Ling, who had been incarcerated for the murder. Wong was understandably less than happy at the way he was being portrayed on screen: a cold-blooded killer, pervert and perjurer to boot.

Whatever the film's moral and legal ramifications — re-trial by celluloid is a pretty contemptible concept no matter which way you look at it — it must be said that *Legal Innocent* is a brutally effective gore thriller. It belies its low budget and breakneck production schedule with some inventive use of Steadicam and a glacial blue gloss redolent of Argento's *Tenebrae*. Whilst the screenplay has a tendency to dissolve into melodrama, particularly during the patently unbelievable 'seduction' scenes in gaol, director Cha Chuen Yee manages to surmount these shortcomings through inventive editing, cutting to flashbacks when you least expect it and only revealing the details of the murder in piecemeal fashion. As a result, the film manages to build an atmosphere of dread that successfully counterbalances the often amateurish acting and overly florid dialogue. From the initial scenes of a young boy discovering the dissolving remains of a human corpse in a steamer trunk to the climactic re-enactment of the crime itself, *Legal Innocent* has you flinching at every cutaway shot, never quite sure whether you are going to get another look at a dog being boiled on a gas cooker or a tender love scene.

The murder sequence itself owes more than a little to Luc Besson's *Nikita*, with Wang pouring acid into his girlfriend's mouth before she suddenly snaps awake and begins to struggle to escape. The subsequent chase, however, culminating in Wang hurling her semi-nude, acid burned body down a flight of stone stairs before dragging said body back to the bathtub to finish the job, has a sadistic edge seldom seen outside of South-East Asian cinema.

Is this a recommendation? The jury's still out on that one.

David Taylor

PHARAOH'S CURSE.
USA 1956.
Dir: Lee Sholem. With: Mark Dana, Ziva Shapir, Diane Brewster, George Neise, Alvara Guillot, Terence de Marney.

Filmed under the title *Curse of the Pharaoh*, this is a surprisingly effective low budget mummy movie from the producers of *The Black Sleep* and *Voodoo Island*. Set during an uprising against British colonial forces at the turn of the century, an archaeological expedition into the Valley of the Kings discovers a sealed tomb and accidentally releases the spirit of a royal priest, who possesses the body of one of their guides. The horribly withered creature (dressed in what looks like striped pyjamas) shuffles through the ancient corridors, seeking a regular supply of fresh blood to restore its youth.

Pouting Ziva Shapir (aka Rodann, aka Blackman) gives Faith Domergue serious competition as a sexy priestess, director Sholem uses the eerie desert locations to good effect, and Jack Rabin and Louis DeWitt are responsible for the photographic effects. Producer Howard W. Koch went on to better things.

Stephen Jones

Hams investigate slab of Pharaoic meat.

IT CAME FROM THE DEAD!
IT FEEDS ON BLOOD!
IT KILLS FOR A CAT-GODDESS!

SEXPLORER.
UK 1975.
Scr & Dir: Derek Ford. **With:** Monika Ringwald, Andrew Grant, Mark Jones, David Rayner.

As opening credits appear against a night sky, a voice-over intones: "Space, the infinite frontier..." and goes on to tell us that this is a mission to investigate the age-old mystery of the planet Dong. The camera zooms down past the lights of Piccadilly Circus, a grape-sized silver ball plops into a puddle, and voices complain that they've landed in strange waters. But duty is duty, and a point of light emerges to grow, through homely special effects, into a naked girl — the Surveyor.

Not every film can boast a star who appeared on the cover of *Health and Efficiency*, but this one can and Monika Ringwald did (12 July 1975, if you're interested). Somehow avoiding notice in the streets, the Surveyor wanders into a health club. Seeing a man being massaged, she thinks he must be a mutation, her race being, apparently, sexless. Lots more naked ladies parade on screen. The club, thinking the alien's had her clothes pinched, kits her out, and off she goes to observe mankind, accompanied by a particularly tedious soundtrack song, 'The Girl from Starship Venus', sung by Don Lang, poor chap.

The rest of the picture predictably concerns the emotionless alien's encounters with people whose motives she/it can't fathom and who assume she is the sex kitten she looks. A groper in a sex cinema, a porn shop proprietor who gets her a modelling job, a doctor who finds she has no heartbeat, and so on. There's a visit to a strip club so some screen time can be used up on an interminable routine by one Tanya Ferova, and eventually a good guy introduces the Surveyor to the pleasures of Earth sex. Furnished with a full set of new sensory organs, she decides to stay on with Mr Right and the spaceball leaves without her to the sound of that bloody song.

As British sex comedies of its time go, *Sexplorer* is probably above average, which isn't saying much. The script, by director Ford, contains some passable jokes and at least he didn't write that song. Terms such as 'women's lib' and 'permissiveness' breathe a sort of friendly optimism long since overtaken by feminism and AIDS. It's all very good natured and even the stereotyped character of a gay photographer (Rayner) is silly rather than offensive. The sex, of course, is restricted to the uncomplicated nudity and mild softcore gropings allowed in 1975, but Monika Ringwald is certainly attractive and even manages to act about as much as she needs to. If you should catch the Bob Godfrey cartoon *Henry 9 'til 5*, you'll hear a sexy off-screen voice supplied by Ringwald, under the name Marylyn Rickard. Anyone who wants to know more about her, Derek Ford and other denizens of the tepid waters of British sex cinema, should head for David McGillivray's informative and hilarious volume *Doing Rude Things — The History of the British Sex Film 1957-1981*.

The idea of an alien spacecraft turning out to be tiny and landing in a puddle might have been taken from Katherine MacLean's much anthologised 1951 SF story 'Pictures Don't Lie', and the silver ball itself recalls the excellent Childrens' Film Foundation effort *The Glitterball*. Wait a minute, though...that was made in 1977, after *Sexplorer*. Can it be that the makers of our films for kiddies had been watching sex movies?

Colin Davis

SPACE IS THE PLACE.
USA 1974.
Dir: John Coney. **With:** Sun Ra and His Intergalactic Solar Arkestra.

Sight and Sound also requested that we run more gratuitous nude shots with facetious captions. Happy to oblige...

Unlike the Sun Ra short *A Joyful Noise*, John Coney's remarkable film centres not so much on the music of the great man but his notoriously eccentric behaviour. Sun Ra (aka Herman Sonny Blount) professed to come from another planet, bringing his music to the culturally starved minions of Planet Earth who were, in his opinion, righteously screwed up. Sun Ra and his Arkestra performed jazz in the style of Duke Ellington and Fletcher Henderson that would suddenly veer off into the free-blowing void that became tagged 'new wave' or 'avant-garde'. Dressed in flowing King Tut robes, Ra and his Arkestra would blow horns and minds in their quest for perfect interplanetary spiritual harmony.

Coney grasps this nettle firmly and attempts to introduce Ra's philosophy into a crazed plot that is half blaxploitation and half Jodorowsky-style psychedelic western. The action inexplicably opens on Ra's 'planet' (a world where the trees are draped with cellophane and what looks like the bubble machine from *Robot Monster* has landed), where he spouts some words of warped cosmic wisdom before flashing back in time to a 1920s Chicago club. There he plunks away at a piano, wearing a cheap plaid suit, bug-eyed sunglasses and a woollen hat. "What do you think of the piano player?" asks the club's host to the resident king pimp. "Shit!" exclaims the pimp, "Get him off and bring on the girls!" Ra then blasts into a keyboard solo which causes a space storm to rip through the establishment, a sample of his musical powers (or so we're led to believe).

The struggle between Ra and the pimp continues throughout *Space is the Place*, most of which is set in some desert, where the combatants sit around a gambling table and punch it out over a game of tarot cards. Interspersed with the 'action' are some rare shots of the Arkestra in performance mode, "playing such classics as 'Watusi', 'Outer Spaceways Inc' and 'The Satellites are Spinning'."

But what really makes *Space is the Place* so memorable is the sighting of Ra's spacecraft — a floating fibreglass monolith with two crudely painted flaming eyeballs, out of which zap the cheapest of ray gun effects, a classic piece of space junk if ever there was. Imagine *Close Encounters* colliding straight into the back of *Sweet Sweetback's Badasssss Song* and *El Topo* — that only hints at the insane genius that pulsates through Coney's masterpiece. Praise be to the video demon who beamed this one down.

Edwin Pouncey

TOMB OF TORTURE
(aka METEMPSYCHO).
Italy 1963.
Dir: Antonio Boccaci. With: Annie Albert, Thony Maky, Mark Marian, Elizabeth Queen, William Gray, Bernard Blay.

Surprisingly well-shot, this decidedly minor horror-thriller starts out on an impressively eerie note with a slow tracking shot towards a large door. The soundtrack's echoing footsteps are suddenly replaced by a piercing scream, and the title is superimposed in huge, rippling letters before we are plunged into a credit sequence which ends with a slow zoom into the eye socket of a skull. There then follows more tracking and panning around the cluttered rooms of an old castle, where something indistinguishable moves in the shadows and a rat scurries across the mantelpiece. A woman's hand brushes across a windowpane and outside we see two girls climbing the castle steps. From then on the spell is broken, crushed by the mundane mechanics of the hokey plot and the jarringly inane dialogue. The story centres on the mysterious death of Countess Irene, the castle's owner. Her fiancé is still searching for her missing corpse, and her crazy cousin, Elizabeth, is still hunting for hidden jewels. Bruno, the Countess' grotesquely deformed but loyal manservant is also lurking around, murdering the two bimbos from the opening scene in a fully-furnished basement torture chamber. Reincarnation, that stifling old horror potboiler standby, rears its unwelcome head with the introduction of Anna Darnell, Irene's double. Suffering nightmares in which she is lanced to death by someone wearing a suit of armour, she sets out to solve the mystery with the aid of her reporter boyfriend. The quaintly frenetic climax reveals — surprise, surprise — loony Elizabeth to be the Countess' killer, and she perishes herself when a rat nibbles through the string of a loaded crossbow. An absolute non-starter in terms of a 'whodunnit', *Tomb of Torture* nevertheless exerts a certain degree of charm through its striking monochrome visuals and Armando Sciascia's weird psychotronic score. The monster make-up is suitably outlandish and the scenes in the dungeon provide an adequate touch of Grand Guignol. Little seen in its native Italy, it was particularly successful in France. In the US, schlockmeister Richard Gordon distributed a sepia-tinted version which later resurfaced on tape. Italian production catalogues don't even list the real names of most of the cast and crew, and although Boccaci — here calling himself Anthony Kristye — does a competent enough job, he doesn't appear to have done much else. Some sources wrongly list the year of production as 1966.

Mark Ashworth

TRANCE.
Germany 1982?
Scr & Dir: Eckhart Schmidt. With: Désirée Nosbusch, Bodo Staiger. Music: Rheingold. A Barbara Moorse Workshop Production.

A schoolgirl waits for the postman. He shakes his head, and hers hangs miserably — still no reply from the pop singer she worships. A monotone voice-over reveals the thoughts scarcely displayed in her sullen face: the singer *must* know how she adores him. Perhaps her letters are kept from him by jealous minions. She runs away from home and contrives to meet her idol, who takes her to a remote house he owns. After the nude love scene he dresses to leave — the affair is over. Unable to accept this, the girl embeds a handy statuette in his skull, dismembers him with an electric carving knife and, over the next few days, cooks and eats the corpse. Finally she returns to her family, unsuspected of the crime.

Summarised thus, packaged in a video box bearing a close-up of a feminine tongue licking blood from a blade (which indeed takes place), *Trance* sounds like a nifty little exploitation job. In fact, it is a slow, serious

An exercise in political incorrectness: facially challenged basement lurker molests prostrate bimbo.

ANNIE ALBERT/THONY MAKY/MARK MARIAN/ELIZABETH QUEEN
A RICHARD GORDON Presentation Produced by FRANK CAMPITELLI Directed by WILLIAM GRACE Screenplay by ANTHONY KRISTYE and JOHNNY SEREMENTI
A TRANS-LUX RELEASE

art movie, occupied for most of its length with the numb wanderings of the girl, who cannot relate to her respectable family or her classmates. The singer's zombiefied performance is echoed in his offstage behaviour. The nude love scene is 'lyrically' filmed, but the detached manner of the protagonists avoids a TV ad effect. The dismemberment is not detailed: little gore, no prosthetic raw stumps. When the girl carries a limb across the kitchen, there is obviously an offscreen actor attached to it.

Summarised *thus*, the film sounds like pretentious tedium. In fact, though not superficially entertaining and sometimes heavy going, it is, particularly in retrospect, genuinely disturbing. The first hour's misery effectively sets up the final unhinging of the girl's mind. The delightfully named Désirée Nosbusch is good, slipping convincingly from lack of contact with the everyday world into a world of her own. While the singer (Staiger) is unlocking the door of his hideaway, the camera zooms in on the girl, waiting in the car. She opens her mouth, engulfing us as the screen goes black. This presumably symbolised her avid possessiveness — unless someone has been watching too many Italian horror movies.

We last see the cannibal girl writing in her journal in the oversized hand of the screen mad person, having just watched a TV appeal for information on the vanished singer:

I know where you are. Don't worry — I'll never give you away. I missed my period. I shall give birth to you...we'll be very happy together.

Désirée Nosbusch, by the way, hosted the Eurovision Song Contest when it came from Luxemburg in 1984. Not, I suspect, stark naked and brandishing a carving knife. Pity.

    Colin Davis

Sometimes, even tedium can be effective. The first hour of this film fully lives up to its title, as we observe a catatonically uninvolved teenage girl's obsession with a zombie-like German zero-rock star who calls himself 'R'. She refuses to be drawn into arguments with her parents, glumly wanders around the industrial hell she lives in and has a miserable time at school. Then, she runs away from home and loiters outside the TV studio where 'R' is taping a show. From the point our heroine picks up her hero onwards, the film turns into a horrifically cool dissection of the fan mentality that goes beyond even the misanthropy of *The King of Comedy*, the straight splatter of *The Fan* and the real life murder of John Lennon in getting to the mangy heart of the rock idol craze. After the girl has had unemotional, unexciting sex with 'R', she bludgeons him to death with a statue, calmly dismembers him with an electric carving knife, eats him cooked over a period of weeks, and grinds his bones into flour which she scatters. Having thus consumed the object of her desires, she shaves her head and returns to her parents to settle back into the monotony of her life. According to the credits, this was mostly improvised by the cast, so young Désirée Nosbusch — a strikingly attractive girl who looks a little like Zoe Tamerlis in *Ms. 45* — should be complimented not only for her frighteningly convincing performance but with being sick enough to come up with the whole idea. Director Schmidt, like Ulli Lommel before him, seems to be adapting the lessons of the so-called New German Cinema as represented by Fassbinder and Wenders towards a new

kind of gloomy exploitation horror. Since much of the film is without dialogue, the inevitable poor dubbing job on the video release doesn't hurt it too much. Very, very strange.

    Kim Newman

UNCLE MEAT.
USA 1967-1987, released 1993.
Dir: Frank Zappa. With: Phyllis Smith, Don Preston, Frank Zappa, Carl Zappa, Aynsley Dunbar, Ray Collins, Meredith Monk, Massimo Bassoli, C. Mercedes Lewis, Francisca Fisher, Billy Mundi, Stumuk.

We were the Mothers and this is what we looked like...

'Admittedly, this is sort of a weird movie,' confesses Frank Zappa on the cover blurb for his long-awaited Mothers movie. 'And, for some viewers, helpful hints on how to watch it might be in order. As with many of my other projects, *Uncle Meat* and its themes derive from 'folk lore'. Part of the problem with this technique lies in the fact that the 'folks' involved are 'non-standard behavioural types' and their 'lore' tends to be somewhat arcane. In spite of this, just as folk songs and legends record people and events deemed 'unworthy' of consideration by Serious Historians, this film provides a record for future generations that during this part of the twentieth century there actually were people who did not think or act like the plasticised caricatures that will survive to represent us in TV re-runs or 'Real World' history books.'

Amen to that, Frank, although it is hard to imagine anybody but a dyed-in-the-wool Mothers of Invention fan sacrificing nearly 100 minutes of precious computer gaming time to watch this fascinating underground movie that goes 'beyond time, beyond space, beyond reason.'

Uncle Meat was first announced as forthcoming on the US-only release of a Mothers compilation entitled *Mothermania*. That was in 1968, and the next year the soundtrack for 'The Mothers movie of the same name which we haven't got enough money to finish yet' hit the stores in the shape of a double album with accompanying booklet. Hardcore Mothers fans held their breath in anticipation and wondered how on earth they would manage to sit through the promised twenty-four hours of footage without nodding off and missing some vital piece of Zappa's cinematic jigsaw. In the end, it took some twenty years to complete, and the running time has been cut to a more reasonable 99.38 minutes. However, it is still one hell of a strange movie to struggle through, and it is advised that the viewer watch it in bite-sized chunks rather than swallow the entire wriggling, screaming thing down whole. *Uncle Meat* makes the later *200 Motels* look as sharp as *Blade Runner*: a hodge-podge of concert footage, home movie material and Zappa-controlled freakery that turns Don Preston into a 'monster' and uses props such as hamburger meat, a plastic duck and a rubber chicken to their very limit. For Mothers fans it offers several opportunities to catch the band in action at one of the most productive periods of their soon-to-be-terminated career. The Royal Festival Hall footage from '68 is splendid stuff, the on-stage theatrics captured here giving the best representation yet of how entertaining and musically competent the Mothers really were. Those who have already invested in the *Ahead of Their Time* CD may be somewhat disgruntled to discover that the very same soundtrack is featured.

Equally entertaining is the occasional flash of 8mm footage from Motorhead Sherwood's home movie archive. Here such intimate and hilarious scenes as Jimmy Carl Black (the Indian [drummer] of the group) being fake doggy-humped by another Mother, or saxist Bunk Gardner suddenly and mysteriously dropping his hippie flares to moon his unit at the camera, are key developments in *Uncle Meat*'s warped plot. Add to this the scene in a supermarket — inhabited by artist Cal Schenkel and Motorhead 'in concert', a (literally) red-faced Meredith Monk and British blues drummer Aynsley Dunbar, who is looking for someone to beat him with a toilet brush — and the picture goes even more wildly out of focus. Zappa and his 'freaks' at play may scoff at the 'Serious Historians' Zappa refers to in his cover notes, but something far more twisted and interesting is being enacted in *Uncle*

Exactly who were the Young America Horror Club? And what else did they recommend?

Meat. A perverse kind of voyeurism oozes from the film, as Zappa urges his leading lady (Phyllis Smith) to get naked with Don Preston and his hamburger for a massage in the shower. She resists, and the plot is instantly re-written before your very eyes, but the goading and subtle torture of his 'victim' by the director never stops. For this alone, *Uncle Meat* is worth your money, an underground movie in the tradition of Warhol's *Flesh*, Conrad Rooks' *Chappaqua*, Yoko Ono's *Number 4* ('Bottoms') and the Palmer/Weisman *Ciao! Manhattan*. In short, a classic of strange '60s cinema.

Edwin Pouncey

THE VAMPIRE
(aka EL VAMPIRO).
Mexico 1957.
Dir: Fernando Mendez. With: Abel Salazar, Ariadna Welter, Germán Robles, José Luis Jiminez, Mercedes Solar, Alicia Montoya. Abel Salazar/ Cinematografica ABSA/American International.

THE VAMPIRE'S COFFIN
(aka EL ATAUD DEL VAMPIRO).
Mexico 1957.
Dir: Fernando Mendez. With: Abel Salazar, Ariadna Welter, Germán Robles, Yerye Beirute, Alicia Montoya, Guillermo Orea. Abel Salazar/Cinematografica ABSA/American International.

From the opening vampire's eye shot of an aerial attack on a female victim, director Mendez stamps his style on the wonderfully atmospheric *The Vampire*.

It owes much to the look of the Universal horror films of the 1940s, and there are specific echoes of the underrated *Son of Dracula*, particularly in the opening scenes set in a railway station.

Producer Salazar plays the light-hearted Dr Enrique, who arrives at a lonely hacienda to investigate a series of strange deaths. He discovers the culprit is the sartorially elegant Hungarian Count Karol de Lavud (Robles) and the film becomes a duel of wits between the two protagonists, until Enrique finally stakes the suave vampire.

The Vampire proved so successful that the sequel went into production just six months later. Count de Lavud returns when the stake piercing his heart is removed by a body snatcher. It's up to Dr Enrique (Salazar again) to track the vampire back to his spooky waxworks lair, where he finally spears the Count through the heart, just as the latter is transforming into a bat.

Although the sequel doesn't quite contain the same intensity as the original and Salazar is allowed to overplay the comedy relief (a recurring problem in Mexican horror movies), it still benefits from an impressive performance by Robles (who prefigures Christopher Lee's sensual Count) and some striking photography by Mendez, particularly a scene where the vampire's shadow stalks heroine Welter through the twisting backstreets.

Taken together, these two films represent a high point in Mexican horror movies which has rarely been equalled since. For their release to American television (by AIP), new footage and inferior dubbing were added. If you have the opportunity, see the originals.

Stephen Jones

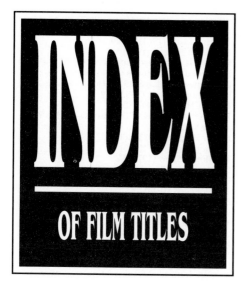

INDEX
OF FILM TITLES